Medieval Academy Reprints for Teac.

Medieval Academy Reprints for Teaching

Gerd Tellenbach
translated by R.F. Bennett

CHURCH, STATE AND CHRISTIAN
SOCIETY AT THE TIME OF THE
INVESTITURE CONTEST

Published by University of Toronto Press
Toronto   Buffalo   London
in association with the Medieval Academy of America

© Medieval Academy of America 1991
Printed in Canada
ISBN 0-8020-6857-X

Translated from *Libertas: Kirche und Weltordnung in Zeitalter des Investiturstreites* published by W. Kohlhammer, Leipzig 1936
Translation first published in 1940 in the series Studies in Mediaeval History edited by Geoffrey Barraclough and published by Basil Blackwell Publisher Oxford
This edition reprinted from the 1948 printing by arrangement with Basil Blackwell Publisher

Canadian Cataloguing in Publication Data

Tellenbach, Gerd, 1903–
    Church, state and Christian society at the time of
    the investiture contest

    (Medieval Academy reprints for teaching; 27)
    Translation of: Libertas: Kirche und Weltordnung in
    Zeitalter des Investiturstreites.
    Reprint. Originally published: Oxford: B. Blackwell,
    1940 (1948 printing)
    Includes index.
    ISBN 0-8020-6857-X

    1. Church and state – History.   2. Investiture.
    3. Liberty.   I. Medieval Academy of America.   II. Title.
    III. Series.

    BX1790.T45 1991   261.79'09'021   C90-095928-2

INTRODUCTION

WHEN historians write and speak of the "Investiture Contest" they are thinking of much more than the narrow issue which the phrase implies—a contest about investitures, a struggle fought out, principally in Germany, to decide whether lay princes might or might not continue to invest with ecclesiastical benefices, a struggle which ended in compromise at the concordat of Worms (1122). It has recently been shown[1] that the question of investiture came only relatively late to dominate the conflict of Church and State at the end of the eleventh century, while more than a decade ago an important publication[2] had already turned the attention of scholars away from the issue of investitures[3] to the problem which claimed the lively interest of churchmen in the days of Gregory VII: the problem of canonical election. The term "Investiture Contest" is unfortunate, because it obscures the breadth of the controversy which centred round Gregory; but it is a term which has come to stay, and it can do no harm provided that we understand the full meaning of the revolutionary movement it is used to describe. Far from being concerned solely with the narrow issue of investitures, the Investiture Contest was in reality a conflict between two violently opposed conceptions of the nature of Christian society. The two parties to the conflict were agreed—as, indeed, were nearly all Western European thinkers until the later middle ages—upon certain fundamental assumptions; both desired the structure of society to be hierarchical, and both wished it to be based on the principles laid down in the Gospels.

[1] Z. N. Brooke, *Lay Investiture and its relation to the conflict of Empire and Papacy*, in *Proceedings of the British Academy*, xxv. (1939).

[2] Paul Schmid, *Der Begriff der kanonischen Wahl in den Anfängen des Investiturstreites*, (Stuttgart, 1926).

[3] On investitures, see A. Scharnagl, *Der Begriff der Investitur in den Quellen und der Literatur des Investiturstreites*, (Stuttgart, 1908).

At that point, however, agreement ceased, and the older conception, resting on long tradition and the vested interests of centuries, was bitterly attacked by a newer conception which, entirely novel in that its political implications represented a catastrophic disturbance of the old order, was yet equally traditional in so far as it rested upon accepted Christian doctrines and drew its main force from the purely religious and Catholic nature of its thesis. In the words of an English historian whose death we have recently had to lament, " The investiture struggle was an attempt to study "—and, we may add, still more to revalue—" human society and to arrange its parts in the light of Christianity and Christian law."[1]

There could scarcely be a better brief definition of the true significance of the Investiture Contest than this; but Professor Whitney, to whom we owe it, never himself set out to apply his definition to the whole history of the controversy and of the reforming movements from which it sprang. Professor Tellenbach, however, has attempted to do so, and the result is to show up the Investiture Contest clearly against its historical background and to make its inner meaning plain; this is the great merit of his book, and the reason why it is here translated. In all probability, more has been written about the Investiture Contest than about any other aspect of medieval history—even in English alone there is an abundant literature[2]—but it would be safe to assert that no single work performs quite the same service as Professor Tellenbach's book, and it has therefore seemed desirable to put it at the disposal of English readers.

If a history of histories of the Investiture Contest and the Hildebrandine movement were to be written, it would be found that several divergent points of view have successively dominated the minds of historians. The first was pure partisanship, Catholic writers defending Gregory and

---

[1] J. P. Whitney, *Hildebrandine Essays*, (Cambridge, 1932), p. 57.

[2] Besides works referred to in the notes and appendices, *infra*, see in particular Whitney, *op. cit.*, R. W. and A. J. Carlyle, *A History of Mediaeval Political Theory in the West*, vols. iii and iv (London, 1928, 1932), Dr. Z. N. Brooke's chapter in *Cambridge Medieval History*, v. 51–111, and A. J. Macdonald, *Hildebrand*, (London, 1932).

Protestant writers attacking him.[1] Later, more objective arguments were adopted; an attempt was made to relate the struggle itself to earlier reform movements, in particular the Cluniac reform,[2] and the Investiture Contest was seen as the last and inevitable stage of a long process of historical evolution. Again, Hildebrand was pictured against a background of the contemporary revival of canon law,[3] and his policy was seen as a struggle against abuses and for the enforcement of law. Finally, after the publication of Stutz's work on *Eigenkirchenrecht*,[4] the Investiture Contest appeared as a conflict of the old (Roman) canon law with the " Germanic "[5] proprietary church law of the early middle ages.[6]

Readers of Professor Tellenbach's book will see that none of these explanations—nor some others which are less deserving of specific mention[7]—can be considered adequate by themselves. The theory that the Hildebrandine policy was directed solely against abuses, though still commonly held, ignores the widespread reform movement of the

[1] E.g. O. Delarc, *Grégoire VII et la réforme de l'église,* (Paris, 1889), and H. H. Milman, *History of Latin Christianity,* (4th edn., London, 1872), iv. 138–141.—A notable exception is J. Voigt (*Hildebrand als Papst Gregorius VII,* Weimar, 1815), the first of Gregory's modern biographers, who, though a Protestant, treated his subject so sympathetically that the Catholic bishop of La Rochelle wrote to him that one who so fully entered into the spirit of the medieval papacy should himself be a Catholic, and attempted to convert him to the Roman Church: see the correspondence printed in the preface to Voigt's second edition (Weimar, 1846).
[2] See Appendix V, *infra,* p. 186.
[3] Cf. P. Fournier et G. Le Bras, *Histoire des collections canoniques en Occident depuis les fausses décrétales jusqu'au décret de Gratien,* (Paris, 1932), and P. Fournier, *Un tournant de l'histoire du droit,* in *Nouvelle revue historique de droit,* xl. (1917), 129–180.
[4] See the works quoted, *infra,* p. 72, note.
[5] On the question whether *Eigenkirchenrecht* was Germanic or not, see in particular P. Fournier, *La propriété des églises dans les premiers siècles du moyen-âge,* in *Nouvelle revue historique de droit,* xxi. (1897) 486–506.
[6] Cf. G. Kallen, *Der Investiturstreit als Kampf zwischen germanischem und romanischem Denken,* (Cologne, 1937) ; but see also C. Erdmann's review in *Deutches Archiv,* ii. (1938) 591–2. Kallen's thesis is an exaggeration.—Cf. further H. von Schubert's important work *Der Kampf des geistlichen und weltlichen Rechts,* in *SB. d. Heidelberger Akad., phil.-hist. Klasse,* 1926–27 Abh. 2.
[7] For instance E. Bernheim, *Mittelalterliche Zeitanschauungen in ihrem Einfluss auf Politik und Geschichtsschreibung,* (Tübingen, 1918), vol. i.—a work which for a time had a wide influence—where the struggle is seen as a working out of Augustinian ideas; but cf. H.-X. Arquillière, *L'augustinisme politique,* (Paris, 1934).

eleventh century, which was led by princes and bishops after the end of the confusion caused by the Danish and Magyar invasions—themselves the ultimate cause of disorders in Church and State alike.[1] The theory that the struggle was one between ancient canon law and the proprietary church system ignores the fact that the papacy was not opposed to the latter when its effect was to produce greater cohesion of ecclesiastical organisation;[2] on the contrary, *Eigenkirchenrecht* made its contribution to the cause of reform, for it was partly through the use of the papal proprietary rights over great reforming houses like Cluny and Hirsau that reform was propagated.[3] In the hands of the Church it was of great value in linking one centre of reform to another at a time when other unifying forces were weak; and earlier still, the proprietary system had assisted the Church when the inducement which it gave to great lords to found churches on their estates was a potent factor in the spread of Christianity in the West.[4]

While, therefore, it cannot be maintained that the Church took exception in principle to the proprietary system, it can equally little be argued that Hildebrand's object was to enforce a conception of canon law and canonical election which his enemies knew but refused to recognise. Doubtless his intention was to assert such a conception, in so far as he understood it; but it has recently been shown[5] that his legal learning was small, and in any case—what is far more important—neither of these terms can be exactly defined for the period in question:[6] Hildebrand's contemporaries habitually used them, but could not agree about their meaning. Anti-Gregorians as well as Gregorians sought to secure the observance of law and the " right order " in the Church,[7] but each side had a different interpretation of the words which they used. To deny this is to accept the propaganda of the Gregorians at its face value; and here it is worth emphasising the well-known fact that the eleventh century was the first great age of pro-

[1] Cf. *infra*, pp. 76, 83.
[2] Cf. *infra*, pp. 117–119.
[3] Cf., for instance, *infra*, pp. 93–4, 96–7.
[4] Cf. *infra*, pp. 73–4.
[5] By Caspar, HZ. 130 (1924) 22.
[6] Cf. *infra*, pp. 100, 102.
[7] Cf. *infra*, p. 144.

paganda in world-history.[1] Again, only an equally un-
critical acceptance of party arguments can lead to the
statement that the royal position in the Church was based
solely on force and usurpation; on the contrary, until the
middle of the eleventh century, saints, popes and bishops
all approved the domination of devout princes,[2] and the
royal headship of the Church had a tenable theoretical
justification.[3] The reformers themselves were divided on
the matter; some of the most important among them—for
instance, Peter Damian—wished to work hand in hand with
the monarchy, and realised that administrative change
unaccompanied by spiritual rejuvenation would have very
poor results.[4] Finally, the Gregorian movement was
neither a simple fusion of two earlier and hitherto distinct
processes of reform—the Italian and the Lotharingian[5]—
nor a direct continuation of Cluniac policy. To maintain
either of these views is to underestimate the novelty of the
movement, to allow for nothing new and to misunderstand
the rôle of the great pontiff, who has been called " der
grosse Anfänger, der auf sich selbst allein steht."[6] It is
one of the marks of Professor Tellenbach's book that he is
not afraid to admit the emergence of novel principles and to
maintain that the year 1058 saw " a great revolution in
world-history . . . which even those most closely concerned
had only dimly foreseen."[7]

This, however, does not mean that Professor Tellenbach
rejects the modern approach to the problem of the Investiture Contest--the method of looking back. On the contrary,

[1] Cf. C. Mirbt, *Die Publizistik im Zeitalter Gregors VII*, (Leipzig, 1894),
and E. Voosen, *Papauté et pouvoir civile à l'époque de Grégoire VII*,
(Gembloux, 1927).
[2] Cf. *infra*, pp. 90–91.
[3] Cf. *infra*, pp. 57–60, 70–71, and F. Kern, *Gottesgnadentum und Wider-
standsrecht im frühen Mittelalter*, (Leipzig, 1914), pp. 2–139 (trans. S. B.
Chrimes, *Kingship and Law in the Middle Ages*, pp. 1–68).
[4] Cf. *infra*, pp. 82, 111, 191.
[5] This is the thesis of A. Fliche, *La réforme grégorienne*, ii. (Louvain-
Paris, 1925) 174, 183, 188–9, 197–8, etc. ; see also E. Voosen, *Papauté et
pouvoir civile*, pp. 60–64.—On the question of the " Lotharingian
law-schools," see *infra*, pp. 101–2.
[6] " The great Innovator, who stands quite alone "—E. Caspar (the
editor of Gregory VII's letters) in HZ. 130 (1924) 30.
[7] *Infra*, p. 111.

he only demands that it shall be rightly applied, and shall not lead to a facile explanation of the whole movement by its origins, combined with the suggestion that it was no more than a fusion of the parts from which it sprang. It is not enough simply to analyse Gregory's policy and to suppose that he took one aim from Cluny, another from Humbert, and so on; the method is the right method, if rightly applied, but it must not be allowed to direct attention away from the movement itself and to focus it upon the origins alone.

The Investiture Contest was, as Professor Tellenbach says, "a struggle for right order in the world,"[1] and it therefore becomes necessary to discover what, to the mind of the eleventh century, this " right order " was. The idea that a " right order " existed and that it should be recognised and put into effect by man was widely held, but there was no agreement as to the precise nature of the " order " itself; there was no common tradition, but several points of view. The question at issue, therefore, was not whether a " right order " ought to be attained—for on this all were agreed—but how it was to be attained and which of the rival conceptions of " right order " was to be victorious. In order properly to explain these rival conceptions, Professor Tellenbach goes back to the first principles of Christian society, as they had been laid down by Christ, developed in contact with Roman philosophy and moulded by historical circumstance. His first two chapters are, in consequence, devoted to an examination of what are in a sense preliminary matters, and some readers may think that sixty pages constitute an excessively long introduction to a short book whose confessed purpose is the discussion of something else. This is, however, to misconceive their true purpose; Professor Tellenbach is not moved by the old desire to apportion blame or praise, to laud Hildebrand or to defend monarchy—indeed, his impartial appreciation of the views of both parties makes it very difficult to see on which side his own sympathies lie—but he attempts instead to understand the movements of the age: an age which, as he says,

[1] *Infra*, p. 1.

is " the greatest—from the spiritual point of view perhaps
the only—turning-point in the history of Catholic Christendom."[1] The fulfilment of this object necessarily involves
a thorough study of the time when the seeds of the ideas
expressed during the controversy were sown and grew
gradually to maturity.

It is no part of the purpose of this introduction to recapit-
ulate what Professor Tellenbach has to say. It is sufficient
to remark that he distinguishes three main attitudes on the
part of the Church: (i) the ascetic, based on withdrawal
from the world; (ii) the sacerdotal, based on conversion of
the world by the priestly hierarchy; (iii) the monarchic,
based on the conversion of the world by the action of a
divinely-instituted kingship to which the clergy should be
subordinate—here, of course, it comes into conflict with
the sacerdotal outlook—and not by a clerical hierarchy
subject to the bishop of Rome.[2]

The attitude of withdrawal, which was dominant in the
early centuries of Christianity, could be reconciled with the
conception of monarchical control; devout men, withdrawing from a world which did not interest them because
they regarded it as fundamentally evil, were content to
leave secular society to be ordered by the kingship.[3] The
sacerdotal point of view, which exalted the power of the
priest and regarded it as his duty to convert the world and
lead it to the Kingdom of God, could not accept the
monarchy in this way. There are, then, in reality only two
lines of thought: withdrawal, which is reconcilable with the
theocratic monarchy, and conversion, which is not, because
it must involve the subjection of lay society to the priestly
authority. The interaction of these two tendencies in
Christianity, writes Professor Tellenbach, has at all times
been of vital importance, and they ultimately determined
the course of the reform movement in the tenth and
eleventh centuries.[4] The chief interest of the pontificate of
Gregory VII is the fact that it marked the final rejection
by the official Church of the old attitude of mistrust

[1] *Infra*, p. 164.　　[2] Cf. *infra*, pp. 55, 60.
[3] Cf. *infra*, p. 61.　　[4] Cf. *infra*, pp. 25, 56.

towards the world.[1] To Gregory, this attitude had no meaning; his historic rôle was to enunciate logically and unequivocally the opposite principle, the conversion of the world by the priesthood.

This was the positive side of his task, and for its successful execution there was one indispensable prerequisite: that the world should be ready to accept the claim of Christianity to be the moral basis upon which its affairs should rest.[2] This is an aspect of the age of Canossa which is sometimes too little stressed; both parties approached the quarrel from a high ethical standpoint, neither grounded its actions solely upon considerations of power-politics (this applies with particular force to the argument that, in view of the governmental system set up by Otto I, the emperors needed complete control of Church appointments within their territories lest the government itself should collapse —an argument which is sometimes accorded an importance greater than it deserves), both really felt that they were right in the fullest sense of the word and that their claims were in accordance with the will of God. Many things had contributed towards the attainment of this situation—the first victory of the principle of conversion in St Augustine's *De Civitate Dei*,[3] the theocracy of Charlemagne and the wide extent of the proprietary system, to mention only a few—and even something approaching a dissolution of society, caused by the invasions of Saracens, Norsemen and Magyars in the ninth and tenth centuries, had been unable to prevent its development: the popularity of the reforming movement with all classes of the laity amply demonstrates the truth of this statement. In one way, then, the interest of the Investiture Contest lies in the fact that it deserves to be set beside the missionary journeys of St Paul and Constantine the Great's edict of Milan as one of the few notable steps in the long process by which the Christian religion has sought to lead the world to complete acceptance of its principles and to incline it towards the canons of conduct laid down in the Gospels. This is a process which Catholic and Protestant have equally at heart, and it is of

[1] Cf. *infra*, pp. 157–8.   [2] Cf. *infra*, p. 88.   [3] Cf. *infra*, pp. 28–30.

particular interest at the present time, when it seems to many that the root cause of our ills is the very incompleteness of the process; there is a painful abundance of force in the contention that a new step forward is needed—a step forward by the whole of society, akin to that which not only made possible the work of Gregory VII but also set the tone for the arguments used on both sides throughout the earlier part of the Investiture Contest.

On the negative side, Gregory's task could only be the destruction of the hitherto dominant régime in Church and State; and this involved, as its primary object, the attempt to deprive princely dominion over the Church of the divine and sacramental character in which it had so long appeared. The " right order in the world " could not be established until this object had been secured, since, in Gregory's eyes, the " right order " implied the existence of a " free " Church in a reorganised society. This part of his programme clearly amounted to an attack upon the political institutions of his time, and the question at once arises, " Was Gregory a ' politician'?"[1] The answer can only be " No." Reform in its widest sense was undoubtedly the ideal Gregory set before himself—a reform of the whole of society was the thing which he most desired to see—but reform in the narrower sense was at most a part of his object; he was not concerned solely with the condition of the Church in the sense of an ecclesiastical organisation, and was not opposed only to monarchy if—or because— monarchy prevented the eradication of abuses. The theory[2] that Gregory set out to establish the primacy of Rome because the weakness of the Church had led to its " enslavement " by temporal princes, whose control had in turn resulted in simony and nicolaitism—so that from an attack on simony and clerical incontinence the rest of the Gregorian programme follows logically—is attractively simple, but it quite fails to do justice to Gregory. He was indeed deeply concerned about simony and the marriage of priests,[3] but these things were not the core of the movement

[1] Cf. *infra*, pp. 155-6.
[2] Advanced notably by Fliche, *op. cit.*, ii. 185, 189-190, etc.
[3] Cf. *infra*, pp. 128-132 and index, *s.vv.*

to which he has given his name, nor the explanation of the struggle with kings and emperors. If it is true, as we have said, that the real issue was the establishment of the " right order in the world," and if this meant the supremacy of priests over laymen—and the supremacy of the pope in particular, as the chief of all priests—then one conclusion alone can follow: Whether the results of royal control were good (as they were under Henry III), or bad (as they may be admitted to have been under Henry IV), it still remained true that, for Gregory, royal control was in itself an evil.[1] There could be no compromise on this principle, though doubtless there had to be *de facto* compromises in certain cases, like that of William the Conqueror.[2]

This analysis shows how truly Gregory VII deserves to be called " the great Innovator;" his outstanding quality was his ability clearly and directly to assert first principles and to apply them to the practical requirements of the situation in which he found himself. At the same time, the fundamental importance of Professor Tellenbach's careful distinction between Gregory and his supposed precursors[3] is revealed: only such a distinction brings to light the essential novelty of Gregory's position—which is otherwise in danger of being obscured in the shadows cast by the great reforming movements which preceded him—and throws his real greatness into bold relief.

In what sense may we speak of the " novelty " of Gregory's position? The following pages will make it clear that there was in his programme a relatively small proportion of new ideas; there were precedents for most of Gregory's actions, and all arguments to the contrary must fail. Gregory drew upon tradition, yet made a new use of it. He took the oldest of traditions—that of the Catholic Church, with the irrefutable claims its sacramental doc-

---

[1] Compare Gregory's attitude towards Henry III (*infra*, p. 101) with the general respect for Henry's great personal merits and his services to the Church, which had led to an almost universal acquiescence in a reversal of the canonical order of papal elections during his reign: cf. A. Michel, *Papstwahl und Königsrecht*, (Munich, 1936), and *Journal of Theological Studies*, 39 (1938) 317.

[2] Cf. *infra*, pp. 120, 123–4.

[3] Cf. *infra*, pp. 102, 110, 120–121, 141, 166, etc.

trines gave to the demand of the priesthood that their
supremacy should be recognized—and showed how no true
Catholic could resist the entirely novel construction he
placed upon it.[1] While there are strong reasons for denying
that, at the time of the synod of Sutri, for instance, the
alliance of the monarchy with reform was already foredoomed to turn into opposition, a more wide-ranging view
must reveal the truth of the assertion that the dogmatic
structure of the early Church made the emergence of the
Gregorian programme a logical necessity. Gregory was the
completest and most ruthless Catholic who had yet held
office in the Church, and yet he was a revolutionary ;
innovation and an obstinate refusal to abate one jot or
tittle of the law met in him to form a paradoxical and yet
entirely consistent whole.

Gregory attained a very considerable measure of success,
but his victory was far from complete. During his pontificate, we have said, the Church finally abandoned the old
attitude of withdrawal and turned to attempt the conversion of the world; in spite of this, however, the old
outlook persisted: the next century saw a monastic revival
on a hitherto unprecedented scale, and generations of
historians have agreed in awarding to St Bernard, its
leading figure, the title of " the ideal monk "—in describing
him, that is to say, as the chief exponent of some of the
ideas against which Gregory VII had fought. So, too, it
proved impossible to confine the laity to a purely passive
rôle in Church matters, because more settled and more
prosperous conditions gave many of them leisure to ponder
upon spiritual truth, and led to the conclusion that all men
were called to play an equal part in religious activity.
Accordingly, the twelfth and thirteenth centuries saw a
wide development of popular religion, which frequently
ended in heresy and was often tainted with anti-sacerdotalism;[2] and this last is, of course, no less than a denial

[1] Cf. infra, p. 167.

[2] On these religious movements of the twelfth and thirteenth centuries,
see the very important work of H. Grundmann, Religiöse Bewegungen im
Mittelalter, (Berlin, 1935). Anti-sacerdotalism had already raised its head
even before the Investiture Contest, in the form of the common dispute
whether the sacraments were valid when administered by an impure

of the sacramental principles for which Gregory stood and upon which the subordinate position assigned to the laity was based. Even when the " conversion " *motif* appeared again with new force in the mendicant movements of St Francis and St Dominic, it was in the end unable to deal effectively with the problem of the layman's religion. Finally, despite the creation of a papal monarchy in the thirteenth and fourteenth centuries,[1] the " national church " tendency persisted with undiminished force;[2] Divine Right itself lasted many hundred years more[3]— the long continuance of the practice of touching for the King's Evil shows how difficult it was to eradicate the feeling that the king was more than an ordinary layman—while the reign of Philip the Fair, the Gallican movement and the concordats of the fifteenth century, for instance, show that princely control of the Church had lost little of its theocratic dress, if it was also beginning to clothe itself in a more secular garb and to appeal to expediency and the new conception of the sovereign State.

For a short time, Gregorianism may have conquered both Church and World, but from early in the thirteenth century at latest the old tendencies of episcopalism, non-resistance and royal control raised their heads again. If the lessons taught by the conflict of ideals in the Investiture Contest of the eleventh century are of permanent value to a world which aspires to arrange its affairs according to Christian principles, it is equally clear that contemporary society failed properly to learn them; and this failure in its turn—at least in so far as its unintended effect was to drive the papal monarchy to an ever more intransigent assertion

priest, and similar questions had been debated in the curia of Leo IX (cf. *infra*, p. 98); it is worth pointing out, however, that the official Church was bound always to decide that it was office and not personal morality which mattered, since otherwise the idea of *ordo* and the entire clerical hierarchy would be destroyed (cf. *infra*, p. 49). Later on, when the heretical view had gained wide acceptance, St Francis adopted a similar attitude: cf. I Celano, 46, II Celano, 146, 201 (ed. E. d'Alençon, Rome, 1906, pp. 48, 279, 319–20).

[1] The best sketch of the development of the monarchical organisation of the Church is in J. Haller, *Papsttum und Kirchenreform*, (Berlin, 1901).

[2] Cf. K. Schleyer, *Die Anfänge des Gallikanismus im dreizehnten Jahrhundert*, (Berlin, 1937), and EHR. 53 (1938) 532.

[3] Cf. Kern, *op. cit.*, esp. pp. 118–122 (trans. Chrimes, pp. 58–60), and Marc Bloch, *Les rois thaumaturges*, (Strasbourg, 1924).

of its authority, and in the end to separate it from the religion of the world which it set out to convert—was in some way responsible for the occurrence of the next great crisis in Christian history, the Reformation.

The pages which follow contain a full translation of the text of the book *Libertas: Kirche und Weltordnung im Zeitalter des Investiturstreites*, (W. Kohlhammer, Leipzig, 1936). The Appendices have been selected from the seventeen printed at the end of the German edition, and in some places have been slightly condensed; Appendix I, *infra*, corresponds to the author's IV and VI, II corresponds to VII, III to XI, IV to XVII and V to III (in the case of the last, as I have explained, *infra*, p. 187, with considerable additions by myself). The notes represent only a selection from the large body of references and illustrative material collected by the author. Professor Tellenbach has seen and approved the whole of the present text with the exception of the Epilogue and the Appendices, which could not be sent to him because of the war. I should perhaps explain why I have retained a few German words—Eigenkirche, Eigenkloster (plural, Eigenklöster), Eigenkirchenrecht—in this translation: their English equivalents—proprietary church, proprietary monastery, proprietary church law—are rather unfamiliar and are exceedingly unwieldy from the stylistic point of view, and I have in consequence preferred to use the German words on some occasions if it seemed that the construction of a sentence would thereby be simplified.

I owe the warmest thanks to four people: to Professor Tellenbach, for permission to translate; to the General Editor of this series, Mr. Barraclough, who has read every word I have written and has saved me from a number of mistakes, besides giving me a great deal of other help and encouragement; to my wife, for making the Index; and to Mr. H. L. Schollick of Messrs. Basil Blackwell and Mott, for passing the book smoothly through the press under the strain of war-time conditions.

Magdalene College, Cambridge.   R. F. BENNETT.
June, 1940.

CONTENTS

CHAP.   PAGE

INTRODUCTION   v

LIST OF ABBREVIATIONS   xxiii

I. FUNDAMENTAL PRINCIPLES.   .   .   .   1–37

     I. The principle of religious order and the early
      Christian concept of liberty: Freedom and
      dependence, 2.—Freedom can be increased: the
      hierarchy of free beings, 7.—Heavenly and
      earthly rank, 9.
    II. The structure of medieval law and its concept of
      liberty: Freedom in Roman law, 10.—Its in-
      fluence in the middle ages, 13.—Roman and
      medieval ideas of freedom compared, 15.—Privi-
      lege, 16.—Differentiation of privilege, 17.—
      Things (e.g. churches) as possessors of *libertates*,
      20.—*Libertas* means subjective right, 21.—
      Natural law as the guarantee of *libertates* and of
      the hierarchy, 22.
    III. The attitude of early Christianity towards the
      world: The two tendencies: withdrawal from
      the world, conversion of the world, 25.—Influence
      of St Augustine's *City of God* on Christian political
      theory, 28.—The Roman empire becomes Chris-
      tian: Church and World drawn closer together,
      30.—Pope Gelasius I's theory of the Two Powers,
      33.

II. THE MEDIEVAL CONCEPTION OF THE HIER-
    ARCHY   38–60

     I. Mystical and hierarchical philosophy: its concept
      of liberty and its hierarchical system, 38.—The
      freedom of the Redemption: Pauline ideas fami-
      liar to the middle ages, 40.—Possibilities of ad-
      vancement, 42.
    II. The ascetic (i.e., monastic) conception of the
      hierarchy: Withdrawal from the world, 42.—
      Dualistic asceticism and pantheism, 43.—The
      doctrine of merit, 44.—The monastic conception
      of the hierarchy is based on the next world, 45.—
      Individualism, 46.
    III. The sacramental (i.e., priestly) conception of the
      hierarchy: The clergy as the servants of God, 47.
      —Distinction between office and person, 49.—The
      sacramental conception of the hierarchy is mainly
      an affair of this world, 50.

CHAP.   PAGE

IV. Both conceptions highly honoured in the middle ages, 50.—Both were current at the same time: comparison of the two, 54.

V. The conception of the hierarchy as a royal theocracy: The position of the laity in Christian thought, 56.—Special position of kings: Divine Right, 57.—Conflict of opinion, 58.

III. THE TRANSFORMATION OF SOCIETY BY THE CHRISTIAN CHURCH: ROYAL THEOCRACY, PROPRIETARY CHURCHES AND MONASTIC PIETY 61–88

I. Church and State before Gregory VII: Ultimate conflict between opposed conceptions of the hierarchy inevitable, 61.—Theocracy draws Church and State together, 62.—Various interpretations of the "Two Powers" theory, 62.—The Church does not claim supremacy in the ninth century, 65.—The duty of non-resistance, 67.

II. Royal theocracy and the proprietary system: General considerations, 69.—The proprietary system: the laity no longer a purely passive order, 71.—Development of ecclesiastical organisation, 73.—Evils of the system, 74.—Attempts at reform, 75.

III. Monastic piety and its influence in the West: Monastic reform, 77.—Acquisition of merit on behalf of others, 78.—Care for the dead, 78.—General adoption of the monastic outlook,.79.—Monastic reformers and the reform of the Church, 82.—Personal influence of leading figures, 83.

IV. Henry III and reform: His character and his opposition to simony, 85.—His conception of Divine Right, 87.—The synod of Sutri, 87.

IV. THE STRUGGLE AGAINST LAY DOMINATION OF THE CHURCH: THE INVESTITURE CONTEST 89–125

I. Power of the laity before the middle of the eleventh century: its general acceptance by the Church, 89.—Proprietary legislation in the tenth and early eleventh centuries, 91.—Monastic reformers accept the proprietary system, 93.—Connections between reformed monasteries, 96.

II. Origins of the revolt against lay domination, 1047–1059: Henry III's reforms not a political mistake, 97.—The pontificate of Leo IX, 98.—Leo's attitude towards lay domination, 99.—

Opinions in the curia, 101.—The " Lotharingian law-schools," 101.—Wazo of Liège and the Auctor Gallicus, 103.—Territorial policy of the popes, 106. —The third book of Humbert's *Adversus simoniacos*, 109.—The Easter synod of 1059, 111.

III. Extension and success of the new programme of Church reform : Developments before Gregory VII, 112.—Prohibition of lay investiture with bishoprics and abbacies, 113.—Measures against minor proprietary churches, 114.—Propaganda and canon law during the Investiture Contest, 115.—Policy of Urban II and Paschal II, 116.— Clerical *Eigenkirchenrecht* protected and systematised, 117.—Radical tendencies, 119.—Strength of the opposition, 120.—Tactics of the reformers, 120.—The extent of their success : the lay princes lose their spiritual authority, 124.

V. LIBERTAS ECCLESIAE : THE STRUGGLE FOR RIGHT ORDER IN THE CHRISTIAN WORLD . 126–161

I. The freedom of the Church and its servants : The freedom of God and the freedom of the Church, 126.—The Church as the Body or the Bride of Christ, 127.—Simony, 128.—Part played by bishops and priests in the mystical marriage of Christ with the Church, 129.—Dogmatic character of simony, lay investiture and nicolaitism, 130.— The priests' share in the omnipotence of Christ, 132.—Their service of Him the root of their freedom, 134.—Arguments of the traditionalists, 135.

II. The struggle for the primacy of Rome : Developments before the eleventh century, 137.—The pope as " universal Ordinary " from Leo IX to Gregory VII, 140.—Episcopal opposition before 1076, 142.—Opposition at the synod of Worms, 1076.—Later opposition, 145.—The Anonymous of York, 146.

III. The struggle to compel the monarchy to accept the " right order " : Modification of the theory of the Two Powers : Attacks on the sacramental conception of kingship, 147.—The royalist defence, 148.—The deposition of Henry IV, 151.— Extension of the power to bind and loose to earthly affairs, 152.—Infallibility of the Roman church, 153.—The world drawn into the sphere of the Church, 154.—Disciplinary power of the pope and his claim to obedience, 154.—Basis of Gregory's claim to political authority, 155.— Means by which Roman authority was extended, 156.—Change in meaning of the " Two Powers "

CHAP.   PAGE

theory, 158.—Abandonment of the doctrine of
non-resistance, 159.—Caused by the new position
of the papacy, 160.—Revolutionary results of
Gregory's papacy, 161.

EPILOGUE   162–169
Theme of the Investiture Contest, 162.—Its causes,
163.—Character of Gregory's VII views, 164.—
Their religious basis, 166.—Catholic and Protestant attitudes towards the State, 167.

APPENDIX I : HENRY III's CHURCH POLICY.   .   169–177

APPENDIX II : PROPRIETARY CHURCH LEGISLA-
TION, 900–1039   178–179

APPENDIX III : VICTOR II AND STEPHEN IX   .   180–182

APPENDIX IV : THE GREGORIAN IDEA OF FREE-
DOM IN RECENT LITERATURE   .   .   .   183–185

APPENDIX V : CLUNY AND GREGORY VII   .   .   186–192

INDEX   193–196

ABBREVIATIONS

AA.SS.	*Acta Sanctorum Bollandiana.*
AUF.	*Archiv für Urkundenforschung.*
Barraclough	G. Barraclough, *Mediaeval Germany*, vol. ii.
Bouquet	M. Bouquet, *Recueil des historiens des Gaules et de la France*, (1869).
Bruel	A. Bernard et A. Bruel, *Recueil des chartes de l'abbaye de Cluny*, (1876 sqq.).
Calmet	A. Calmet, *Histoire ecclésiastique et civile de Lorraine*, (1728).
Carlyle	R. W. and A. J. Carlyle, *A History of Medieval Political Theory in the West*, 6 vols. (1903 sqq.).
Chrimes	S. B. Chrimes, *Kingship and Law in the Middle Ages* (trans. of Kern, q.v., *infra*).
CSEL.	*Corpus scriptorum ecclesiasticorum Latinorum*, Vienna, 1866 sqq.
EHR.	*English Historical Review.*
Harnack, DG.	G. C. A. Harnack, *Lehrbuch der Dogmengeschichte*, 3 vols. (1905–10).
HJ.	*Historisches Jahrbuch der Görresgesellschaft.*
HPM.	*Historiae Patriae Monumenta*, Turin, 1836 sqq.
HZ.	*Historische Zeitschrift.*
JL.	Ph. Jaffé, *Regesta Pontificum Romanorum*, 2nd. ed., ed. S. Loewenfeld, F. Kaltenbrunner and P. Ewald, 2 vols. (1885–8).
Kern	F. Kern, *Gottesgnadentum und Widerstandsrecht im früheren Mittelalter*, (1914).
Mansi	J. M. Mansi, *Sacrorum conciliorum nova et amplissima collectio*, (1759 sqq.).
MGH.	*Monumenta Germaniae Historica.*
	Auct. Ant. Auctores antiquissimi.
	Capit. Capitularia regum Francorum (Legum sectio II).
	Conc. Concilia (Legum sectio III).
	Const. Constitutiones et acta publica imperatorum et regum (Legum sectio IV).
	D with initial of king. *Diplomata regum et imperatorum Germaniae* (DO I = *Diplomata Ottonis I*, etc.).
	Epp. Epistolae.
	Epp. sel. Epistolae selectae.
	Lib. de lite Libelli de lite imperatorum et pontificum saec. xi et xii conscripti.
	LL. Leges.
	Poet. lat. Poetae latini.
	Script. rer. Germ. Scriptores rerum Germanicarum in usum scholarum.
	SS. Scriptores.
MIÖG. *or* MÖIG.	*Mitteilungen des Instituts für oesterreichische Geschichtsforschung* or (since 1923) *Mitteilungen des oesterreichischen Instituts für Geschichtsforschung.*
Mirbt	C. Mirbt, *Die Publizistik im Zeitalter Gregors VII*, (1894).
MPG.	J. P. Migne, *Patrologia cursus completus, series Graeca.*
MPL.	J. P. Migne, *Patrologia cursus completus, series Latina.*
NA.	*Neues Archiv der Gesellschaft für ältere deutsche Geschichtskunde.*

QF.   *Quellen und Forschungen aus italienischen Archiven und Bibliotheken.*

S B. d. Bayr.
   A k.
S B. d. Preuss.
   A k.   *Sitzungsberichte der Bayrischen [Preussischen] Akademie der Wissenschaften.*

Scheeben-   M. J. Scheeben, *Handbuch der katholischen Dogmatik,* ed.
  Atzberger   L. Atzberger (1898).

Thiel   A. Thiel, *Epistolae Romanorum Pontificum,* (1868).

ZKG.   *Zeitschrift fur Kirchengeschichte.*

ZRG.   *Zeitschrift der Savigny-Stiftung für Rechtsgeschichte.*

CHAPTER I

FUNDAMENTAL PRINCIPLES

THE Investiture Controversy, the examination of which is the purpose of this book, was a struggle for right order in the world. To justify this assertion we shall have to go far afield, and study first of all the medieval principles of world-order and universal rule. They originated in early Christian times and can, like so much of the spiritual side of early medieval civilisation, only be grasped when regarded as a development of late classical and early Christian cultural traditions. Our first object, therefore, is to understand the religious conception of the hierarchy as a purely spiritual order, to show how the extent of an individual's subjection to God made him either ruler or subject, and how, in this way, the whole of Creation was thought of as a series of grades or degrees.

From the earliest times there is noticeable a tendency to claim validity for hierarchical distinctions on earth as well as in the Hereafter. It was easily admitted that the servant of God may be considered to have a special aptitude for the leadership of his fellow-men, and that a special rank should therefore be accorded him even on earth. Such a connexion between religious and secular status was promoted by the structure of medieval law, with its peculiar differentiation of subjective rights, formally corresponding to the gradations of religious worth. Further, the sacred character of the medieval conception of justice must at the same time be kept in mind, for only so does the force of the demand for the right ordering of the world become comprehensible.

The inconsistent attitude which Christianity had at first taken up towards the world had long prevented the extension of the Church's hierarchical doctrine into the secular sphere. No one who regarded the world as something that must remain alien to the kingdom of God could demand the

dominance of His servants in it; but if the world were
regarded as Christian, then the validity of Christian
principles had to be claimed for it as well. Before proceeding further, therefore, we must explain the divergent views
of the world which are to be found in primitive Christianity,
since we shall have, at a later stage, to study their subsequent development.

Three preliminary sketches, then, are necessary before
we can turn to a description of the hierarchical idea in the
early middle ages and of its historical influence in the
eleventh century:

    I. The principle of religious order and the early
       Christian concept of liberty.
   II. The structure of medieval law and its concept of
       liberty.
  III. The attitude of early Christianity towards the
       world.

I

Freedom has always been regarded as something
supremely worthy of human contemplation and endeavour.
Men have boasted and proclaimed their freedom, whether
it idealised a beautiful body or a moral sense, whether it
dwelt in a community of men or whether they longed for
and seemed to have found it, under the guise of religious
freedom, in the ultimate problems of human existence.
Though seldom very clearly understood, it has been visual-
ised in many shapes. It has often been negatively defined,
as that which it is *not*: that man is free, it might be said,
who does not blindly follow nature, impulse or passion, and
who is not at the mercy of tyrants, evil spirits or demons.
But wherever deeper thought has been given to the matter,
the conclusion has always been reached that this is to miss
the essential point that freedom from something always
goes with dependence on something else, and that this
dependence forms the positive content of freedom. The
attempt, therefore, to discover what freedom in its highest
sense really is, involves deciding what we are ultimately
dependent on.

Of the twin concepts, freedom and service, it is service which has dominated the Christian conscience, while freedom has been regarded as its magical reflex, as the glory contained within it. The devout have striven to surrender themselves in limitless obedience to their God, to follow His will so entirely that the sinful force of the private will, driving them away from Him, ceased to exist.

"My yoke is light, my burden is easy:" these words have been a source of consolation in all Christian ages. The fact that the Synoptics often speak of imitation, service and surrender, but never of freedom, harmonises well with the feeling of many classical and early medieval minds. Their hope is in that subjection to Christ which shall be at the end of time, their desire is to realise the image of it here and now. Of it Origen wrote: "What manner of subjection is this? I believe it is that state in which we should desire to be subject to Him, even as the Apostles are, and all the saints who have followed Christ."[1]

St John's Gospel treats the idea of freedom seriously, but mentions it only once (viii. 31 sq.), and this passage may well be dependent on St Paul, the real creator of the Christian conception of freedom. This conception is repeated again and again in St Paul's letters. The Epistle to the Romans says: "Know ye not, that to whom ye yield yourselves servants to obey, his servants ye are to whom ye obey; whether of sin unto death, or of obedience unto righteousness? But God be thanked, that ye were the servants of sin, but ye have obeyed from the heart that form of doctrine which was delivered you. Being then made free from sin, ye became the servants of righteousness. . . . For when ye were the servants of sin, ye were free from righteousness. . . . But now being made free from sin, and become servants to God, ye have your fruit unto holiness, and the end everlasting life."[2] Here we have a formula which is fundamental to the Christian idea of freedom, a formula which, when combined with fragments of late

---

[1] Origen, Περι ἀρχῶν in the Latin translation of Rufinus, I. 6. i. (*Griech. Christl. Schriftsteller*, Origenes v, ed. Kötschau, p. 79.)

[2] *Romans* vi. 16–22; and cf. *ibid.* xiv. 4, I *Cor.* vii. 22, *Gal.* i. 10, I *Pet.* ii. 16.

classical philosophy and reinforced by evangelical piety, became one of the most valuable inheritances handed down either directly or by way of the Fathers (notably St Augustine) to medieval times. If we take this formula as our starting-point it is easy to trace the development of the early Christian idea of freedom and its implications.

The basis of this Christian conception was that every servitude was connected with a corresponding freedom; in short, to every " free from " there corresponds a " bound to." The true content of any freedom is the very dependence of which it is the consequence, and from this derive twin conceptions of freedom—as something false, wretched and fugitive, or as a true, noble and lofty ideal. " And Thou freest us from the chains which we forged for ourselves, if we rise no more against Thee in the wantonness of false freedom from desire to possess more, and with the doom of losing all, loving ourselves more than Thee, the All-God."[1] It is, therefore, possible to possess a certain type of freedom—that, namely, which is the result of being cut off from God and from the divine purpose—through the act of disobedience to the divine command, and this is the freedom of the evil man, who is the slave of unrighteousness. The Christian, however, who is free from sin, and serves righteousness, is God's bondman.

Man desires good; but when, regarding it as the command of the Law, he strives by his own efforts to attain to the good, it soon becomes clear that it is beyond his reach. For he is weak, and instead of doing the good which he desires, he does the evil which he hates. But Christ through His sacrificial death gained divine grace for man, and through grace man obtained the power to do good from inner necessity ; thus Christ overcame the compulsion and bondage of the law by removing the reason for their existence. For one who acts according to an inner sense of law, external law would mean merely a departure from the instinctive standards which guide him. This is fundamental to the ethic of Christian freedom; above all else, the moral revolution implicit in Christianity means that

[1] Augustine, *Confessions*, III. viii. 16 (CSEL. XXXIII. 1, 58).

dependence on lesser loyalties has been replaced by bondage
to God. " Where the spirit of the Lord is, there is liberty."
St John's first Epistle (ii. 4) emphasises this identification:
" He that saith, I know Him, and keepeth not His commands, is a liar and the truth is not in him."[1]

The will is free when it is good and is in harmony with
that of the Godhead.[2] Here we meet the second decisive
and formative characteristic of freedom, through which it
becomes clear how dependence can be regarded as freedom.
The psychology of Christian freedom is closely related to
the ideas of the Stoics, and was influenced by their writings
just as the time when it began itself to assume a more
scholarly form. St Paul himself may, through Philo, have
been acquainted with Stoic doctrine; but its influence was
not decisive, for though, like the Evangelists, St Paul may
have perceived ideas which were later to be more fully
developed, his mission was to bring first principles to
practical realization.

As his goal, as true freedom, the Stoic set before his eyes
life in inner accord with itself, with justice, virtue and
nature. Only so was restraint possible, and with it true
wisdom and happiness, and the control of the passions by
reason. How were these to be secured? The Stoic replied,
" By the wise man seizing on and freely willing that Good
which he perceives in virtue of his participation in universal
reason, and gaining thereby the freedom to do as he will,
because he wills only the Good."[3]

Clement of Alexandria, the first important Christian
student of the philosophy of religion, introduced many
Stoic formulae into his works. He writes, for instance,
" We know freedom, through which alone Our Lord has
freed us, redeeming us from lusts, desires and other passions." Ambrose of Milan recognises willing servitude;

[1] On this section see *Romans* vii; cf. Lietzmann, *Handbuch zum Neuen
Testament*, viii. 74 sq., H. Jonas, *Augustin und das paulinische Freiheits-
problem*, p. 48. Cf. also *John* xiv. 15 and 23; 2 *Cor.* iii. 17; *Gal.* v.
[2] See in particular Augustine, *De civ. Dei*, xiv. 11, in CSEL. XL. 2,
28 sq.: " arbitrium igitur voluntatis tunc est vere liberum, cum vitiis
peccatisque non servit."
[3] Cicero, *De officiis*, i. 70, says expressly: " . . . libertate . . ., cuius proprium est sic vivere, ut velis." Cf. *Paradoxa*, v. 1: " Quid est libertas?
Potestas vivendi ut velis."

Augustine often shows the influence of Stoic thought. The Christian philosophers felt themselves in many ways related to the Stoics and identified many of the latters' ideas with their own.[1] In fact, however, similarity of verbal expression was frequently greater than real similarity of thought. The Stoic wise man wills the laws of philosophically abstract universal reason, even if he grants them an almost religious character, whereas the Christian wills the commands of a personal God, whose Son became flesh, appeared on earth, redeemed the world, and made it obedient to the Father. For the Stoic, freedom is the independence of his inner self from everything external and not willed by him; for the Christian it is absolute dependence on God. The Stoic's will is passionless, governed by the intellect, calm, moderate and finely-balanced. The true Christian wills with an intensity of feeling which extinguishes self and unites him with God; his will is love.

The wonderful freedom of the children of God, secured by God's love and in its turn producing love, is an idea for the introduction of which to the Christian consciousness the often-quoted sentences of St John and St Paul are mainly responsible. Nearly all the rapturous outbursts of later times make explicit reference to the two Apostles. Through love alone does bondage become the free and joyful obedience of children to parents, which, in comparison with slavish subjection, means an increased obligation and a greater reverence. " The truly devout man lets himself be led by love to Him who is really worthy of love and to that which must come to pass." Fear is changed into love ; this is the new life-giving law of freedom (*vivificatrix lex*). " This is free service before the Lord, where love and not necessity serveth."[2]

[1] Clemens Alex., *Strom.* III, v. 44, 4. (*Griech. Christl. Schriftsteller,* Clemens Alex. ii., ed. Stählin, p. 216.)

[2] *John* xiv. 15 and 23; 1 *Cor.* xiii; *Gal.* iii. 26, iv. 7, v. 1 and 13; 1 *John* ii, etc. See also: Irenaeus, *Contra haereses,* IV. xvi. 5 (MPG. 7 col. 1018 sq.) and IV. xxxiv. 4 (*ibid.,* col. 1085): " vivificatrix lex, libertatis lex;" Augustine, *Enarr. in Psalm.* 99, 7 (MPL. 37 col. 1275): " Libera servitus est apud Dominum; libera servitus, ubi non necessitas, sed charitas servit;" Augustine, *De mor.* i. 30, 63 (MPL. 32 col. 1336): " Tu parentibus filios libera quadam servitute subiungis, parentes filiis pia dominatione praeponis."

These ideas underwent important developments in St Augustine. He sees the ability to love directed towards many objects. Our minds are not shaped by what we know, but by what we love. The only true virtue is to love that which we ought to love. " And what," asks Augustine, " can we more worthily make the object of our love than God? Let him who rejoices in freedom strive to be free from the love of transitory things, let him who takes pleasure in ruling become subject to God, the ruler of all, and love Him more than himself. For this is full righteousness, to love the higher more than the lower." Augustine's insight here unerringly seizes upon the multiplicity of freedoms which has already been indicated. Love produces dependence upon that towards which it is directed; there are as many dependences as there are objects of love, and as many freedoms as dependences.[1]

These dependences can be distinguished according to their strength, and the degree of freedom corresponds naturally to the degree of closeness in the relationship. Freedom can be increased, and it is this fact which shows how rich the early Christian idea of freedom was in potentialities of development, in spite of its essential homogeneity. The degree of nearness to God, the intensity of freedom, differentiates the merits of individuals. Perfection is no more to be obtained on earth by the Christian than is pure wisdom by the Stoic, but the closest possible approach to the final happy state is the goal of each. Since the vital importance of free-will was admitted, the relative goodness or badness of a man's moral conduct showed how near he had approached to the ideal; but the gift of faith was not necessarily bestowed equally on every believer, for Christ himself had said that its amount might vary. And so the question " Who should be the greatest in the kingdom of God? " was not merely raised but was also definitely answered.[2]

[1] Cf. Augustine, *Ep.* 155, 13 (CSEL. XLIV. 443).

[2] On the differing degrees of grace, cf. *Matth.* xviii. 1, *Mark* ix. 34, *Romans* xii. 3 sq., 1 *Cor.* xii. 4 sq., *Ephes.* iv. 7, and Lietzmann, *Handbuch*, viii. 108 and ix. 62. Also Augustine, *Ep.* 157, 2, 8, (CSEL. XLIV. 454): " Haec enim voluntas libera tanto erit liberior quanto sanior, tanto autem sanior quanto divinae misericordiae gratiaeque subiectior."

It was in the search for an answer to this question that the stream of classical mysticism, of Neo-Platonic and Neo-Pythagorean philosophy, mingled with that of Christian thought, permanently affecting both its direction and its colour. Christian philosophers regarded Plato as the pupil of the prophets, or at least believed that he had come nearer to a true knowledge of God than any of the other heathen philosophers. The two great Alexandrians, Clement and Origen, together with St Augustine, and, following him, pope Gregory I, must be given a place of honour among those who remodelled Platonism and transmitted it to later Christian thought. Next to them in influence were the writings attributed to Dionysius the Areopagite. In particular the metaphysical doctrines of the creation and the salvation of the created were by this means introduced into Christian thought. " God is the fire and the angels are the flames.of the fire, and the saints glow at His breath, but they who are fallen away from the love of God, are become cold in their love toward Him." God creates the world out of His own will, and the angelic hosts are in immediate subjection to Him, while His creatures surround Him in ever-widening circles, enslaved to demons and to a transitory life in penance for their sinful backsliding. But His grace creates love, which aspires again to Him, and the end is the freeing of all from punishment and slavery. The whole of creation will once more, as at the beginning, be at one with God. " From love man returns back into God, seeking to bring himself into subjection to God, not to make himself equal with Him. . . . The more he directs his utmost efforts towards this end, the more blessed and the more exalted will he become, and he will be boundlessly free (*liberrimus*) under the sole domination of God."[1]

[1] This section is mainly based on Origen, Περι ἀρχῶν, I. 5 sq. (ed. Kötschau, p. 68 sq.). The first quotation comes from *ibid.*, II. 8, 3 (p. 156). Augustine's famous polemic against Origen (*De civ. Dei*, xi. 23, CSEL. XL. 1, 544) shows the main ground of difference between them: Origen had falsely taught, says St Augustine, that this world was not created as something good in itself, but only as a punishment for sin; in reality, however, the whole creation is good, including the sinners, just as a painting has dark colours in the right places. The second quotation in the text is from Augustine, *De mor.*, i. 12, 21 (MPL. 32 col. 1320). On Augustine's Platon-

Thus there emerges the picture of a pyramidal structure of free existences, in which the parts are linked not only to God but also to each other. It is God's will that peace shall rule, peace which is a foretaste of the eternal peace which shall be when all things have returned back into God. A double relationship is therefore set up: the superiority of the higher beings, the guardians of the more lowly-placed, and the obedience of these latter to their superiors. "Men should rule the beasts, the angels men, and the archangels angels" (Gregory I). This God-ordained hierarchy is still more highly-articulated, however; even among men on earth it is natural that those who are spiritually more advanced should be entrusted with power over those who are in need of their guidance. It fitted in well with the general development of Catholic thought to identify this metaphysically-conceived and purely spiritual order with the actually existing gradations of society. And this identification was made with increasing frequency, especially in regard to the priesthood, which was particularly concerned with the business of salvation and endowed with grace-giving powers. Throughout the whole middle ages a story was constantly repeated from the ecclesiastical historian Rufinus, to the effect that Constantine had told certain bishops, who were accused before him, that they were gods, ordained by the true God, had quashed the proceedings, and thrown the indictment in the fire. Gregory I repeats this tale in a passage where, as was so often done after him, he was laying stress on quotations from the Bible in which priests are called gods and angels.[1]

A metaphysical evaluation of earthly merit was reached in yet another way. Jesus had commanded; "Whosoever

ism cf. H. Fuchs, *Augustin und der antike Friedensgedanke*, in *Neuphilol. Untersuchungen*, iii. (1926). pp 59 sqq., and H. Leisegang, *Der Ursprung der Lehre Augustins von der civitas dei*, in *Arch. f. Kulturgesch.* xvi. (1925), pp. 127 sqq.

[1]Cf. Origen, Περι άρχων, I.6,2 (ed. Kötschau,pp.79 sqq.). On St Augustine's conception of peace, see H. Fuchs, *ut supra*. The quotations from Gregory the Great are from *Moralia*, iv. 29, 55 (MPL. 75 col. 665) and *Reg.*, v. 36 (MGH. *Epp.*, i. 318).—It is fully in accordance with the general development of ideas that clerical-hierarchical influence falls into the background with the Alexandrians (cf. Harnack, DG. i. 413 and note 3) and becomes dominant again later, e.g., under Gregory I.

will be great among you, let him be your minister, and whosoever will be chief among you, let him be your servant."
The words " great among you " were naturally meant in
relation to the future kingdom of God, and were understood
in that sense.   Devout Christians strove not only to be the
servants of God, but to earn the title of " servants of the
servants of God " as well; and yet at the same time they
demanded that a man's rank on earth should correspond
to his rank before God.   Admonitions were constantly
directed to kings and princes, calling upon them to serve
their subjects as Christ had commanded, and thus to prove
themselves rulers by true divine right.   On the other hand,
a position of rank and dignity was demanded on earth for
the trusted servants of God.   To be submissive in the service of God was no disgrace, but a mark of the highest
nobility.   " Why should man also not serve, since the
Lord of Lords hath served us? "   St Augustine had already
expressed this idea clearly and proudly: " We bishops are
indeed your servants, but in Jesus. Through Him we are
servants, through Him we also are free. The bishop, who
is set over many, is a servant in those things wherein the
Lord Jesus Himself serveth."[1]

But many centuries were to pass, changing the face of a
world still foreign to the kingdom of God, before the world's
" true emperor " should be that bishop whose proudest
title was expressed in the words *servus servorum Dei.*

II

Liberty, according to Cicero, consists in living as one
wills.[2]   This involves a freedom from all restraint: for the
individual, freedom from bodily want, from prison and
slavery; for the body politic, freedom from the dominance
of alien races.   This primitive conception of freedom is the
same in every language, for it takes no account of the

---

[1] *Matth.* xviii. 1, xx. 25 sq., xxiii. 11, *Mark* ix. 35, x. 43, *Luke* xxii. 25.
On the spiritual position of secular rulers, see Kern, pp. 53 sq. (= Chrimes,
pp. 27 sqq.) and G. Morin, *Discours inédit de S. Aug. pour l'ordination d'un
évêque,* in *Rev. bénédictine,* xxx. (1913) 398 sq.
[2] *De offic.* i. 70: " cuius proprium est sic vivere, ut velis." Cf. note 3,
supra, p. 5.

positive content of freedom, and is satisfied with a simple absence of restraint. Everywhere and in all ages blood has been shed and battles fought for the " freedom of the fatherland."

On the other hand, the freedom which men have sought to realise within a human society, and which is shared by all the individuals forming the society, is a many-sided freedom; in it, a balance has to be struck between right and duty, and there are many ways of doing this. Freedom of this kind is always the solution of a cultural problem; in its solution each people reveals its cultural values, and the many-sidedness of the idea itself is reflected in the different ways in which it can be expressed both in thought and in language.

A short sketch of Roman ideas on the subject is a necessary preliminary to an examination of the medieval conception of freedom, for a comparison of the two will help us to understand the latter; and to observe the influence of classical tradition is the medieval historian's constant duty.

Cicero, in the *De Re Publica*, showed clearly what he understood by a free people: " freedom, " he wrote, " dwells in no state where the people does not possess supreme authority; nothing is more to be prized than freedom, but when it is not the same for all, then it is in nowise freedom." The Romans dated their freedom from the expulsion of the kings and the assumption of authority by the people. Legal differences of status gradually disappeared, so that classical Roman freedom meant the equal participation of all citizens in self-government. Freedom consisted in each man surrendering to others as much power over himself as others for their part surrendered to him, and this found practical expression when each citizen had his turn in office and his share in legislative action. All were free, for none was bound more than another by the self-imposed law.[1]

---

[1] Cicero, *De re publ.*, i. 47, and *De lege agraria*, ii. 102: " vos quorum gratia in suffragiis consistit, libertas in legibus, honos in iudiciis et aequitate magistratuum." In general see T. Mommsen, *Römisches Staatsrecht*, iii. (3rd ed., 1887) 63, 458, 655 and *passim*. On the equality of duty, see esp. Cicero, *De re publ.*, i. 69: " aequabilitatem . . . qua carere diutius vix possunt liberi."

Equality before the law is something quite familiar to the modern world, but a long development, in which the reception of late Roman law marked an epoch, was necessary before the present position was reached, for in no age before the present was the principle of equality so widely realised as in the later Roman republic and the empire. The reason for this lies in the Romans' gift for logical thought, which made it possible for them to systematise individual cases and regulate them according to abstract norms. Such rules could then conveniently be brought into logical harmony with each other, and were admirably suited for the creation of a system. This abstract, objective system of law was self-sufficient, and, backed by the state's authority, imposed an order and a pattern upon daily life. It had before it a plurality of equal citizens, each possessing the same subjective rights, the same freedom and—in principle at least—the same share in government and the same capacity at private law. " The objective order defined the boundaries of freedom abstractly and equally for all; within these bounds the free individual will could mark out its own territory."[1]

In practical political life, however, equality of constitutional rights can never be maintained: fate distributes political talents with unequal hand. The Roman realised this fact, and accepted it, without fundamentally undermining his position as a citizen—his *dignitas*, his *libertas*—when, out of independent conviction, he put his trust in the best qualified, recognised his *auctoritas*, and in his own interests freely surrendered a part of his power, without thereby permanently binding himself in principle. *Auctoritas* has long been recognised as the strongest moral principle in Roman political life.[2]

The senate was the repository of political authority *par excellence*. *Senatus auctoritas populique Romani libertas* are practically inseparable ideas. But individuals also based their power on *auctoritas*. It was not felt to be a

---

[1] Cf. O. Gierke, *Das deutsche Genossenschaftsrecht*, ii. (1873) 27 sq., 130 and iii. (1881) 36 sqq.

[2] R. Heinze, *Auctoritas*, in *Hermes*, lx. (1925) p. 363

diminution of freedom if the people voluntarily recognised authority and surrendered some of its share in government; tyranny and slavery were only seen where an individual or a party seized power without the tacit consent of the people and the latter were ruled against their will. Thus submission to authority was the basis of the Roman principate, for in theory the *princeps* was no monarch, but only an official, to whom the people had voluntarily handed over its power. Even in the days when the Roman emperors were absolute monarchs, their power was still held to be based upon the autonomy of the Roman citizens, for the people, in the *lex regia*, had surrendered them its whole power.[1]

This imperial Roman conception of freedom was also familiar to the Christian Fathers. Ambrose writes to Theodosius I: " Nothing so well becomes an emperor such as you, as when you love the liberty of those who are bound to you by the obedience of a soldier. This indeed is the difference between good and bad princes, that the good love liberty, and the wicked love slavery." Gregory I's words are even clearer: " For this is the difference between the kings of the barbarians and the Roman emperors, that the former are the lords of slaves, the latter of freemen."[2]

Citizenship in the Roman sense, however, made little impression upon the early middle ages. The medieval state grew from essentially different roots. The notion of equality of rights and the transference of authority were in origin foreign to medieval thought, which took a far simpler view of the grounds of political obligation. Among occasional remarks, however, which show the influence of Roman ideas of freedom, may be noticed the quotation, in

---

[1] See the article *Auctoritas* in *Thesaurus linguae latinae*, ii., esp. pp. 1225 sqq. on *senatus auctoritas*. On the theory of delegation in the Corpus juris civilis, cf. *Inst.* I. 2, 6 (ed. Mommsen): " Sed et quod principi placuit, legis habet vigorem, cum lege regia, quae de imperio eius lata est, populus ei et in eum omne suum imperium et potestatem concessit."

[2] Ambrose, *Ep.* xl. 2 (MPL. 16 col. 1148)—note his reliance on Cicero, *De lege agr.*, ii. 9; Gregory I, *Ep.* xi. 4 and xiii. 34 (MGH. *Epp.*, ii. 263 and 297), and, in conjunction therewith, Livy, *Ab urbe condita libri*, xlv. 18. See also Leo the Great, *Sermo* lxxxii, (MPL. 54 col. 425 sq.).

the late eleventh century treatise *De unitate ecclesiae conservanda*, of the words of Gregory I quoted above; John of Salisbury, too, seems to have been indebted to Roman thought when, in his comparison of the good prince and the tyrant, he wrote: " the prince defends the laws and the freedom of the people, but the tyrant thinks he has done nothing unless he destroys the laws and brings the people into slavery."[1]

In a more indirect way, the Roman conception of political freedom forced itself upon the middle ages through a prayer in the royal and imperial Mass, where God's assistance is asked " so that, the enemies of peace being over- come, Roman liberty may serve Thee in security." The Romans were certain that their freedom was peculiar to them: " other nations can suffer slavery, but freedom is natural to the Romans." Even if others are free, only the Roman people possesses true freedom—the freedom of a civilised and cultured race in contrast to the merely communal life of the barbarians. It was in this form that *libertas romana* was accepted into the liturgy, and, since *imperium romanum* was identified with Christendom, *libertas romana* came to mean the free civilised community of the Christian Roman Empire.[2]

[1] *Lib. de unitate eccl. conserv.*, i. 2 (MGH. *Lib. de lite*, ii. 185); John of Salisbury, *Policraticus*, iv. 1 and vii. 17 (MPL. 199 col. 513 and 777; ed. C. C. J. Webb, i. 235 and ii. 160–6). Cf. also Lambert of Hersfeld, *Annales*, ad ann. 1076 (ed. Holder-Egger, MGH. *Script. rer. Germ.*, p. 270): " Hanc regis ac tiranni esse distantiam, quod hic vi atque crudelitate obedientiam extorqueat ab invitis, ille legibus ac more maiorum moderetur subiectis praecipiatque facienda." Also *ibid.* ad ann. 1073 (p. 152): " Si ita faceret, se promptissimo animo ei sicut hactenus servituros, eo tamen modo, quo ingenuos homines atque in libero imperio natos regi servire oporteret." The quotation from a letter of Gregory I is also included in the collection of canons of Cardinal Deusdedit, *lib.* iv. c. 105 (ed. Wolf von Glanvell [1905], p. 446).
[2] Cf. Cicero, *Phil.*, vi. 19: "Aliae nationes servitutem pati possunt, populi Romani est propria libertas." The prayer known as the " secret " in the *Sacramentarium Gelasianum* (ed. H. A. Wilson, *The Gelasian Sacramentary*, 1894) shows Frankish influence even in the oldest manuscript (*Cod. Vat. Regin.* 316, late vii cent.), and runs: " Suscipe Domine, preces et hostias ecclesiae tuae, pro salute famuli tui illius supplicantis, et protectione fidelium populorum antiqua brachii tui operare miracula; ut, superatis pacis inimicis, secura tibi serviat Romana libertas." Cf. Tellenbach, *Römischer und Christlicher Reichsgedanke in der Liturgie des frühen Mittelalters*, in *Sitzungsb. d. Heidelberger Akad. d. Wiss.* (1934–35), Heft 1, p. 14 sq.

From its place in the liturgy, the Roman conception of freedom exercised an influence upon literature. Prolonged research would bring much evidence to light, but a few instances may be cited in passing. In one of his poems, Gerbert (pope Sylvester II) says that *libertas romana* has perished through the fury of the Gothic sword. Benzo, a publicist of the imperial party during the struggle over investitures, seems to be thinking of this freedom when he records that God intervened in a battle between the supporters of Alexander II and Honorius II, and brought victory to the latter, who were fighting *pro libertate imperii*, by sending the Apostles with white banners to their assistance. An interesting combination of this conception of freedom with that of the Roman church occurs in the *Liber de unitate ecclesiae*: " The Roman church is the mother of all the churches that make up the One Catholic Church, and the *dignitas Romani nominis* "—a term which, incidentally, is liturgical in origin—" is said to be the head and mistress of the peoples who belong to Rome; because it is free, it secures the freedom of all those who are under its rule (*civilitate sua*)."[1]

Subjective right, the freedom of the individual, is often described as ability, as strength, as the indwelling *virtus* of a man. But it can also be defined by its limits; the realm of possibility, in other words, becomes most clear when its frontiers are considered. Law for the Romans is a boundary enclosing and protecting an area which it does not occupy, and which is therefore free; freedom exists where no limitations are imposed. Roman thought did not entirely ignore the conception of freedom as an indwelling force, but was nevertheless content to accept the view that the chief qualities of freedom are negative. The limits, in this view, are the same for all. If therefore these limits, and not differences in individual power or merit, beget the conception of freedom, then the amount of freedom must also be

---

[1] MPL. 139, col. 287 : " . . . gladio bacchante Gothorum Libertas Romana perit;" on the other hand Cardinal Humbert, in a work of which only fragments are preserved, contrasts the false Roman freedom (cf. 1 *Pet.* ii. 16) and the true freedom which is reached through the Church: cf. Schramm, *Kaiser, Rom und Renovatio*, ii. (1929) 130.

the same for all. Consequently, freedom to the Romans had a general and abstract character which to some extent disregarded concrete relationships.

The middle ages, on the other hand, could not conceive the freedom of the individual as part of an objective legal system, because the latter, in its modern or Roman sense, was at best only partially realised in the medieval state. Medieval law, coloured by its Germanic origins, is nothing more than the totality of the rights of individuals. There is no abstract conception of law, and, as Gierke says, " an abstract conception of freedom is equally lacking."

In common with other periods, the middle ages sought to define freedom as independence; but the correlative dependence was special or individual, not general, and defied conceptual definition. The *libertas* of a church, for instance, might consist in its independence of the diocesan bishop—but this is not to say that it was not subject to some other ecclesiastical authority. A man may be free (*liberrimus*) in regard to all others, but the serf (*servus*) of a particular lord.[1]

Yet the positive characteristics of freedom were more important to the middle ages than its negative limitations. The *libertas* of the clergy can mean not only freedom from lay control, but also the capacity and the mission of " ruling angels and men." Moreover, *privilegium* is often used in the same sense as *libertas*; and it must here be remarked that *privilegium* must not be given its original meaning of " exception from the law." The medieval sense becomes clear if we consider the theory of privilege advanced by cardinal Humbert, one of the greatest reformers of the eleventh century, and we can at the same time see how easily the middle ages regarded not only men, but also things, land, buildings, villages or churches, as

---

[1] On the following, see Gierke, *Genossenschaftsrecht*, ii. 30 sqq. and 127, esp. note 1; Kern § 5 (= Chrimes, pp. 70 sqq.); and Kern, *Recht und Verfassung im Mittelalter*, HZ. 120 (1920) pp. 1 sqq. (= Chrimes, pp. 149 sqq.). Humbert speaks of a villein who is free of all other lords in *Lib. adv. simoniacos*, iii. 10 (MGH. *Lib. de lite*, i. 210): ." Nam quamlibet vilis laicorum servus aut mercennarius nulli praeter eum, cuius est, famulari cogitur eique soli subiacet cum suis rebus, ab aliis liberrimus."

the bearers of privileges, the possessors of *libertates*.[1]

Humbert's purpose is to illustrate the connection between the spiritual office and the church as a material complex—a complex of buildings, goods, and serfs. He heads his exposition " A proof that a possession is worth nothing without its *privilegium*." The privilege of land, he says, is that of possessing and cultivating it (*cultura = licentia habendi et colendi*). If a man acquires cities, provinces or kingdoms, he demands with them the right to hold them and to rule them. In the case of a horse, "privilege" is the right to ride upon it and to make any desired use of it. Similarly, in the case of a bishopric considered as a material concept, episcopal consecration gives the right to rule and administer it.

It is plain that this intimate connection of the idea of *privilegium* or *libertas* with an individual or a thing results in an endless differentiation of privilege. The modern conception of freedom is seldom bound up with an attribute, and if so, the purpose is purely analytical. On the other hand, it was both usual and necessary in the middle ages to speak of my *libertas*, the *libertas* of the church of Mainz, of the city of Worms, of the *ministeriales* of a count, etc. The words *honor, dignitas, status, ius* are used in a similar sense to *libertas* or *privilegium*, and these synonyms must be kept in mind if the medieval conception of freedom is to be rightly understood. When a medieval charter speaks of the *libertas* of a church, it does not mean either that it may not have been the property of a lord or that it was exempt from the exercise of episcopal authority; rather the clerk who drafted the document was referring to a subjective right or to a totality of subjective rights, the status of the church.[2]

The middle ages, it is true, were not altogether incapable

---

[1] Cf. Peter Damian, *Opusc.* xxviii. (MPL. 145 col. 513), where the clerical conception of freedom is also noticeable; Odo, *Sermo* iii. (MPL. 133 col. 724): " Et hoc equidem privilegium utrisque [*sc.* Moses and Benedict] est commune, quod ambo sunt legislatores; " Humbert, *ut sup.*, iii. 2 (pp. 199 sq.); cf. also H. Böhmer, *Das Eigenkirchentum in England*, in *Festgabe fur F. Liebermann* (1921), p. 304, note 1.

[2] Compare with these the class " liberties "—the " liberty " of the nobility, etc.

of equating the *libertates* of different persons or things.
As has been said, it is possible to perceive the beginnings of
an attempt to clothe the conception of freedom in more
abstract and general forms; there is, for example, a *libertas*
of the tribes—the ancient freedom of the Saxons is a case
in point—a *libertas* of churches in general, of the clergy, of
the *ministeriales*. On the other hand, the *libertas* of the
ministerialis Hugo, for instance, is not limited to his share
in the general privileges of the *ministeriales*, but may also
include certain personal claims or duties which distinguish
his *libertas* from that of all the other servants of his lord.

Medieval liberty was ultimately based on the complementary nature of rights and duties. Thus membership
of the folk gave a particular freedom, and this had something of the modern meaning. It is the freedom of those
who are subject only to the king, and only to him in so far
as he fulfils his duties towards them. This comes out
clearly in a story of duke Ernst of Swabia. The duke was
in revolt against his step-father Conrad II, and urged his
vassals to give him the obedience they had sworn. Two
counts raised an objection: " We will not deny that we
swore fidelity to you against all men, but not against him
who placed you over us. Were we the serfs of our king and
emperor, given by him to you, it would not be lawful for us
to separate ourselves from you; but since we are free, and
have our king and emperor as supreme defender of our
freedom on earth, we lose our freedom as soon as we desert
him, and every good man, as a certain writer says (*ut ait
quidam*), loses freedom only with his life." There are difficulties in the way of a complete understanding of this
story, for the term *libertas* is here used without qualification; but the last sentence is quoted from Sallust (*ut ait
quidam*), and Bruno, who wrote about the war between
Henry IV and the Saxons and quoted the same sentence,
changed *libertas* into *libertas mea*, showing, therefore, that
liberty at that time could only be conceived of subjectively.
The real point of the story, therefore, is the idea of a
reciprocal obligation, the conviction that *libertas* would
disappear with the breach of the duty of fidelity to the

emperor, together with the clear opposition, so common in the middle ages, between full freedom—freedom of blood—and bondage.[1]

However, the right of the fully free was, in the middle ages, at bottom essentially the same as the right of the partly free, whereas in antiquity freeman and slave stood in sharpest contrast to each other, the one a person, the other a thing. In the middle ages both were persons, and the rights of both had a similar legal structure. Each possessed a concrete bundle of rights, with corresponding duties. Differences were largely quantitative. The unfree lived under the most widely varying laws, but even the lowest had some rights and were not at their lord's arbitrary disposal. Though bound to the soil, the villein had a claim to his land and could not be separated from it; frequently he had the right only to be judged by his fellow-villeins; and he could only be called upon to do a fixed amount of labour in the fields. Similarly, those who were unfree but not bound to the soil were only liable for limited dues in money and labour. It is characteristic of medieval freedom that it is frequently mentioned in relation to men who were in law either unfree or only partly free; it is common to find the rights of *ministeriales, censuales* or *cerocensuales* described as *libertates*.[2]

One qualification must, however, be made to the statement that from the legal point of view there was a certain resemblance between the states of freedom and unfreedom.

[1] Wipo, *Gesta Chuonradi imp.*, c. 20 (ed. Bresslau, MGH. *Script. rer. Germ.*, p. 40) and Paul von Bernried, *Vita Gregorii VII* (ed. J. M. Watterich, *Pontif. Rom. Vitae*, i. [1862] p. 530): " nec se illi plus quam illum illis alicuius fidelitatis vel subjectionis obnoxios, ut liberi homines. . . ."

[2] Legal historians were long without an adequate picture of the meaning of liberty in the middle ages, and many controversies and laborious hypotheses were the result. It is only in recent years that the relativity and differentiation of the concept of freedom have gradually become clear. Cf. the extremely important remarks of H. Fehr, *Zur Lehre vom mittelalterlichen Freiheitsbegriff, insbes. im Bereiche der Marken*, MÖIG. xlvii. (1933) 290 sqq.—An absurd but revealing use of the word *libertas* occurs in a charter of Archbishop Engelbert of Cologne, dated 1221, and setting forth the unfree status of the villeins of the Abbey of Marienfeld: " litones et homines eidem monasterio quocumque iure pertinentes a condicione et *libertate*, que opido Widenbruke *imposita* est, omnino nostra auctoritate fecimus *liberos* et absolutos." (J. Ficker, *Engelbert der Heilige*, [1853] p. 336, no. 23).

The relationship between king and count was entirely personal; it was a moral obligation upon each to keep faith with the other, and could only be dissolved by mutual consent. On the other hand, while a lord could not interfere with the rights of his villeins, he could, without their consent, transfer to a third party his rights in and duties towards them. In this power of alienation is preserved the original chattel-like character of the unfree, though in a form modified by the development of a sense of personal right.

Yet the analogy of the chattel was far from prejudicing the existence of a *libertas*, for we have already seen that inanimate objects had as many different *libertates* as persons. Among them churches take the first place. Churches had in the middle ages a right which was really *sui generis*; it most closely resembled that of the great estates, though their love of comparisons sometimes tempted medieval writers to compare it with personal, rather than property, rights. Clerical *libertates* were, like all others, susceptible of wide variations. Each church had its own, and this liberty was called " ancient," " proper," " noble," " entire." Yet it was not necessarily complete in our sense; a " proprietary monastery," for example, the private property of its owner, may have come into its lord's hands with certain liberties attached to it, but it remained nevertheless an *Eigenkloster*, and could be transferred from the hands of one owner to those of another without the consent of the monks. Nevertheless episcopal and lay *Eigenklöster* had *libertates*, and so did monastic *Eigenkirchen*. A church could be made more free—the comparative form of the adjective is noteworthy—that is, it could be raised to a more privileged position (*privilegiare, libertare, nobilitare*). To the *nobiles libertates* belong the *libertas* of the imperial monasteries and the *libertas romana* of the churches and monasteries under papal protection. But even their rights were very various; some of the imperial monasteries were alienable, some inalienable, while among the Roman churches some were closely bound to the papacy, others were bound merely in name.

A corresponding use of the word *libertas,* which makes clear its characteristic sense of subjective right, is found in its application to states.   We have only to recall the famous sentence in a letter which Gregory VII wrote to the Hungarian duke Geisa in 1075, where the word *libertas* appears as an attribute of *status* and is qualified by the adjective *propria,* and where in addition the dignity of certain kingdoms is designated *nobilissimus: Notum autem tibi esse credimus, regnum Ungariae, sicut et alia nobilissima regna, in propriae libertatis statu debere esse.*[1]

When the point has been grasped that to the middle ages *libertas* simply means subjective right, and that law is nothing more than the sum of all individual *libertates,* the meaning of a privilege as the reduction to writing of this right becomes fully comprehensible.   A privilege does not —as one might suppose from the modern use of the term— create exceptions to a generally prevailing law; rather it is the precise formulation of an actual and concrete subjective right, that is, of a *libertas.*   The weak and undeveloped state of the objective legal system provides an explanation of the fact that in the middle ages grants of privilege—and under this term are included such different things as the rights of cities, marks or *ministeriales,* and even manorial custom —were far more common than general state legislation.

It is not immediately clear to the modern mind how this multiplicity of varying subjective rights was held together. To-day we have a positive law, through which the subjective rights of every individual can be established.   We have learnt that there must be a positive law, even though it may appear to us in many respects to be a bad law.   To our way of thinking, the public interest demands that this law be applied and maintained.   Each individual is disposed to admit the rights of others, for they are at bottom the same as his own.

What is it, then, which makes for the observation of subjective rights, where there is no feeling of the necessity for positive law, no sense of the " public interest," and

[1] *Reg. Greg. VII,* ii. 63 (ed. Caspar, p. 218), and see Appendix IV.   For a parallel, cf. Suger of St Denis, *Vita Ludovici,* c. 31 (ed. Molinier, p. 118): " regnum nobilissimum Francorum."

no consciousness of equality in rights? It is the ever-present force of the idea of justice. In the middle ages, for instance, the expression "bad law" which we have just used, would have appeared a contradiction in terms. Bad law is no law, but injustice. The law is eternal and indestructible, and the most deeply-rooted evil customs cannot alter it. "The law is a part of the world-order." It exists independently of human observance and human action; nature will automatically avenge any contravention of it. Thus it comes about that law is observed, and the *libertas* whose sheet-anchor it is cannot vanish. It is most significant of the medieval attitude to law that positive law was not made but discovered. The king collects around him the great men of his court and inquires of them what the law is; they reply by giving their opinion, but in so doing they do not feel themselves to be making a decision, but only to be revealing what has always been.

The middle ages had a "public interest" in the law, because it was sacred for everyone. This at least was the main reason. Not only, for example, had the king a sacred right to govern, but the meanest servant of the manor had the sacred right to be free of labour-services on one day in the week. Further, there is a selfish motive behind this public interest. One of the fundamental propositions of medieval natural law was the sentence : " All things whatsoever ye would that men should do to you, do ye even so to them" (Matt. vii. 12). But even when these words were explicitly quoted, contemporaries were thinking more of the sanctity of subjective right than we should readily suppose. Each man's *libertas* was, to their minds, protected by natural law. It was the law of nature that different men and things should have different *libertates*. Natural law is that which should be, in small things as well as in great. It is called a " return to the law of nature " when a rebellious vassal renews his due fealty to his lord; it is contrary to nature when a king violates the rights of his subjects, and looses the bonds of mutual loyalty.

Libertas is the right of every individual. The very foundation of natural law is that every individual's rights must be maintained and defended (*suum cuique ordinem, suam dignitatem, suas leges tutas inviolatasque manere pati*). This is the basis of world-order and stands high above earthly affairs; and the idea of *libertas* is rooted in it.[1]

The principle " to each his own " was not discovered in the middle ages. It was formulated in Roman times; and whatever might be the strength of the positive law, it is of course not to be supposed that natural law ever died out among the Romans any more than among us. It found expression in statements about unjust laws and in the occasional recognition of the competence of the individual conscience to judge the laws, even though political farsightedness demanded the observance of laws which stood condemned by this examination. The Romans were familiar with the distinction between positive law and natural law, and they had also a conception of a law which was common to all peoples, the *jus gentium*. Isidore's *Etymologies* had made all this known to the middle ages long before the study of Roman law was revived, but despite the strength of classical tradition the idea of natural law soon suffered profound modification. For the Romans, natural law is the abstract principle of order in the world and is to be comprehended through reason. Nature is still order in the middle ages, but its creator is God; God and nature were therefore equated, and the commands of both understood through the religious instinct. Lawyers called the eternal order *aequitas*, and the will which directs it *justitia*. God himself is in the fullest and most complete sense *justitia*; men share this *justitia* when they are guided by the divine will, and to be thus guided is " justice " or

---

[1] Augustine, *De civ. Dei*, xix. 13 (CSEL. XL. 2, 395): " ordo est parium dispariumque rerum sua cuique loca tribuens dispositio "; Lambert of Hersfeld, *Annales*, ad an. 1073 (ed. Holder-Egger, MGH. *Script. rer. Germ.*, p. 152): " Sacramento se ei fidem dixisse, sed si ad aedificationem, non ad destructionem aecclesiae Dei rex esse vellet; si iuste, si legittime, si more maiorum rebus moderaretur; si suum cuique ordinem, suam dignitatem, suas leges tutas inviolatasque manere pateretur. Sin . . . pro aecclesia Dei, pro fide christiana, pro libertate etiam sua dimicaturos "; Manegold, *Ad Gebehardum*, c. 47 (MGH. *Lib. de lite*, i. 391): " ad hoc unum aliquem super se populus exaltat, ut . . . cuique sua distribuat . . . omnibus videlicet iusticiam impendat." These examples are intended as illustrations, not as proofs, and could easily be multiplied.

" righteousness."[1] Medieval literature is full of statements
that God is the author of nature, the law or the beginning
of all law, the eternal and true law, the very truth and the
sun of righteousness. Like God, Christ too is eternal
justice, the righteousness of the Father. The earthly ruler,
if he is wise, does well always to consult the eternal law.[2]

All positive law is dependent upon eternal law, from
which it draws its authority, but there are certain legal
rules whose dependence is particularly close, namely those
of " divine canon law." They have been revealed by God,
and the guarantee of their rightness is stronger than that of
any other law, which has only been discovered by human
endeavour. " It is sure and undoubtedly true that the
authority of the canons is the law of God."[3] Even at the
present day, canon law is more in Catholic eyes than mere
law; it is a part of religion. But such a distinction between
law and religion was foreign to the middle ages, despite all
the distinctions which were made between secular and
ecclesiastical law. Secular law, too, was considered a gift of
God, and was felt to have a religious sanction, for in the
middle ages no difference between law and morality was
admitted. It is easy for us to see the difficulties to which
such an attitude leads: how hard it is to understand a law
which derives from a religious and moral consciousness,
and how indefinite such a law must be, finding clear
expression as seldom as religious convictions. Objections
like these, however, were never entertained in the middle
ages. It was an accepted fact that law in general remains
eternally the same and must rule unchallenged, though its
demands in any particular case were less easily defined.

---

[1] *Dig.*, I. 1, 10 (ed. Mommsen, p. 1): " Justicia est constans et perpetua
voluntas ius suum cuique tribuere." Cf. Carlyle, i. 36 sq. on the *ius gentium.*
Fragmentum Pragense, iii, 9, (ed. H. Fitting, *Juristische Schriften des
früheren Mittelalters*, [1876] p. 215): " Est autem iustitia voluntas ius
suum cuique tribuere. Que quidem in Deo plena est et perfecta, in nobis
vero per participationem iustitia esse dicitur."

[2] Cf. *Fragmentum Pragense*, iv. 2 (ed. Fitting, p. 216): "Nihil enim aliud
est equitas quam deus;" and Humbert, *Adv. simoniacos*, i. 21 (MGH.
Lib. de lite, i. 135): " O Deus et domine Spiritus sancte, qui es iustitia
sempiterna. . . ."

[3] From a letter from abbot Siegfried of Gorze to abbot Poppo of Stablo,
written in 1043 (ed. Giesebrecht, *Kaiserzeit*, ii. 714 sqq.).

But it is plain that an ideal must have had overwhelming force when based on that strict and holy law which was God Himself, through observance or contravention of which a man might win or lose immortality.

Thus we see that there were two kinds of order; the eternal order of all creatures round God, and the earthly order of men and things. The inner relationship between them is unmistakable. In the mind of medieval man they often overlap and mingle. To have a standing before God and the law was the positive meaning of *libertas*, and implied taking the place assigned to the individual by the first law of creation: " to each his own." If a definite connection between religious and legal *libertas* did not exist from the very beginning, it was easily forged, as a natural corollary to the relationship between life eternal and the sensual world.

III

From the very beginning, the attitude of Christianity towards the world was determined by various considerations, the application of which was not always consistent. Christ's command had been to preach the kingdom of God to all men, but it was certain that His kingdom was not of this world. His kingdom was a supernatural power working in the world, a law, an order, visible in its fulness only to Himself, and remaining for all others a matter of hope and expectation. Out of Christ's attitude to the world there arose among the early Christians a tendency to withdraw from temporal affairs and to concentrate on the kingdom of Heaven; it was only by slow degrees that there developed the missionary spirit and an attempt to organise this world on the basis of the next. The way in which each Christian century has combined these two primitive tendencies of withdrawal and conversion has been of vital importance.

The life of Christ and his disciples was raised above the world, since they prized nothing that it could give or take away. They rendered to Caesar, the ruler of this world, whatever he might claim, thinking neither of opposition to him nor of his conversion.

Although the first congregations after Christ's lifetime were far more closely bound to the world by ties of family and business, and by the use of the property which they held in common, yet their attitude was fundamentally the same. They awaited the appearance of the promised kingdom of God, and the vicissitudes of this life could not touch them closely. St Paul, however, found it necessary to give directions for temporal behaviour (Rom. xiii). These are governed in the first place by belief in the omnipotence of God and by the conviction that since state and society do actually exist, they must serve some divine purpose. The state's action in maintaining the law and punishing the evil-doer is recognised as having some value for the Christian community. If an earthly ruler acted tyrannically, the early Christians passively accepted him as a punishment from God. The Pauline phrases have lent support to the theocratic state at all times; they were not used in the middle ages simply to defend the state against the Church, as is often thought, but were also accepted by the Church in the very sense which made them so precious to theocratic rulers.

Among the thousands of converts which the Christian religion soon made, people of wealth and political or social eminence were constantly increasing in numbers. The hope of an imminent Second Coming began to disappear, charity decreased and austerity became softened. As a result it became ever more necessary, in spite of a continued concentration on the Hereafter, to come to terms with the earthly life in some way, for both the generation then living and many generations to come would have to live in the world and be concerned with its affairs.

At the same time Christian ideas upon the world and the state were given clarity and precision through contact with contemporary political philosophy, especially Stoicism. The Stoics taught that in the Golden Age men had been obedient to the pure law of nature, until wickedness, crime and war came into the world and compelled the establishment of new rules for the guidance of corrupt humanity. These were not identical with the laws of nature, but approached them as closely as the conduct of man allowed. It was not even this " relative natural law " which ruled, however, but man-made laws, the goodness or badness of which was to be judged according to the degree of their coincidence with the law of nature.

It needed only slight modifications to bring these ideas into correspondence with the Christian view of the world. Thus the eternal law of nature was identified with the divine command, which guided the first man in Paradise. After the Fall weak and vicious humanity was driven out into the world of death, evil and war, for the direction of which new rules and new authorities were set up.

Yet it would be far from the truth to suggest that the first centuries saw the unchallenged rule of tolerant indifference and passive obedience to the world's commands. The very determination to hold fast to eternal truths,which, in the one case, produced indifference to the world, might, in another case, result in bitter hatred of everything worldly. Asceticism, reacting against the increasing moral laxity of the general public, sought to represent the sensual world as dangerous to the soul's health and deserving of contempt, while the divine honours which the state demanded for the emperor, together with the periodical persecutions, fanned the flames of revolt.

It is sufficient simply to mention these tendencies here, for there was no distinction of principle between the obedience and the disobedience of Christians to the state. Whichever attitude was adopted, interest in the life to come was overwhelmingly greater than that in the present. While the heathen for the most part approved the state and even set out to improve it by bringing its laws into closer approximation with reason, to the Christian it appeared a transitory thing, in the shadow of eternal death, and very different from the Kingdom which was not of this world.

As we shall see, it was a curiously long time before Christianity freed itself from this attitude towards state and society, from indifference and the feeling that neither had more than a limited worth. It was not until a hundred years after the Roman Emperors had accepted Christianity that it underwent, in St Augustine's *City of God*, a modification which was to be decisive for the future.

The City of God, according to St Augustine, is the community of all reasoning beings, both angels and men, whom the divine providence has chosen. The angels have always been members of the eternal Church, but that part of the Heavenly City which dwells upon earth is no more than the reflection of the eternal Church and of hope grounded in faith, since it is entangled with the *civitas terrena*. It is still unknown who will be saved and who damned at the Last Judgment; the Church in its earthly form includes false friends, and there are true believers among its persecutors. Only at the Last Day will the Church be made pure from all stain and the chaff be separated from the wheat.[1]

Here on earth all men, even the true citizens of the Heavenly City, suffer from the consequences of original sin; unlike the angels, they have a mortal body and are only as perfect as is possible on earth. They all need the gifts which are granted to fallen humanity—earthly peace and earthly justice. It cannot be doubted that Augustine held the state to be a consequence of sin whether men govern it justly or not. It is a manifestation of sin and therefore its final collapse is certain; even the most Christian state cannot, according to Augustine, belong to the future kingdom of God.[2]

Yet such a state can be of some assistance in the right direction of a guilt-laden life. Those who use it for this purpose, but keep their eyes fixed on eternity, will one day receive the pearl of great price. All men belong to the *civitas terrena*, all have need of temporal goods, all are afflicted by the same evils, but their faith and their hope may vary. For some the state, serving present needs only,

---

[1] I accept the view of those scholars who seek no theory of state and society in our sense in Augustine's *De civitate Dei*, but treat it rather as a discussion of mankind and human affairs from a metaphysical and eschatological point of view.

[2] Cf. *De civ. Dei*, ix. 14 (CSEL. XL. 1, 428): " Utrum et beatus et mortalis homo esse possit."

is an end in itself; they are its true citizens, and rejoice and
are glad in it.   Hence they share only in it and not in the
things eternal, and at the end of time they will go down
with it to destruction; both they and it form part of the
company of the damned.   The others long for God and
belong through faith to the Heavenly City; they are
strangers on earth, the captives of the *civitas terrena*.[1]

   Where Augustine was thinking purely in terms of the
ultimate realities, his attitude towards the world corresponded to the older " indifferentism."   For him, too, a
great gulf was fixed between the Kingdom of God and the
kingdoms of this world.   Earthly goods were of no value in
Heaven, and human virtues as nothing before God.   But
whereas in the Apostolic age the imminent approach of the
Kingdom of God alone seemed to possess reality and scant
attention was paid to the merely present, Augustine's
doctrine of *usus* and *fruitio* builds a bridge between the
two: in his conception, the citizen of the Heavenly Kingdom belongs to both worlds, and should make use of the
earthly state and even co-operate faithfully with it.

   Indeed, Augustine went further and even had an ideal
of the state—a proof how little eschatological repudiation
really implied a negative judgment of the state as such.
It is, however, noteworthy how sceptically Augustine
treats the almost christianised Roman Empire.   Far from
regarding a Christian empire as a realisation of God's
kingdom on earth, he doubts whether there is any possibility
of realising the Christian postulates in it: " If the kings of
the earth and all nations and people would hear and give
heed to God's commands regarding honesty and integrity,
the state would give to earthly life that happiness which it
is capable of giving.   But since one obeys and another does

---

[1] *De civ. Dei*, xviii. 54 (CSEL. XL. 2, 362): " Ambae tamen temporalibus
vel bonis pariter utuntur vel malis adfliguntur, diversa fide, diversa spe,
diverso amore, donec ultimo iudicio separentur." See also *ibid.* xix. 17 (p.
403): " Civitas autem caelestis vel potius pars eius, quae in hac mortalitate
peregrinatur et vivit ex fide, etiam ista pace necesse est utatur, donec ipsa,
cui talis pax necessaria est, mortalitas transeat." On the necessary
participation in earthly goods, see in particular *Expos. quorundam proposi-
tionum ex ep. ad Rom.*, 72 (MPL. 35 col. 2083): " Cum enim constemus ex
anima et corpore . . ." and *Enarr. in Psalm.* 55, 2 (MPL. 36 col. 647).

not, and men love the flattery of vice above the roughness
of virtue, Christ's children must suffer, whether they be
kings or whether they be of some lower condition." Augustine, then, not only admitted the necessity of the state,
but even recognised the theoretical possibility that it
could be of real assistance on earth to the scattered members of the Heavenly Kingdom, and looked upon the
services which the state's officers rendered to the Church
as the service of God.[1]

This utilization of the state becomes the more important
because less absolute standards and diminishing religious
fervour soon produced a tendency to overlook the final
worthlessness of the state, and because, on the other hand,
the affinity of Christianity to the world, once it became an
accepted fact, was bound of necessity to increase, so that
the best possible use might be made of the state's potentialities for good. Augustinian ideas, then, created an
atmosphere favourable to the development of close relations between Church and world; while already in Augustine's time external circumstances were highly conducive
as such a development.

A century earlier, Constantine the Great had made an
alliance with the Church in order to use its inherent
tendency towards universality to strengthen the declining
cohesion of the empire. From this there arose the task
which he and later emperors carried out with considerable
success, that of protecting the catholicity of the Church
from provincialism and divergent trends in dogma. In
this way, at least one pre-condition for the agreement of
Church and empire was fulfilled. Yet at the beginning of
the fourth century the Church included but a fraction of the
population, and until the end of the century heathenism
was a power to be reckoned with in the perpetual wars and
disputed successions; put at first on an equal footing, it had
its privileges reduced and was finally deprived of them, but

---

[1] *Enarr. in Psalmum* 136 (MPL. 37 col. 1762) : " Habet et haec civitas
quae Babylonia dicitur, amatores suos consulentes paci temporali et nihil
ultra sperantes totumque gaudium suum ibi figentes, ibi finientes, et
videmus eos pro republica terrena plurimum laborare . . . non eos sinit
Deus perire in Babylonia. . . ."

maintained itself until the laws of Theodosius II and Valentinian III made it the citizen's duty to profess the Christian religion, and membership of Church and State was at least in principle the same thing. Here a point was reached at which catholic Church and catholic State could grow together into the single body of Christendom.

When Constantine became the friend of the Christians he had no intention of weakening either the priestly authority or the religious foundations of imperial power. It is true that he no longer claimed the divine honours accorded to his heathen predecessors, but as the ambassador of the Christian God he wished to be regarded as the " bishop for all non-spiritual things." [1] It is significant that he built and was buried in a church in which the tombs of the twelve Apostles surrounded his own. [2] As the divinely-appointed emperor he took a hand in everything, even purely spiritual matters. It was he who founded the Roman imperial theocracy, and his successors followed his example; they wished, one and all, to make the Church great and to make the peoples of the earth subject to it, but they themselves intended to direct the Church.

The Church thus fell into the extremely peculiar position of having the world, to which it felt itself alien and against whose apparently contrary principles it had directed its missionary endeavours, knocking at its doors and demanding admission. Admittedly, it set out to convert the whole world and all its inhabitants, but it was itself only prepared to be involved to a very limited extent in worldly affairs, as is plain from the fact that, in spite of its acceptance of Christianity, St Augustine still regarded the Roman Empire as far from satisfactory from the Church's point of view, and never even drew a clear distinction between the heathen and the Christian Empire. This had, however, already ceased to be a matter for the Church alone, since it was the world which was forcing its way into the Church and demanding the means of salvation, thus compelling it

[1] τῶν ἐκτὸς ὑπὸ θεοῦ Καθεστάμενος ἐπίσκοπος: Eusebius, *Vita Constantini*, iv. 24 (ed. Heikel, *Griech. Christl. Schriftsteller*, Eusebius, v. i. p. 126).
[2] On Constantine's tomb, see A. Heisenberg, *Grabeskirche und Apostelkirche, zwei Basiliken Konstantins*, ii. (1908) 100.

to abandon its attitude of indifference. But neither state
nor society was either able or willing to accommodate itself
to all the other-worldly regulations the Church had drawn
up. They allowed themselves to be outwardly christianised, but brought many heterogeneous conceptions into the
new alliance. The conquest of some of these alien elements
by the Church and its assimilation of others is the main
theme of medieval history.

In Constantine's own reign the Church and its leaders—
persecuted and tormented a few years before, now blinded
by the brilliance of the imperial mercy—wonderingly
respected their mighty defender's lightest wish. Later they
slowly came to a truer realisation of the position, and
attempted to define and maintain inviolate an area within
which the Church's supremacy should be unquestioned.
On the one hand, the Church now took the whole *imperium
romanum* for its province and established itself therein, and
on the other it refused to become submerged in it, thereby
reflecting the earlier divergent tendencies towards converting the world and withdrawing from it. So far from attempting to make itself a political factor of importance, the
Church is usually found on the defensive against the
emperors. Constantius II, whose policy was similar to that
of his father, if less skilful, had to be told by Hosius of
Cordova not to interfere in Church matters; it was not his
place to give commands, but rather to let himself be in-
structed: God had given the empire to him and the Church
to the bishops; just as anyone who deprived him of the
empire would be contravening the ordinance of God, so
he should beware lest he burden his soul with guilt by
concerning himself overmuch with the affairs of the
Church. Ambrose of Milan treated the emperors with still
greater bluntness, at least in his later years, when he made
it clear to them that they were set, not over, but in, the
Church, were not its lords but its sons. His famous words
served as a useful weapon in all medieval struggles for
clerical power. Nor was the dictum of John Chrysostom
forgotten: the spiritual power stands as high above the
secular as the heaven does above the earth, or even higher.

Similar expressions were constantly repeated—an indication how little fruit they bore. The rulers had no intention of giving up their claims, although these were rejected by the Church. It was in vain that the popes forbade the Eastern emperors to call themselves kings and priests; the Byzantine rulers became and remained supreme over the Eastern Church.[1]

In the year 496, during the Acacian schism, pope Gelasius I wrote a letter to the emperor Anastasius I, in which he set out at length the principles underlying the relations of Church and state. It re-states the objectives which Christianity had always set before itself, and shows the effect of the Church's experience of the world during nearly five centuries. Its phrases exercised an enormous influence on later times; scarcely any passage from papal letters or decretals was so familiar to the middle ages as these decisive sentences of Gelasius: " There are two things, most august emperor, by which this world is chiefly ruled: the sacred authority of the priesthood and the royal power. Of these two, the priests carry the greater weight, because they will have to render account in the divine judgment even for the kings of men."[2]

There had been no doubt of the unity of the Christian world in the minds of the emperors since Christianity became the state religion, and they themselves imposed no further limitations upon it. The leadership of mankind lay for them in the hands of king and priest, the final word being, at least in practice, with the imperial power. A famous passage in the *Corpus juris civilis* shows how the state understood the relationship of the two powers: " The

---

[1] On Hosius of Cordova, see E. Caspar, *Gesch. des Papsttums*, i. (1930) 179 sq. On the imperial *sacerdotium* of the Eastern emperors, see Theodosius II's summons to the Patriarch Cyril of Alexandria to attend the Council of Ephesus, in Mansi v. 531; cf. further Mansi, iv. 1111, and John Chrysostom, *In ep. II ad Cor. Homil.*, iv. 4 (MPG. 61 col. 508).

[2] Thiel, i. (1868) 349, no. 12. The phrase is repeated in Gratian's *Decretum* (c. 10, D. 96). The idea of giving account at the Day of Judgment derives from *Hebrews* xiii. 17; on this Epistle, all earlier work is now replaced by E. Caspar, *Geschichte des Papsttums*, ii. (1933) 64 sqq. and 753 sqq.—where an entirely new basis for the understanding of the Gelasian theory of the two powers is given—and H. X. Arquillière, *L'augustinisme politique*, (1934) p. 72.

noblest gifts of the divine clemency to mankind are the
priesthood and the empire, the one providing for the service
of God, the other watching in love over human affairs; both
proceed from the same source and lend adornment to life."[1]

Clerical theory itself had as little doubt of the divine
origin and divine mission of the imperial power; anything
else would have run counter to the current ideas of Christian
theocracy. By the end of the fifth century the Church, too,
had come to recognise the identity of the communities
ruled over by king and priest. Gelasius I's remark that
hic mundus was ruled by them both shows how much
nearer to the world and its affairs the Church had
approached since its foundation. In actual fact, the Church
had long been compelled to accept the imperial theory of
unity if it wished to fulfil its task of influencing the world.
Had it at this stage pointed to the supernatural character
of the heavenly kingdom and turned away from the world,
like many ascetic movements, it would at once have lost all
influence. Moreover, the emperor would have been bound
to regard this withdrawal as a doubt cast upon his own
religious mission, would have rejected this—quite rightly,
from a Christian theocratic standpoint—as unbelief, and
the prelates' words would have fallen on deaf ears. The
Church had, therefore, to pay heed to this world and yet
to preserve itself from contamination by it.

It is clear that the formulation of the theory of the two
powers by Gelasius I was a defensive measure, designed to
resist the pressure of a presumptuous world. With almost
tedious repetition, partly in long-familiar phrases, he
informed the emperor that he was supreme only in secular
matters, and that in the Church his duty was to obey, not
to command. In the existing circumstances it was courage-
ous of Gelasius to deny the emperor active participation in
clerical affairs and to demand that he submissively obey
the Church's decisions. This is shown by the careful com-
position of his letter. Despite its strictness where principle
is involved and its allusions to the fundamental truths of
Christianity, the tone of the letter is respectful. The

[1] *Corp. iur. civ.*, iii. (ed. Schoell and Kroll, p. 35), Nov. VI.

emperor is begged not to charge the pope with presumption. As Roman *princeps* he ought not to be offended if men tell him the truth. But the very expression *auctoritas sacrata pontificum et regalis potestas* contains within itself the nicely-calculated comparison of the two offices which comes immediately afterwards. The *auctoritas* of the priesthood, here qualified by the adjective *sacrata*, is created by God, and is the epitome of the unlimited authority with which Christ had endowed the priests; reverence and awe are therefore its due. To call the imperial power simply *regalis potestas*, on the other hand, is a tendentious undervaluation. For the Roman emperor holds no mere *potestas*, no office whose commands are satisfied by a purely outward obedience. Even the heathen empire had rested upon an authority which Hellenistic and Oriental ideas had long ago raised into the quasi-religious sphere. And it was this authority, the real basis of the emperors' claim to rule the Church, which Gelasius now proceeded to ignore.[1]

In a no less important expression of opinion, contained in the fourth of his treatises, Gelasius explained how the emperors' claim to rule the Church had arisen. More justice is done to the imperial position in this case, both the *imperium* and the priesthood being referred to as *potestates*. Melchizedek, prefiguring Christ, was both king and priest. The Devil copied this and caused the heathen emperor to be called *pontifex maximus*. Christ, however, the true priest and king, recognised human weakness and separated the two offices; henceforward the Christian emperors should be beholden to the priests for eternal life, the priests to the imperial government for earthly goods.[2]

The letter to Anastasius follows the same lines but makes more of the greater metaphysical eminence of the priestly office. Gelasius here calls the emperor's attention to the extreme reverence he owes to the priest from whom he receives the means of salvation. The same argument recurs in a less cleverly conceived letter of Gelasius'

---

[1] Symmachus seems to go even further in equalizing the two powers. He says: " Quia his praecipue duobus officiis regitur humanum genus. . . ." (Thiel, p. 703).
[2] Thiel, p. 567 sq.

successor, Symmachus. " Let us compare the dignity of the
emperor with that of the priest," he writes; " the difference
consists in the fact that one is concerned with earthly, the
other with heavenly things. The emperor receives baptism
and accepts the sacraments at the priest's hands, requires
his prayers, hopes for his blessing and asks for the imposition of penance. Finally, the one wields human, the other
divine authority: the latter is, therefore, if not higher in
dignity, at least equal."[1]

The last sentence is plainly a piece of diplomacy. Both
Symmachus and Gelasius were as convinced as John Chrysostom of the superior dignity of the priesthood. Yet the
sole purpose of these remonstrances consisted in preventing
the emperors' interference in religious matters, and if
the pope equated himself with the emperor in the leadership
of " this world " he thought of his functions as limited to
purely ecclesiastical affairs, and had no intention of laying
claim to a share in secular government. It was equally far
from his mind to constitute himself a court of appeal from
the emperor. A sharp distinction must be drawn between
mere precedence and actual superiority, and the assertion
that the Church of the early middle ages claimed authority
over the state must be eliminated from historical works
wherever it is found. Gelasius writes: " If even the prelates
obey thy laws respecting public order because the empire is
given thee by heavenly dispensation, . . . with what devotion, I ask you, must one obey those to whom it is committed to serve the sublime and holy mysteries? " The
priest's dignity, then, is immeasurably high in comparison
with that of the earthly ruler, but the latter still has his
own independent province, for which he is responsible to
God alone, and within which he may demand obedience
from all men.

Gelasius I was extremely conscious of his sublime dignity, but neither he nor the Fathers of that age had yet
reached the idea that on earth the Church was supreme over
princes and emperors. The discrepancy between the

---

[1] Thiel, p. 703, no. 10, 8. Cf. also the letter of Felix II to Zeno, in Thiel,
p. 250, no. 8, 5.

actual political power wielded by each precluded the development of such thoughts, but an even stronger influence was the feeling that it could not be the business of the servant of God to interfere in the affairs of the princes of this world. The Church naturally took an interest in the world, which was identical with the dominions ruled by the Roman emperor, but there still persisted the idea of a gulf fixed between Heaven and earth, which had taken shape in the writings of St Augustine, and the original Christian doctrine that God's kingdom was not of this world. This hindered the development of the idea of one united Christian world. It meant that it was still only admitted with reserve that the world belonged to the Church, and so held the Church back from asserting its superiority and demanding the recognition of it. But this demand was bound to arise once the ideal of a united Christian world approached realisation in actual fact. If the world were once really conquered by the Christian religion, then its supreme ruler could only be the head of the Church on earth.

CHAPTER II

THE MEDIEVAL CONCEPTION OF THE HIERARCHY

FREEDOM in its deepest sense is subjection to God, oneness with Him, service for Him; there are many ways in which men can share it. There are countless stages and gradations between the freedom of God, which is absolute, and that of the being who is most Godless and therefore least free. We have shown how such views developed from the body of mystical ideas current in the late classical period. The chief agents in their transmission were Augustine, Dionysius the Areopagite—whose relations with Neoplatonism were even more direct than Augustine's —and John Scotus Erigena, and it was just these men who were the most widely-read of all western medieval authors. However, the mystical and hierarchical philosophy of this period was more than a mere legacy of early Christian times, handed down by the writings and traditions of the Fathers; it is one of the forms in which human thought about the problems of the world has always found expression, though it has never been so thoroughly exploited as it was during the middle ages. Men read Augustine, Gregory and Dionysius because of their existing spiritual needs, and then naturally allowed themselves to be guided by them, rapidly assimilating the ideas which they had formulated.

The hierarchical forms which linked all things together, but also classified and graded them, were applied to super-human and sub-human beings as well as to the relation of man to God; all creation was divided into rational or spiritual, animal or inanimate beings, and metaphysically one group was always superior to the other. Psychology taught an hierarchical relation of soul and body, or even of the spiritual faculties, and this had an influence on the social and economic structure. People pictured to themselves nine ranks of angels in Heaven, the most diverse kinds of demons in Hell, and the world in the midst, related to both.

"As no spirits exist between God and the Seraphim, so between heretics and the Devil no man."[1]

Moreover, it is the will of the Creator that in Heaven and on earth the higher shall always rule over the lower. Each individual and each class should stay in its place, perform its assigned tasks and enjoy the favours and rights proper to it. World-order is assured by the fundamental principle of natural law :" to each his own. " To rebel against this rule is a grievous sin which brings confusion into the world and wrongs its Ruler.[2]

In religious matters the station and dignity of every creature were determined, according to the prevailing doctrine, by the measure of its participation in God. He alone has absolute Being, in Him alone all things have their highest fulfilment. Only He truly exists; in comparison with His Being, all other Being is no Being. He, as the source of all Being, gives of it in accordance with grace and works. It is the aim of human life to imitate Him more and more closely, to become as far as possible like Him, to draw ever nearer to Him, to strive for union with Him, and so in the next world to participate in His, the absolute freedom. Much indeed can be attained here on earth, but it can never be more than a reflection, a promise of future blessings.

In Paradise, man was free. But, writes abbot William of St Bénigne, a pupil of Majolus of Cluny, he used his inborn freedom of choice to sell his freedom in exchange for the forbidden fruit. Has God, he asks, lost His right over man as a result of this bargain? No; for He has also bowed the Devil beneath His yoke. But since He had once bestowed freewill on man, He could not recall the unwilling to the freedom into which they were born. Adam's descendants had to remain in the bonds of a servitude until such

---

[1] Humbert, *Adversus simoniacos*, ii. 13 (MGH. *Lib. de lite*, i. 153).
[2] Cf. Adalbero of Laon, *Carmen ad Robertum regem*, v. 215 sq. (ed. G. A. Hückel, *Les poèmes satiriques d'Adalbéron*, in *Bibl. de la Fac. des lettres de l'Univ. de Paris*, xiii. 150), appealing to Augustine, pseudo-Dionysius, and Gregory I; Odo of Cluny, *Sermo* i (MPL. 133 col. 709); Urban II, in JL. 5370 (MPL. 151 col. 290); canon 15 of the Synod of Arras (Mansi, xix. 455 sq.), *De ordinibus ecclesiastici regiminis*,—described according to the doctrines of Pseudo-Dionysius and Gregory I, which are quoted.

time as God Himself, at the price of His blood, restored them to the old state of freedom.[1]

This freedom is gained in the form of redemption through baptism, the second birth which makes a man a Christian. It is significantly called Christian freedom, and is distinguished from the bondage of those who are not baptised. Thus Gregory VII exhorts William the Conqueror to honour God, Who has changed him from a wretched and miserable bondman of sin—for as such were we all born—into a mighty king.[2]

But even after baptism, redemption is not yet complete. Feebleness of the soul and the corruption of the flesh remain. " The grace of baptism secures that earlier trespasses (i.e. original sin) work no further harm, and that we are born into the estate of the children of God. But it does not bestow immunity from the penalties of future sin, and man is thus still left open to the assaults of the forces of evil. All men without exception must eat their bread in the sweat of their brow. Here and now, not only is a busy secular life bound of necessity to be a life of bondage, but even the contemplation, by which we are led to heights above ourselves, does not fully attain the freedom of the spirit."[3]   This is the teaching of Gregory the Great; and bishop Fulbert of Chartres, who died in 1028, supposed that we shall only be really free when we have been united in eternal communion with the author of our freedom. The freedom of the redemption can, however, be increased

---

[1] William of St Bénigne, *Tract. sup. Rom.*, vii. 15, 19 (ed. E. De Levis, [1797] pp. 125 sqq.).

[2] *Reg.* vii. 23 (ed. Caspar, MGH. *Epp. sel.* ii. 501); Fulbert of Chartres, *Ep.* v. (MPL. 141 col. 199): " nos prima nativitate captivos secunda nativitate liberos"; Odilo of Cluny's Sermon for Easter-Day (MPL. 142 col. 1007): " Servitus hodie daemoniaca pellitur, libertas dominica hodie christianis conceditur "; Gregory II to the Saxons, *S. Bonifatii et Lulli epistolae*, no. 21 (ed. Tangl, MGH. *Epp. sel.* i. 35): " ut a diabolica fraude liberati mereamini adoptionis filiis aggregari, et ut ab aeterna damnatione liberati vitam habeamus aeternam."

[3] John Scotus, *Expos. super coel. hier.* viii. 2 (MPL. 122 col. 204).   See also Gregory I, *Hom. in Ezechielem*, i. 3, 13 (MPL. 76 col. 811); William of St Bénigne, *ut supra*; Fulbert of Chartres, *Tract. in Act. Ap.*, xii. 1, c. 22 (MPL. 141 col. 306). The complete dogmatic system may be found in Scheeben-Atzberger, iii. (1882) 641, Abschn. 23, L. Lercher, *Institutiones theologicae dogmaticae*, iv. (1930) 306 sq., or B. Bartmann, *Lehrbuch der Dogmatik*, ii. (1930) 263.

through grace and good works, and with it the hope of eventual liberation and an exalted position in the world to come.

The middle ages were quite familiar with the conception of freedom which we have found in early Christian literature. Archbishop Hincmar of Reims has much to say, in his work on predestination,[1] on the Pauline form of the idea of freedom—that he alone is truly free who subjects himself to righteousness, and so on. He cites passages to this effect from the works of Augustine, Remigius of Lyons and Alcuin, and his quotations are important in that they furnish a measure of the dissemination of these ideas. They were known to abbot Odo of Cluny, who did much to spread the Augustinianism which he derived from Gregory I. It is unnecessary to multiply instances, but medieval sources are full of references to ungodly, slavish and abhorrent freedom on the one hand, and on the other to true freedom, free service and sublime subjection. So, too, we meet with repetitions of the idea that freedom is loving service and is sharply distinguished from service for fear of punishment. But, it must be repeated, the thought of service under God and of His mild yoke is more frequent in the middle ages than consideration of the freedom resulting from such service. It is the aim of all the devout to be as subject to Him as possible; subjection or humility, that is, the renunciation of selfishness and the sinking of self in God's will, is the supreme virtue. It is said in praise of saints and other devout men that they ascended the steps of humility and that the greater and more honoured they became on earth, the more humble did they become in heart.

For all men, the highest aim of life must be to emulate the saints in their surrender to God. The extent to which they fulfil their aim determines their position (*libertas*) in the celestial hierarchy. Yet even in the first centuries of Christian history it was decided after bitter disputes that all men were not capable of acting up to the same moral standards, and that they ought not to be called upon to

---

[1] Hincmar, *De praedestinatione*, praef. (MPL. 125 col. 62).

do so. In the middle ages this conviction remained unshaken. Lay-folk must be on their guard against mortal sin, lest they lose the state of grace obtained through baptism, but from them only the strict fulfilment of the principal commandments of God can be required. Catholic theology to-day still takes up roughly the same position: " Man must avoid sin and do the work which God commands; but over and above this, he may also perform the good works (*opera supererogatoria*) which God suggests to him." This latter precept, however, is particularly applicable to the clergy. The laity, on the other hand, stand in relation to the clergy and monks as the child to the adult; they cannot bear the strong meat of the adult, but " need the gentle nourishment of milk. " Although laymen are never regarded, from the religious point of view, as fully adult, no reproach is cast upon them on account of their moral and religious weakness; on the contrary, they are as necessary as are the more exalted classes.[1]

II

It is the business of monks and hermits in especial to attain on earth that perfection of life and that union with God which is possible for mankind. It is they who still preserve the life of the primitive Church. As a class, they share the honourable name of the saints, since they are God's servants and handmaids. They have withdrawn into solitude or into the cloister, and their whole life is directed vigorously towards the service of God. They have chosen, as their vocation, war against demons and the lusts of the flesh; since no one who lives in the world is free from the assaults of the Devil, and there is an ever-present danger of stumbling and a thousand allurements attack the flesh, they entirely avoid the earthly life, that they may not

[1] On the different moral demands made upon different classes, see Harnack, DG. i. 456 sqq. On the *opera supererogatoria*, which are highly important for the whole doctrine of justification by works, see Scheeben-Atzberger, iv. 92 sqq., Abschn. 715 sqq.—Bernold, *Apologeticus*, c. 13. (MGH. *Lib. de lite*, ii. 73), explains that St Paul's command that everyone should take a wife (1 *Cor.* vii. 2) is only meant for the laity: " et his non solidum cibum sed lacteum potum ministra, utpote neophysitis. . . ." (based on 1 *Cor.* iii. 2.)

jeopardise the heavenly. The stormy seas of this life frighten them, and they believe that they can only escape shipwreck by fleeing to the safe haven of the cloister. They come thither and renounce the freedom of the world to take upon themselves the servitude of Christ; the more gladly they do it, the freer their service is, and the more pleasing to God. They win freedom; from being the slaves of the world they become the freemen of God. They renounce money, property, worldly renown and comforts. Freest of all is the hermit or the simple monk. Even an office in the cloister or still more in the secular church is only undertaken by the true monk with sighs, because it draws him back into the world from which he had fled. They rejoice in their servitude and in " the emancipation of poverty; " because the world is the essence of all that is material and burdened with sin, they seek to die to earthly things that they may gain eternal life. They wish to be " alive to God and truly crucified to the earthly existence, " to be buried with Christ by mortifying the flesh, that they may rise again with Him. Death itself is lauded as the accomplishment of all these desires; one account of a bishop's death runs: " This was indeed a year of jubilee for the bishop, for, delivered from temporal and eternal guilt alike, he was restored to the glorious freedom of the children of God."

When asceticism reaches a high degree of abhorrence of everything sensual and earthly, it reminds us of the dualistic asceticism of antiquity, which contrasted God and World, Spirit and Nature, as the good and the evil principles, and which therefore recognised the putting off of the material and the ascent to pure spirituality as the only method of salvation.[1] The Church, of course, rejected these ideas as unchristian, but it could not prevent their influence from continuing beneath the surface. Similar conclusions can be drawn from the teaching of Christian mysticism, which was pantheistic in tendency. If God is the highest existence, the most universal Being, Who unfolds and

---

[1] On dualistic asceticism, see A. Harnack, *Das Mönchtum*, 8th ed. (1921) pp. 12 sqq.

expresses Himself in all particular existences, if all that comes from God must struggle back again to Him, then it was precisely through mortification of the flesh that a separation of spirit and body could be brought about, and man could reach a higher plane of existence and thereby a closer approach to God. To cling more and more completely to God and Christ, to be united with Them as intimately as possible, was the passionate desire of religious mystics of this type; but their final hope was so to be carried away out of themselves in ecstasy that they could share in the pure contemplation of God. The ascetic's aim, it was said, was continually to come nearer to Christ " through the fire of spiritual contemplation. " Not only did men, encumbered here by the flesh, seek a spiritual home in Heaven, but God Himself, they hoped, would graciously descend and dwell in their spirit. By contemplation it was possible to save one's soul at the last Judgement, for " the contemplation of God is the only thing to which all works of justification and all striving after virtue are inferior. "[1]

At the same time, the establishment of a claim to reward in the next world by means of works which are meritorious in the sight of God is, next to actual asceticism, the highest aim of monastic life. The other two orders, priests and laymen, can, it is true, also acquire merit by good works, but for monks and nuns this task is in the fullest sense their life. The renunciation of goods and family counted as a most meritorious act in itself, and through it Christ was said to become the real debtor and the holy man the creditor, whose capital bore heavy interest. Endowments for religious purposes were, in the later middle ages, quite regularly referred to as business transactions of a particularly exalted and sacred character, through which earthly possessions were exchanged for heavenly ones. A brief glance at the modern doctrine—which is, of course, identical in structure with that of the middle ages—may perhaps

[1] William of St Bénigne, *Tract. in Rom.*, vii. 15 sqq. c. 1 (ed. De Levis, p. 119): " una ergo et sola est contemplacio Dei, cui merito omnia iustificationum merita, universa virtutum studia postponuntur."

explain how the Catholic conception of merit is to be understood. " Merit in the concrete sense is an act which one man performs for the benefit of another, and which calls forth, as a matter of right, a reciprocal action on the part of the latter." In the strict sense, Christ's sacrifice is the only merit worthy of reward (*merita de condigno in sensu stricto*). Men can only accomplish actions deserving reward through the grace of God, and in consequence what they do is their own act only in so far as their voluntary collaboration is necessary (*merita de condigno in sensu mitiori*). Finally, there are lesser acts, which cannot in any proper sense be called merits at all, because they stand in no direct relation to the corresponding gifts of God, but which are nevertheless accepted by God in consideration of the good will which they reveal (*merita de congruo*). The reward to be obtained is pre-eminently an increase of grace; and "the final goal which is to be reached or earned through grace is everlasting life." [1]

The aims of monasticism are high, but it strives only, as we have seen, for the treasure which is laid up in Heaven. The monk and all who accept his ideals wish finally to rise to the glory of the Father, and, thirsting for the promised freedom, are firm in the belief that " there will be just as little servitude among the servants of God in the glorious freedom of the life to come, as there is of freedom among the children of God amidst the tribulations of this life. " Wishing to become co-heirs with the heavenly citizens, they have renounced the world in order to reign with Christ in eternity and to take a high place in the holy hierarchy of those who are subject to God. It is, however, extremely important to stress the fact that every dignity and every rank gained through asceticism or works of justification will only become reality in the next world; here on earth there is no need for them to be expressed in any way, or at least it is quite immaterial whether they are so expressed or not. The hierarchical conception of monasticism, in short, is based on the next world.

[1] *Matth.* vi. 19 sqq., *Luke* xii. 33 and xvi. 9, and *Prov.* xiii. 8 are frequently quoted in this connection. On the doctrine of merit, see Scheeben-Atzberger, iv. 104 sqq., Abschn. 721 sqq., and Bartmann, *op. cit.* ii. 116 sqq.

Individualism is the second characteristic of the monastic type. For the pure hermit, the impulse of love for one's neighbour is of small value; he loves God and the angels and those—with whom he is himself united—who are sure of salvation when the earthly life shall have passed away. The aim of asceticism is the eternal salvation of the individual, and it is not too gross an exaggeration to speak of this as egoism.[1]

In the Christian West, however, ascetic groups rarely pushed their flight from the world to such extreme limits; their close connection with the Church, to which the two other classes, the secular clergy and the laity, also belonged, and with its work of salvation, was enough to deter them. The idea that moral perfection and the capacity for mystical ecstasy made the sacraments of the Church superfluous remained largely foreign to the West, though common in the East. Yet there must have been a revival of asceticism of a strange kind in the eleventh century, especially during the ferment of the Investiture Contest, if there were people whom Bernold of St Blasien had to attack with the words: " Let those who believe that they are excepted from the pains of excommunication, because, being monks and religious and having fled the world, they are not subject to the spiritual shepherds and their discipline—let them, I say, see what the Council of Chalcedon has to say on this matter." In this case, however, there was as yet no doubt of the sacramental power of the priesthood, but only of the extent of its jurisdiction; even in the cloister it was believed that all the Christian virtues were worthless without the sacraments which only the priest could administer. In every monastery there were many monks who were also priests, and they were regarded as the chief agents through whom the others could grow in the state of grace. It is said, for instance, that at Cluny prayers were ceaselessly offered and Masses celebrated for the state of the Church. This, of course, emphasised the unity of the whole Church,

---

[1] Cf. Troeltsch, *Soziallehren*, p. 107: " Among other things, monasticism and contemplation were the salvation of Christian individualism, in the only form in which it was then possible to preserve it."—*Social Teaching of the Christian Churches*, trans. O. Wyon, (1931) i. 111.

since the sacrifice of the eucharist was always regarded as being primarily offered by the entire Church and not merely by the celebrant and his immediate circle; besides the eucharist, however, contemplation and good works could benefit all the living and the dead as well as the individual performing them, for merit which the individual has acquired for himself can also, in certain circumstances, be of advantage to others. We shall have to return to this point, which is one of the chief reasons why monasticism stood in such high honour during the middle ages.[1]

Besides turning thus positively towards the world, monasticism was sometimes untrue to its ideal and transgressed its chosen principles in slighter and cruder ways, from the pursuit of profane knowledge and useful husbandry to political activity. Further, the demand of the ascetic that he shall be treated on earth with a respect befitting his metaphysical rank is psychologically interesting, since this too is strictly speaking a departure from his true manner of life.

Yet despite the infiltration of other ideals and interests, the peculiar qualities of monasticism remain its relatively highly-developed religious individualism and its predominant concern with the next world, which it tries to approach as closely as possible through a life of contemplation and good works. The more a man succeeds in leaving the world behind him, the higher he climbs in the heavenly hierarchy and the more exalted does he become in the metaphysical sense. This characteristic stands out even more clearly when we compare the monks with the other fully active class in the Church, the priesthood.

III

The priest, as the representative of Christ, is the mediator between God and man; by his consecration he becomes directly the servant of Jesus, Who, through him, communicates to men His gifts, the sacraments. Through him

---

[1] *Virtutes S. Eugenii Bron.*, c. 16 (MGH. SS. xv. 650): " nihil valet christianitas, si defuerit presbiteralis auctoritas." On the Mass at Cluny see E. Sackur, *Die Cluniacenser*, ii. (1894) 88 n. 5 and 227 sqq.

men are made free from sin in baptism, and he alone is able so to strengthen them with the other sacraments and to direct their steps by the jurisdiction which he possesses that they can tread the right road to Heaven and to perfect freedom. By the grace that works within him the priest can save not only himself but also the people under his charge; he passes on what has been given to him, and proclaims the righteousness of the Lord. The Church, in its narrower sense as the ecclesiastical hierarchy, disowns this world, but none the less organises it on the basis of the Hereafter. The Church, in fact, countenances the world in order to convert it. St Peter, the first bishop of Rome, says Florus of Lyons in one of his poems, had power to raise the kingdom of earth into the kingdom of Heaven.[1]

The clergy as a class owe their position in the main to the fact that they are the instruments of Christ. For all clerics, from the lowest of the minor orders to the bishop, the dignity of their task is the reason for the rank they hold in the hierarchy of the Church. Those who occupied the highest offices were sometimes even called angels and gods, and scriptural authority could be quoted in support, but care was taken to explain exactly with what right this was done: as the highest beings share all the characteristics of the lower, it was argued, so conversely the lower share those of the higher, though not in like measure. The priests, it was said, belonged to the same order as the angels, and in consequence possessed all that the angels possessed, at least in so far as it was possible for men to do so; like the angels, they existed for the purpose of communicating the divine decisions to those in their charge; therefore it was reasonable that priests and angels should have the same name, and since they imitated God and performed His works they could also be called gods.[2]

The sacramental hierarchy, and the place which every

---

[1] " Qui terrestre valet in caelum tollere regnum."—*Carmina*, 28, 68 (MGH. *Poet. Lat.* ii. 561). Similarly, a poem of the x cent. (ed. Schramm, *Kaiser, Rom und Renovatio*, ii. 64): " Sub Caesaris potentia purgat papa secula."

[2] Cf. Pseudodion. Areop., *De coel. hier.* xii. 2 and 3 (MPG. 3 col. 297), *De eccl. hier.* v. 1, 6 (*ibid.* cols. 500, 505); John Scotus, *Expos. super coel. ier.* viii. 2 and xii. 3 (MPL. 122 cols. 198 and 233).

cleric obtains in it by the sacrament of ordination is, in contrast to its ascetic equivalent, not primarily concerned with the next world, but holds good in the Church on earth. The hierarchy exists to lead the people of God on earth, and in doing this it is the representative of Christ; hence the metaphysical worthiness of a priest is not of decisive importance. A sharp distinction was always made between office and person; a priest was not necessarily holy because he had been consecrated. Thus Hincmar of Reims, following Gregory the Great, writes: " If you hold us priests to be unworthy, or despise us for any other reason, yet keep in your mind the fear of the Lord, Who calls you to the Heavenly kingdom through our unworthiness." In the same way, Odo of Cluny explains that baptism by a saint is no better than baptism by a sinner, since in reality it is Christ alone who baptises; and similar statements are made about the other sacraments. Bad priests, considers Peter Damian, receive the gifts of God not for themselves but for others.

Ecclesiastics even went so far as to oppose Gregory VII's demands for the enforcement of celibacy, declaring that they would no longer perform their duties if he adhered to his purpose; and if this happened, let him see where he could find angels to serve in his Church. They had no desire, in plain words, to be as holy as the sacraments which they administered. The same distinction between office and person was made in the case of the pope, and use was often made of a celebrated passage from Ennodius taken over by pseudo-Isidore, in which it was said that Peter had left to his successors, as a permanent gift, the merits he had acquired, together with the heritage of innocence.[1]

[1] Hincmar, *Pro ecclesiae libertatum defensione*, i. (MPL. 125 col. 1049), relying on Gregory I, *Hom. in ev.* ii. 36, 2 (MPL. 75 col. 1267); Odo of Cluny, *Coll.* i. 21 (MPL. 133 col. 533); Peter Damian, *Liber gratissimus*, c. 39 (MGH. *Lib. de lite*, i. 72); Lambert of Hersfeld, *Annales*, ad ann. 1074 (ed. Holder-Egger, MGH. *Script. rer. Germ.* p. 199); Ennodius, *Lib. pro synodo*, (MGH. *Auct. Ant.* vii. 52), embodied in Gratian's *Decretum*, c. 1 D. 40.—The moral character of the priest is therefore of secondary import-ance for his dignity. The monk, on the other hand, stands or falls thereby; cf. Odo, *Vita Geraldi*, ii. 8 (MPL. 133 col. 675): " fateor enim vobis, quon-iam incomparabiliter melior est bonus laicus quam sui propositi transgres-sor monachus."

If, then, it is the grace inherent in the office which ultimately determines clerical rank, it remains true that ordination, celebration of the Mass and leadership of the people are by no means without importance in determining a cleric's personal state of grace, i.e. his metaphysical worth as an individual. The idea that he who has the cure of souls must render account to God for those entrusted to his care is in itself a proof that the priestly office will still be effective in the next world. Fidelity or negligence in the performance of official duties in general will be one of the reasons for reward or punishment before the heavenly tribunal. The question of the indelibility of the orders of bishops, priests and deacons was left undecided in pre-scholastic times, but it was already the ruling opinion at that period that the servants of the Church stand personally closer to God than other men. Peter Damian said plainly: " He who rises to the priestly office does not indeed receive the Holy Ghost anew, but he does receive the increase of that which he has already."[1] It may also be assumed that there already existed at this time the feeling that the celebration of Mass brought rewards to the good priest, whereas the evil would not secure them by the same actions.

Thus it is clear that the clergy too, if only in a restricted sense, are as an estate concerned with the next world, and that different ranks in the clerical hierarchy are determined not only by the nature of the part played by individuals in the service of the Lord, but also by the holiness which they may in varying degrees personally acquire, and which endures throughout eternity unless it is lost as a result of sin.[2]

IV

In medieval thought, all means of rising in the religious hierarchy were honoured, and their use recommended. Pronouncements abound in which the active life of the

[1] Peter Damian, *Liber gratissimus*, c. 15 (MGH. *Lib. de lite*, i. 37).

[2] *Ibid.*: " Enimvero ad instar septem donorum spiritus sancti septem nihilominus sunt ordines aecclesiasticae dignitatis." Damian knows no special *ordo* for the bishops; there was, however, no agreement on this point.

secular priest is set as high as the contemplation of the ascetic. Thus we are told that archbishop Anno of Cologne felt it wrong, in spite of his inclination to despise the world, to neglect the secular duties which were bound up with his office. Pope Leo IX is said to have been rewarded with inward gifts for his faithfulness and wisdom in outward matters. Finally, in the *Life* of archbishop Bardo of Mainz there is the highly significant sentence: " Although he was accustomed to a life of contemplation at the feet of God, yet he showed himself to have experience in practical affairs, imitating Him Who, though being of such perfection that angels longed to look upon Him, assumed the veil of the flesh and was manifest in human form."[1]

However, the two ecclesiastical estates differed in their manner of life and in the degree to which they applied the methods they had adopted. This distinction, of course, applies only in a general sense; there were plenty of monks who showed sympathy for the world and felt themselves to be the servants of God on the world's account, and conversely secular priests who vied with the most pious of hermits in all the ascetic virtues. Often, on the other hand, no distinction of rank was made between the two kinds of religious life and activity; monks were simply regarded as the more perfect in morals and the purer in their lives, while priests were the real instruments of God. In actual fact, however, there is plenty of evidence both to support and to contradict this view; the higher rank and the greater nearness to God is sometimes assigned to monks, sometimes to priests.

Clerics are frequently said to have become monks in order to reach a higher degree of humility, to cleave more perfectly to Christ or to lead a more lofty life. Abbo, the famous tenth-century abbot of Fleury, worked out a complete doctrine about the respective rank of the three estates; the state of the laity is good, that of the clergy better, that of the monks best. Only the monks, in their

---

[1] Nortbert, *Vita Bennonis*, ii. c. 10 (MGH. SS. xxx. 2, 877); Wibert, *Vita Leonis*, ix. 17 (MPL. 143 cols. 472 sq.); *Vita Bardonis*, c. 6 (MGH. SS. xi. 325).

life of contemplation, have attained the one thing which is necessary; the more they withdraw from the tumult of worldly affairs, the more like are they to Mary Magdalene, who washed the feet of Jesus with her tears and wiped them with her hair. The clergy, therefore, stand between the monks and the laity, and are as much above the one as they are below the other. More than a hundred years later Hugh of Flavigny, one of the most important chroniclers of the middle ages, suggests the following order of precedence at the Last Judgement; Peter, Paul, John the Baptist, the rest of the Apostles, holy hermits, perfect monks, good bishops, good priests, good laymen, women.[1]

But such ideas were not the only ones; they were indeed hardly the prevailing ones, as is usually assumed to-day; this would be a contradiction at a time when the active life had risen even more in public esteem than the life of ascetism. Thus Anselm, the historian of the bishops of Liège, tells us that bishop Baldrich, having been expelled from his diocese and having entered the monastery of Stablo, one day caused a noise there before the vigil by letting his sandals drop, and was punished by being made to stand by the cross in front of the abbey. No one remembered to call him back, and so great was the humility of his obedience that he remained standing there, became covered with snow and nearly froze to death. Later he became bishop again and devoted his energies to combating heresy; he was even more steadfast in this, says Anselm, than he was when he stood in the snow, for, like a brave warrior, he attacked the heretics with the Word of God, which is sharper than any sword. Further, neither Gregory VII nor Urban II can have prized the ascetic virtues alone and above all else ; Gregory sharply censured abbot Hugh of Cluny for having permitted duke Hugh I of Burgundy to

---

[1] Cf. *Widrici Vita Gerardi*, c. 23 (MGH. SS. iv. 504): " clericus . . . perfectioris vitae requirens statum, . . . iugum Christi expetiit " (i.e., becomes a monk); Sigebert of Gembloux, *Vita Wicberti*, c. 8 (MGH. SS. viii. 511): " Quicumque ex clericali sorte ad altiorem humilitatis gradum optabant ascendere, hic cum Jacob non in somnis, sed revera scalam coelos attn-gentem merebantur videre; " *Gesta abb. Gemblac.* c. 4 (MGH. SS. viii. 525); Abbo, *Apologeticus*, (MPL. 139 col. 463 sqq.); Hugh of Flavigny, *Chron.* ii. (MGH. SS. viii. 384).

take the habit, and Urban forced countess Matilda to marry, a fact which Bernold of St Blasien reports with approval. The overwhelming importance of sacramentalism is further to be seen in the fact that privileges of exemption granted by the pope to monasteries frequently gave immunity from episcopal jurisdiction, but scarcely ever from the bishop's spiritual authority.[1]

The original opposition to western monachism had almost entirely disappeared after the sixth century. Nevertheless, protests were still occasionally made against excessive asceticism even during the middle ages. In a poem in dialogue form written by bishop Adalbero of Laon for Robert of France, the king orders that " no one shall in future go more than once to the church at night; all have ample opportunity for prayer during the day. "[2] The Cambridge Songs, an eleventh-century collection, include a poem which is exceptionally interesting on account of the attitude it adopts against monastic arrogance and egotism. It tells of a monk named John who deserts his friend with the purpose of becoming an angel and living on roots and herbs in the wilderness. Soon he returns hungry, and knocks on his friend's door. The friend decides to give him a lesson, leaves him standing all night outside, and says aloud but as if to himself: " This cannot be John, for

> John to an angel turned him,
> He contemplates the doors of Heaven,
> And men no more concern him."[3]

Reflections of this nature sometimes caused monks to be placed lower than priests in the mystic hierarchy. The Areopagite, who regards the monks as ethically the most perfect of human estates, nevertheless makes the heavenly hierarchy of the angels directly continuous with the

[1] Anselm, *Gesta ep. Leod.*, c. 5 (MGH. SS. vii. 193 sqq.); Bernold, ad ann. 1089 (MGH. SS. v. 449); Greg. VII, *Reg.* vi. 17 (ed. Caspar, MGH. *Epp. sel.* ii. 423).

[2] *Carmen ad Robertum regem*, v. 423 (ed. Hückel, p. 167). On the opposition to monasticism in the West, see Harnack, *Mönchtum*, p. 37.

[3] *Carmina Cantabrig.* (ed. Strecker, pp. 97 sqq.), no. 42 (trans. H. Waddell, *The Wandering Scholars*, p. 90). Compare with this an important essay by B. Schmeidler, *Antiasketische Äusserungen aus Deutschland im xi und beginnenden xii Jhdt.*, in *Festschrift für W. Goetz*, (1928) pp. 35 sqq.

earthly hierarchy of the Church, and makes no attempt to assign the ascetics a place therein. Shortly after 1100, Hugh of Fleury writes that bishops and priests are the very foundations of Holy Church, monks and lower clergy its servants. Most significant of all is the letter which the Chapter of Mainz wrote to archbishop Siegfried (1060–1084)—who had gone to Cluny as a monk—in an attempt to persuade him to return: " We ardently desire, Holy Father, that thou shouldst ascend to something higher, if such exists, but thou shouldst not fall from the higher to the lower; for no estate, no honour, no vow, is so high as the apostolic dignity. Hence there is nothing in the world which surpasses the life of a bishop, nothing which is nearer to God; every monk or recluse, every cloister-dweller and every hermit must, as a being of lesser importance, give way to him." It would be a mistake to suppose that this letter referred to worldly importance. The bishop's rank is metaphysical rather than terrestrial, and bishop Adalbero, in a poem already quoted, declares that bishops " will ascend to the most exalted places in the kingdom of Heaven. "[1]

A review of medieval religious thought makes it clear, therefore, that various conceptions of the hierarchy were current at one and the same time. They often existed harmoniously together in the same mind and were an intrinsic part of the whole outlook of the various classes of clerical society. Yet the intrinsic differences were clearly perceived even by contemporaries, and this perception was occasionally so acute that writers sought to decide which

---

[1] Pseudodion. Areop., De eccl. hier. vi. 1 (MPG. 3 cols. 529 sq.), and in contrast therewith De coel. hier. i. 3 (ibid. col.121) and John Scotus, Expos. super coel. ier., i. 2 (MPL. 122 col. 127); Hugh of Fleury, Tract. i. 13 (MGH. Lib. de lite, ii. 480); Cod. Udalrici, no. 39 (ed. Jaffé, Bibl. rer. Germ. v. 87); Adalbero, Carm. ad Rob. reg., v. 271 (ed. Hückel, p. 154); Anselm II of Lucca, in his Collectio canonum (vii. 116; ed. Thaner, p. 413) quotes the following sentence from Jerome (Ep. xiv. 8, CSEL. LIV. 55), under the heading Quod clerici monachis presunt: " Detrimentum gregis ignominia est magistri, sicut e regione illius monachi vita laudanda est qui veneratione habet domini sacerdotes et non detrahit gradui, per quem factus est Christianus." See also Serlo of Bayeux's impressive polemic against setting an exaggerated value upon monasticism, in his Defensio pro filiis presbyterorum, v. 69 sqq. (MGH. Lib. de lite, iii. 582). St Thomas Aquinas finally established the higher rank of the priesthood.

class was the higher, and even felt the necessity of attacking the exaggerated dignity which had been attached to a lower order.

Such isolated cases of strife between ascetics and priests are, however, only of interest in so far as they reveal more fundamental differences; and it is the existence of these fundamental differences, extending throughout the Church and affecting every phase of religious life, which allow and compel us to make a contrast between the two fundamental conceptions of religious order which we have now surveyed:

(1) The ascetic (i.e. monastic) conception of the hierarchy.

(2) The sacramental (i.e. priestly) conception of the hierarchy.

In order to summarize the essential characteristics of the two distinct conceptions, the following points may be emphasised in recapitulation: The ascetic hierarchy depends on the degree of withdrawal from the world and the vision of God is the height of its desire; it further depends on the accumulation of merit, inclines to religious individualism and places the realisation of a man's true rank exclusively in the Hereafter. The sacramental conception of the hierarchy bases the worth of the individual on the nature of his service at the sacrament, that is, on the measure of Christ's presence within him, and sees the hierarchy as an institution with its face turned towards the world, since its task is to raise the world to eternal life. The sacramental conception of the hierarchy is realised here and now; its existence in the next world is a secondary matter, for the factor which determines rank in the Hereafter is not, as on earth, the grace of God working through man, but the individual's own state of grace.

The two ideal types which we have just elaborated must of course not be conceived in a doctrinaire fashion; they are only intended to express the foregoing ideas in shorter form. To avoid undue generalisation, the two types have not simply been designated "monastic" and "priestly;" but on the whole the statement may stand that the monks were the chief representatives of the first, and the secular clergy of the second, category.

It was these two different religious attitudes and the corresponding different views of the world—withdrawal from it on the one hand, conversion of it on the other— which, as we shall see, ultimately determined the development of the Church and the course of the reform movement in the tenth and eleventh centuries. The aims and the activities of the representatives of the two distinct types of the hierarchy remained radically different throughout this decisive period in the history of the Christian Church. To understand them we must be familiar with the two forms of the hierarchy hitherto considered, and we must know what the Mainz letter-writer whom we have already quoted meant, when he wrote to his spiritual shepherd: " They do well who withdraw from earthly life and deny themselves, who take up their cross and follow Christ; but this a thing which is done only by those who love themselves, and who have been given no task to perform in the vine-yard of the Lord of Hosts. It suffices them if they can but save themselves, for they have none but themselves for whom they must render account. But thou, Father, dost rather govern the world than abandon it."[1]

v

In spite of all differences of opinion about the religious and ecclesiastical hierarchy, there was never any doubt that the laity were the lowest in rank. Within the lay estate itself there were further distinctions: warriors were superior to peasants, men to women; but all alike had to be subject to the priest, to obey his words and to allow no encroachment on his office. A layman who wished to bring a charge against a priest had first to undergo special examination. Originally, only clerics could be buried in a church. Ecclesiastical laws carried greater weight than secular, and under the Carolingians a capitulary laid down that in cases of collision between the count's and the bishop's court the

---

[1] *Cod. Udalrici*, no. 39 (ed. Jaffé, *Bibl. rer. Germ.* v. 81): " Tu autem, pater, melius regis seculum quam relinquis; " cf. also the letter from the diocese of Mainz to Benedict VIII, dated 1024, in *Germania Pontificia*, ed. Brackmann, ii. 1, p. 4 no. 4 (*Ep. Mogunt.*, no. 25, ed. Jaffé, *Bibl. rer. Germ.* iii. 362): " qui primus post Deum in vice sancti Petri orbem terrae regere debes in aequitate . . ."

former should give way. It was maintained that priests and monks reigned with God and were judges with Him over the world, for " they would rather govern the possessors of gold than themselves possess the gold. "[1]

However, until the time of the Investiture Controversy the general conviction prevailed that kings were essentially different from all other laymen. They had a special mission from God and in them God's ruling will was peculiarly active, ennobling their persons. The origins of this veneration of the sovereign prince are manifold; it is a legacy both of ancient conceptions of divine kingship and of Germanic religious sentiment, but is primarily the result of biblical stories and commands, which were the main directive force in the medieval mind. The king's rule is holy, his person sacred; he is set up and put down by God. In pictures of medieval rulers God's hand is sometimes seen over the king's head as a symbol of his religious eminence. The Church took account of this in the ceremony of royal consecration, which was reckoned among the sacraments in the early middle ages, and so drew kingship into its spiritual territory. In the ceremony of consecration, it was held, God gave the king something of His power through His servants the bishops, and as a result the king became " a new man. " At his anointing the emperor was, as an expression of this inner change, received into the ranks of the clergy. The emperor became a canon of St Peter's in Rome, and the kings of Europe usually held canonries in several chapters —Henry II, for example, in the cathedral chapters of Magdeburg, Strassburg and Bamberg.[2]

All Christians felt great reverence towards the God-

[1] Ratherius of Verona, Praeloquia, iii. 4, 8 (MPL. 136 col. 224).
[2] Cf. Kern, pp. 2-139 (=Chrimes, pp. 1-68); M. Bloch, Les rois thaumaturges, (1924) pp. 54 sqq. ; God's hand over the prince's head in P. E. Schramm, Die deutschen Kaiser und Könige in Bildern ihrer Zeit, i. (1928) plates 10, 16, 28 sqq., 64, 85 sqq.; on the sacramental character of the ordination of the king, see Kern, pp. 78 sqq. (= Chrimes, pp. 36 sqq.) and Schramm, Hist. of English Coronation, pp. 115-6; E. Eichmann, Königsweihe und Bischofsweihe, (SB. d. Bayr. Ak., phil.-hist. Kl., 1928 no. 6), p. 13; on the importance of the coronation of Pippin, see in especial E. Caspar, Pippin und die römische Kirche (1914), pp. 14 sqq.—since the anointing was a sacrament, it did not suggest the superiority of the consecrator over the consecrated, nor affect the prevailing doctrine of the direct relation of the king to God.

given prince, but there were many different opinions concerning the place that was to be attributed to him in the hierarchy. Many placed him on a level with the bishops or even above them, others would have nothing to do with conclusions so upsetting to the accepted order; but all were agreed that the king, who ruled on earth, typified the Saviour, who ruled in Heaven. It was admitted that he shared the priestly office. All styled him the illustrious helper and protector of the Church, the head of the people, even the mediator between clergy and people; yet the opinion was widespread that the king remained nevertheless inferior to the priest in dignity, and was bound, like all laymen, to obedience in spiritual matters. In Rome from the tenth century onwards the king was refused the anointing of the head, which was reserved for the bishops as a sign of their higher rank. When we come to deal with the Investiture Contest much will have to be said about contemporary polemical writings, in which such opinions were clearly expressed, but even as early as the ninth century the more extravagant claims of the most passionate venerators of the kingship often called forth sharp opposition, and in the following period opposition was at least spasmodic. The king was told that he was neither a priest nor the representative of Christ.

There were, of course, many who sought to describe the sanctity and the supernatural character of the kingship in such terms. We know that the dignity of certain Merovingian kings was styled " priestly " and that they were compared—e.g. by the poet Venantius Fortunatus—to the Old Testament priest-king Melchisedek. Great inventive skill was applied in Charlemagne's court circle towards finding appropriate words to describe the sublimity of the kingship. Men like Theodulf of Orleans, Paulinus of Aquileia and Alcuin called the king priest, bishop, propagator of the faith, preacher, ruler of the people of God, father of the Church and brother of the priests, representative of Peter or even of Christ. Charles was made the equal of David and Solomon. Naturally, none of these titles must be taken too literally, for no king was ever at the same time

priest, or really possessed priestly orders, but they do show
what men thought about the religious rank of the kingship,
which empowered the ruler to be the representative of God
in the leadership of the Church, not only in external but
also in internal affairs. Later kings were exalted no less
than Charles. Above all, they too were counted as representatives of Christ, and not merely as servants and protectors, but as rulers of the Church. Louis the Pious was
referred to as the leader of true religion ; bishop Fulbert of
Chartres exhorts the French king to protect Holy Church,
the Bride of Christ, which is entrusted to his guidance;
Wipo calls Conrad II and Henry III Vicars of Christ, and
reports that others used the same expression. The importance these views held in the elaboration of the royal
theocracy of the middle ages is shown by a rarely-quoted
passage in the chronicle of Thietmar of Merseburg, where it
is characterised as improper that Arnulf of Bavaria, a mere
duke, had appointed the bishops in his duchy. " Rather, "
explains Thietmar, " our kings and emperors should alone
provide for such things, for they take the place of the
highest Lord in this earthly life, and rightly stand before all
other pastors. For it would be utterly wrong that those
whom Christ has raised to be princes of this world [i.e. the
bishops], who ought to be mindful of Him, should be sub-
jected to any rule save that of those who after the example
of the Lord stand above all other mortals through the glory
of their consecration and the majesty of the crown."[1]

[1] On the king's priestly character, see Kern, pp. 111 sqq. (= Chrimes,
pp. 53 sqq.); Bloch, op. cit., pp. 186 sqq., rightly speaks of a " caractère
presque sacerdotal."—Alcuin writes to Offa of Mercia in 790: " Vos estis
decus Britanniae, tuba praedicationis, gladius contra hostes, scutum contra
inimicos . . .," and in 769: " sapientissime populi Dei gubernator, diligen-
tissime a perversis moribus corrige gentem tuam et in praeceptis Dei
erudi illam, ne propter peccata populi destruatur patria nobis a Deo data.
Esto aecclesiae Christi ut pater, sacerdotibus ut frater et omni populo pius
et aequus. . . ."—MGH. Epp. iv. 107, 147. On the king as vicarius Dei, cf.
Kern, pp. 54 sqq. (= Chrimes, pp. 28 sqq.) and note 98, also Harnack,
Christus praesens-vicarius Christi, in SB. d. Preuss. Ak., phil.-hist. Kl.
(1927), no. 34.— The examples quoted in the text come from MGH. Capit.
ii. 173, no. 248; Fulbert of Chartres, Ep. xxx. (MPL. 141 col. 216); Wipo,
Gesta Chuonradi, c. iii. and v. (ed. Bresslau, MGH. Script. rer. Germ. pp. 23
and 26), Tetralogus, v. 19 and 121 (ibid. pp. 76 and 79); Pez, Thes. anecd.
nov., vi. 1, 235, where abbot Ekbert calls Henry III " caput ecclesiae; "
Thietmar, Chron: i. 26 (ed. Kurze, MGH. Script. rer. Germ., p. 16); there
is a very important parallel to Thietmar in Benzo, Ad Heinricum imp.

It is clear that, from the point of view of religion, royal theocracy was only possible if the king was given a place in the hierarchy above the bishops. In Carolingian times the king was commonly regarded as the equal of the pope, sometimes even as his superior. If, in early medieval royal portraits, bishops also appear, they are always smaller than the king; they show a respectful mien and a humble bearing, and the very arrangement of the figures indicates their lower rank. In the later middle ages this is entirely changed; from this period we possess paintings of arch- bishops of Mainz at imperial coronations, and the prelates are larger than the kings who stand beside them, whereas in earlier paintings the only figures which overshadow the king are those of Christ and the saints. On ceremonial occasions the king took the first place, unless the pope himself was present. The glorification of the king reaches its highest point when, like Christ, he is depicted seated in a mandorla, the symbol of the incarnation, or when the dogmatically impossible assertion is made that the bishop is merely the representative of Christ, the king the vicar of God the Father himself.[1]

To place the king thus, on a level with the priesthood or even above it, implies a conception of the religious hierarchy essentially different from those which we have already described—a conception which we may well call

(3) The conception of the hierarchy as a royal theocracy.

The essential element in it is the idea of divine right, which raises the monarch high above the creatures of earth and lays upon him the duty of leading the people towards God. This conception of the hierarchy as a royal theocracy was the dominant philosophy during the period in which the churches of Europe were still an integral part of the state and still under royal control.

lib., i. 26 (MGH. SS. xi. 609), though this is already polemical. The highest claims are made for the king by the Anonymous of York, Tract. iv (MGH. Lib. de lite, iii. 667).

[1] For examples of this in pseudo-Augustine (Ambrosiaster), Chatwulf, Hugh of Fleury and the Anonymous of York, see Kern, pp. 111 sqq. (= Chrimes, pp. 53 sqq.) and notes 197 sqq.; also Carlyle, i. 150, 215 (on the question of the literary ancestry of Chatwulf), iii. 134 sqq.

CHAPTER III

The Transformation of Society by the Christian Church: Royal Theocracy, Proprietary Churches and Monastic Piety

THE ascetic and the monarchical conceptions of the hierarchy were not foredoomed to mutual enmity, for their interests were in many ways different. The ascetic did not regard the world as worthy of serious attention, and all his efforts were directed towards the future; according to him the hierarchy was something concerned primarily with the next life, and he did not trouble himself greatly with earthly order, accepting any disturbance of it with resignation. From the monarchical point of view, on the other hand, the present world should be led by the temporal ruler to the honour of God, and should be guided by him according to the divine will and towards the heavenly goal. Yet this is exactly the task which the priests claimed as their own; they too wished to " raise the earth up to Heaven. " It can consequently be said that an ultimate conflict between kingship and priesthood was natural and inevitable. In spite of the part which political considerations played in this conflict, we must not approach the question with any doubt as to the truly religious motives of either side, nor with the suggestion that either party acted irresponsibly; in the same way, it is on the whole unjust to describe either royal " encroachments " on the clerical domain or the extension of ecclesiastical authority over what were really temporal matters as the result of personal ambition or moral depravity, however strong the influence of such motives may have been. For both State and Church—to use the terms which are conventional, if not altogether satisfactory—were bound to regard themselves as the supreme body in society, designed by God and comprising and ruling all things. It was only the fulfilment of a resultant duty if the heads of the two institutions each held himself responsible to God for all the activities of human life.

The opposition which had been present in germ since the time of Constantine the Great remained for various reasons in the background during the early middle ages; strife broke out only occasionally, and on the whole it was neither very serious nor very decisive, largely because the Church at that time was still weak. It was only rarely that the episcopate was able, as under Louis the Pious, to secure ascendancy over the ruler, and there were few popes between Gelasius I or his immediate successors and Leo IX who could make much show of resistance to kings and emperors. Apart, however, from its political weakness, the Church only gradually abandoned its old attitude of indifference towards the world. The principle still survived that Christendom had to tolerate the temporal power and accept it as a divine dispensation. The world, it was still said, was not sufficiently Christian to be ruled by the Church. The gulf fixed between the kingdom of God and the kingdom of this world was still unbridged.

So much we are entitled to say, although there is no doubt that the idea of the homogeneity of *ecclesia* and *mundus* gained ground more and more, in spite of many set-backs, and established itself firmly in the minds of men. The increasing decay of the Roman empire and the consolidation of the Germanic states in Europe had also, of course, some part in changing the relations of Church and State. In addition, the cohesion of the whole Church became loosened, and in each country a strong feeling of the independence of the national churches and their close connection with the state had the opportunity to develop. When the Germanic rulers introduced the Church into their territories, and Christianity became the generally accepted creed, the Church assumed an essential place in all the affairs of daily life. King Pippin concluded his epoch-making alliance with the Roman Church, and a bond was created which linked the destiny of the Franks with that of Rome; this alliance was drawn even closer by the empire of Charlemagne. In the empire of Charles and his

successors the Roman imperial tradition was revived and
the idea of Christian unity underwent a new development.
Gelasius I's famous sentences were quoted again and
again, but with a notable change; it was the body of the
Church, and not the world in general, which was now said
to have two heads, the king and the priest. So, too, the
Frankish king issued orders not " to his faithful and those
of the realm, " but " to his faithful and those of Holy
Church; " it is plain, therefore, that from Carolingian
times onwards the words " world, " " empire, " "mankind,"
" Church, " " Christendom, " were often used as synonyms.
Yet it would be quite incorrect if we saw in such expressions
a deliberate perversion of the old idea of unity in favour of
the imperial power; on the contrary, it is entirely in accordance with medieval thought that the City of God—in its
widest sense as the whole of Christendom, the people of
God on earth—should be regarded as the noblest of all
communities, including within itself both State and
Church; to belong to it was for medieval man his first and
most natural duty.[1]

The development of the theocratic idea of office provided
an added reason for Church and State to draw closer together. Even more than the first Christian emperors, the
Visigothic, Anglo-Saxon and Frankish kings regarded their
position as an ecclesiastical office, which imposed on them
the duty of protecting the Church and preserving the purity
of the faith; and this conception of kingship found expression
in the consecration ceremony, where, significantly enough,
the ceremonial was largely modelled on that used for
ordination to the highest spiritual office, the episcopacy.

Yet in spite of all this, the theory of the two powers and
the feeling of unity between Church and State were very
variously interpreted. The monarchists took these ideas
quite literally, and the unity was for them an undoubted and
accomplished fact; the king was the representative of

---

[1] Cf. U. Stutz, *Kirchenrecht*, in *Enzykl. der Rechtswissenschaft* (ed. von
Holtzendorff and Kohler, 7th ed., (1914) v. 298 sqq. The altered form of
Gelasius' words is first found in the *Episcoporum ad Hludowicum impera-
torem relatio* of 829 (MGH. *Capit.* ii. 29), but there are similar expressions
as early as the reign of Charlemagne.

Christ on earth, his dignity the sublimest of all. They did, indeed, admit the separation of the two powers, but felt this as in no sense a limitation upon their freedom of action, and in practice often paid no heed to the rights of the other divinely-ordained authority. The temporal power strove to set itself at the head of the one united Christian society, and the kingship was in consequence the real representative of the idea of unity until the time of Henry IV.[1]

Among the leaders of the Church and all those who could not accept without reservation the monarchical conception of the hierarchy, there were, on the other hand, many discordant and contradictory views about the relation of priesthood and kingship. One thing alone is certain: in the early and çentral periods of the middle ages the freedom of the Church was never understood to mean the separation of the Church from the State. However much it was condemned, the world and its institutions were always felt to have been handed over to the care of the Church by Christ's command to " Go and preach the Gospel, " and separation from them was therefore impossible. Apart from this, the Church made many demands upon the State; protection, provision for its needs, freedom from all burdens and a liberal preference in the enjoyment of all the benefits which the State had to offer. Zealous preachers informed the king that his sovereignty was an office, that he himself was a servant of the Church and that he had to obey the superior wisdom of the priest. The moral laws of Christianity were binding upon him, and even in early times heresy was in itself a ground for deposition. Even the greatest king, it was said, was liable, like every Christian, to punishment by the spiritual authority and to pastoral direction, while their share in the consecration

---

[1] The way in which the theory of the two powers was understood from the secular point of view is well shown in a famous letter of Charlemagne to Leo III, which was written by Alcuin: " Nostrum est: secundùm auxilium divinae pietatis sanctam undique Christi ecclesiam ab incursu paganorum et ab infidelium devastatione armis defendere foris, et intus catholicae fidei agnitione munire. Vestrum est, sanctissime pater: elevatis ad Deum cum Moyse manibus nostram adiuvare militiam, quatenus vobis intercedentibus Deo ductore et datore populus christianus super inimicos sui sancti nominis ubique semper habeat victoriam, et nomen domini nostri Jesu Christi toto clarificetur in orbe " (*Alcuini ep.* 93, in MGH. *Epp.* iv. 137-8.).

and crowning of the king brought the bishops a great increase in their authority.

In the ninth century the bishops of the Frankish kingdom and one or two of the popes made repeated use of their moral influence for political ends; it is only necessary to recall the deposition of Louis the Pious or the actions of Nicholas I. At this period, however, those who wielded the priestly authority had not yet expressly asserted their personal superiority over the king; God alone remained the only Lord and Judge of the king, and the source of his right. When Frankish bishops assisted at the ceremony at which Louis the Pious was divested of his power, and imposed penance on the emperor, they only felt themselves to be executing the judgement which in their opinion had been pronounced by the general defection on the Lügenfeld of Colmar. In particular, the consecration of king or emperor did not make either the officiating bishop or the pope his superior, for the consecration was a sacrament and as such was dispensed by Christ alone; bishop and pope were merely His instruments. The bishop who performed the coronation ceremony was no more superior to the king he crowned than were the provincial bishops superior to the archbishop they ordained; king and archbishop alike owed their consecration only to God.[1]

In spite, therefore, of an awareness, on the part of the priests, of the implications of their office, and of their firm conviction of its higher dignity, the divine origin of kingship was never seriously disputed. The king was always recognised as protector of the Church and supreme lord

[1] Cf. Kern, pp. 228 sqq. (= Chrimes, pp. 105 sqq.) If the imperial title was derived, e.g., by Louis II, from coronation at Rome, such an attitude in no sense implied dependence on the pope. Hereditary right is emphasised in ninth century coronation orders and in other sources—cf. E. Eichmann, *Die Ordines der Kaiserkrönung*, in ZRG., *kanon. Abt.*, ii. (1912) 8. The points made above emerge very clearly in a famous letter of Nicholas I, which has sometimes been misunderstood (MGH. *Epp.* vi. 305, no. 34). The sword which the emperor receives from Peter for use against the heathen must not be confused with the two swords which, according to later theory, were both in the pope's hands (cf. *Luke* xxii. 38); it is the sword used in the coronation ceremony: cf. Eichmann, *op. cit.*, p. 10, n. 1. The limited function of the pope who merely " administers " is here sharply brought out: " imperium suum, quod cum benedictione et sacratissimi olei unctione sedis apostolicae praesule ministrante percepit."

over all temporal affairs, in which even the clergy must be subject to him—indeed, according to strict theory, priests should meddle as little in temporal affairs as secular men in spiritual matters. Ecclesiastics expected the king to endow the Church and its servants with abundant privileges to the glory of God, but they felt themselves bound by earthly laws. Even a man like Nicholas I, who was more active politically than any other pope before the great pontiffs of the eleventh century, held firmly to this principle: " Jesus Christ has so divided the spheres of the two authorities that the Christian emperors need the bishops in order to secure everlasting life, but the bishops ought to obey the imperial law in the use of temporal possessions." Nevertheless we must remember that in practice the pope had already asserted his right to define the limits of his own authority. Hincmar of Reims speaks in a truly Augustinian spirit of the subjection of Christians to the authority of their king, but he adds: " All are commanded to obey the human and earthly authority until at the appointed time the Church shall be freed from the perplexities of the world."[1]

In these words, Hincmar once again expresses the idea which had determined the attitude adopted by Christianity towards the world from the earliest years. It was felt that the only possibility for the State and for all worldly institutions was to make themselves useful to Christians on their road to salvation, but that there would be no further place for them in the heavenly kingdom, since the world and all that belonged to it was felt to be in some way alien to the Kingdom of God. This conviction can also be found in ecclesiastical interpretations of the theory of the two powers, in which the inferiority of the secular power is repeatedly

---

[1] Hincmar, De ordine palatii, c. v. (MGH. Capit. ii. 519) on Gelasius I's letter to the emperor Anastasius, and De divortio Lotharii et Tetbergae, q. vii (MPL. 125 col. 769), where he quotes Gelasius' treatise, iv. 11 (Thiel, p. 567); see also the passages quoted by Caspar, Papsttum, ii. 755. Nicholas I follows Gelasius in Ep. 88 (MGH. Epp. vi. 485 sq.). There are similar expressions in canon 1 of the synod of Trosly (909), printed in Mansi, xviii. 267: " sicut enim regalis potestas sacerdotali religioni se devote submittit, sic et sacerdotalis auctoritas cum omni pietatis officio se regali dignitati subdere debet."

stressed: the Church has the higher metaphysical rank, and the State stands far below it; no king is worthy to take part in the sacred activity of the clergy; human and clerical authority exist for different reasons. Setting these ideas beside St Paul's commands to obey the powers that be, the Church prepared for a painful conquest of worldly abuses.

Hincmar, in whom hierarchical ideas were stronger than in most ninth-century churchmen, drew attention elsewhere in his writings to the Christian duty of non-resistance, and there is nothing strange in finding the same man claiming influence over the world and yet preaching non-resistance. Gregory I, for all his monastic piety, was absolutely humble in spirit: " He who murmurs against the authority set over him," he once wrote, "openly blames the Lord who has given it to mankind." Men like Odo of Cluny or Peter Damian held similar views. Yet Atto of Vercelli, for example, who preached passive obedience in the tenth century, was at the same time one of the most determined defenders of the priestly dignity. A story told by the chronicler of Cambrai shows how the Church could sometimes cover its weakness in face of the king by appealing to the Pauline commands. Henry III, he records, had once demanded something from Lietbert of Cambrai which the latter thought unjust; he refused it, and was in consequence thrown into prison. Thereupon he gave way, " knowing that, according to the Apostle, we must be subject to the king." In acting thus, however, Lietbert seems to have misunderstood the doctrine of Christian obedience; submission to secular commands had always been limited by St Peter's words: " We ought to obey God rather than men."[1]

The question of the duty of non-resistance played an important part in the discussion whether priests should fight or not. In principle this had at first been decided in the negative, for wars were the clearest example of those worldly affairs from which God's servants should hold

---

[1] *Acts* v. 29. Cf. Gregory I, *Moralia*, xxii. 24 (MPL. 76 col. 250): " Qui enim contra superpositam sibi potestatem murmurat, liquet quod illum redarguit, qui eamdem homini potestatem dedit."

themselves aloof. The medieval attitude, however, was not only different in practice, but there was a considerable variation in the strictness of the regulations that were drawn up to deal with the matter. Bishop Gerhard of Cambrai, influenced in all probability by the views current in France at the time, went so far as to declare against clerical participation in the movement to establish the Truce of God, asserting that the preservation of the peace was the king's business, and that the intervention of the bishops constituted a breach of the Gelasian doctrine. Those who were prepared to allow priests to shed blood countered the arguments of Peter Damian by the example of Leo IX, who, they pointed out, had been a fighter and yet a holy man. To this Damian replied by asking whether St Peter attained the primacy because he denied Christ, and whether David received the gift of prophecy because he committed adultery ? The Son of God, he pointed out, had overcome the Devil by His patience, and had taught men to suffer the fury of the world in silence rather than to take up their weapons and meet blows with blows. What, he asks, can be more repugnant to the Christian law than retaliation?[1]

In the ninth and tenth centuries, and even in the first half of the eleventh century, the Church does not yet wish to rule over the world, and will neither judge nor condemn it. A pious feeling that God's decrees are inscrutable leads men to accept the state and the ruler as the gift of either God's grace or of His wrath. Man must not oppose God, whether He bless, try or punish, but must accept what He gives with fortitude, and hope for deliverance through His grace. In spite of many temporary deviations, the decisions about the relations of the two powers which were made by the great popes about the year 500 remained in essentials unaltered until the second half of the eleventh century. Decisive conflicts between the sacramental and

[1] Fulbert of Chartres, *Ep.* 112 (MPL. 141 cols. 255 sqq.); *Gesta ep. Camerac.*, iii. 27 (MGH. SS. vii. 474); *Vita Balderici ep. Leod.*, c. xvi. (MGH. SS. iv. 730); Peter Damian, *Ep.* iv. 9 (*Opera omnia*, i. [1783] 112 sqq.). On the Church's attitude to war, cf. C. Erdmann, *Die Entstehung des Kreuzzugsgedankens*, esp. pp. 68 sqq.

the monarchical conceptions of the hierarchy had not yet arisen, and one of the chief reasons for this appears to lie in the diversity of ideas about the world which had gained currency ; but an increasing uniformity of opinion developed as the middle ages advanced, for the world was coming more and more under the sway of the Church and of Christianity.

II

The idea of the hierarchical pre-eminence of the king was the foundation of the royal theocracy of the middle ages. It laid on the king the responsibility to God for the right direction of the Church, and on the Church the duty of obedience; it christianised the office of the ruler both in his own eyes and in those of his subjects, whether lay or clerical. The acquisition of this theocratic character by the kingship marks the first and most important epoch in the christianisation of the world.

It was because of this theocratic outlook that the rulers of the Germanic states of the middle ages intervened in ecclesiastical matters even more than the Christian Roman emperors had done. They summoned councils and presided over them, founded churches, monasteries and bishoprics, and issued orders on matters of clerical administration; but beside this, their decrees covered the whole field of the canon law, and many bishoprics and large abbacies were filled on their nomination. Through this system, however, the Church was not merely governed, but was also itself educated to the business of government. The chief offices were in the hands of bishops and abbots, who were able to exercise a considerable influence on secular politics, and thereby to some extent to realise clerical ideals; they could often influence the details of administration through their position at the head of local government, and even more through the fact that they themselves were the owners of vast lordships to which extensive political rights were attached. The development of the Church along such lines created a system which led to a mutual and far-reaching

inter-penetration of Church and State, and helped forward
the christianisation of the populations subject to both.

Historically, the rights of the rulers over the Church were
based mainly on theocratic and hierarchical conceptions,
but in this first period of royal theocracy the strength of
their hold was rapidly increased by the system of proprietary churches. With the advance of feudal thought, proprietary right became at least as important a source of
secular authority over the Church as the monarchical
conception of the hierarchy. Two examples will serve as
illustrations. One is the passage already quoted from
Thietmar of Merseburg, to the effect that the bishops, the
princes of the earth, should be subject only to the king, who
after the pattern of Christ surpasses all mortals by virtue
of the glory of the consecration and of the crown. The
second is a story told by the chronicler of St Trond, a
proprietary monastery of the bishops of Metz, situated in
the diocese of Liège. An unpopular abbot had been forced
on the monks by the proprietor of the *Eigenkloster*, bishop
Hermann of Metz, well-known as the recipient of Gregory
VII's most famous letters; they fled, and one of them
persuaded Henry IV, against whom bishop Hermann had
rebelled, to grant him investiture and the help of two counts
to secure him entry. The legal justification for the king's
action, says the chronicler, was the fact that Henry IV
had now the right to administer the see of Metz, since the
schismatic bishop Hermann had now been deprived of it
and it was therefore vacant; hence the king was able to
dispose of St Trond, which pertained to the bishopric.
This story suggests that the monks of St Trond regarded
every bishopric in the kingdom as royal property, to be
disposed of freely by the ruler at each vacancy.[1]

These two examples show the two possible foundations
of royal theocracy in the first half of the middle ages with
unusual clarity. Between the two forces, the one drawing
its strength from theocratic conceptions, the other from the

[1] Thietmar, *Chron.* i. 26 (ed. R. Holtzmann, MGH. *Script. rer. Germ.*,
new series, ix. 16); *Gesta abb. Trud.*, iii. 2. (MGH. SS. x. 240 sqq.). A
similar case, from which the same conclusions can be drawn, is to be found
ibid., v. 4 (pp. 252 sqq.).

system of proprietary churches, stands the canon law of the period; which of them exercised the greater influence upon it would be impossible to determine.

The king's theocratic rights are akin to the proprietary church system in that both constitute a breach in the Church's custom of treating the laity as a passive order. From as early as the third century the division of the ecclesiastical community into active and passive members —that is, into clergy and people—and the subordination of the latter, had been an accomplished fact. The laity had sought to find an outlet for their religious activity in monasticism, which at first was a religious movement parallel to the Church rather than a part of the ecclesiastical organisation, but this was in no way a contradiction of existing hierarchical principles. Similarly, the owner of a proprietary church had no intention of undermining the dogmatically-ordained position of the clergy; but when a man built a church or a monastery on his own land, placed clergy or monks in it, laid down rules governing their activity, prescribed for them the services they should per- form, the rule they should adopt and the good works they should undertake, retained a controlling interest in the life they led, and exercised disciplinary authority over them, then—though all these things might be subject to certain limitations—such a man was no longer a merely passive member of the Church. The exercise of proprietary rights, like the exercise of royal rights, shows the laity taking a more active part in the life of the Church, although the proprietary system, in this unlike the monarchy, did not succeed in destroying the original clerical conception of the hierarchy. Yet the exercise of proprietary rights did, none the less, give to laymen a place in the Church which ran counter to the sacramental idea of the hierarchy; in consequence it could and did lead to serious conflicts, which ended with the revival of the ancient order, the repression of the laity and their return to their old passive position.[1]

---

[1] On monasticism as a movement parallel to the Church, cf. Harnack, *Mönchtum*, pp. 18 sqq., and Stutz, *Kirchenrecht*, p. 289. On *Eigenkirchen-*

This, however, is not the only significance of the proprietary system in the history of the Christian Church. Its nature and the extent to which it prevailed can only be understood against the economic and social background of the early middle ages. Estates were growing both in number and size, and at the same time their legal and social importance was tending to increase; moreover, we must remember that a great deal of land was leased under various forms of tenure, that only a few demesnes which formed the centres of manorial organisations were worked by the landlord on his own account or by his agents, so forming nuclei for large-scale aggregations of property. The rent and the dues of the unfree tenants were paid at these centres, there the labour-services of the villeins were regulated, there too were usually built the mills, bakehouses, etc., which all were bound to use. Lordship of this kind can create a community as easily as can an association of freemen. From the sociological point of view, the medieval estate presents a picture of a society compulsorily formed under the control of the lord, with a tendency both to extend and to become more highly-developed and centralised. On such an estate, the lord would often build a church where he installed a priest of his own choosing, either a serf or some other acceptable man. After the introduction of tithes in the eighth century it was not unusual for landowners to enforce payment to, and prescribe attendance at, the churches which belonged to them. Thus the famous capitulary *De villis* of about 800, dealing with the royal demesnes in S.W. France, orders that tenants on these estates shall pay tithe only to the royal *Eigenkirchen*, and that only the king's own serfs or clerks of the royal chapel shall become priests there. The intimate connection between the church and the estate upon which it was built was in no way broken if the church was alienated to a monastery, a bishop or the king. It was often received back

---

recht, see U. Stutz, *Geschichte des kirchlichen Benefizialwesens von seinen Anfängen bis auf Alexander III* (1895), i. 1, and the same author's *Die Eigenkirche als Element des mittelalterlich-germanischen Kirchenrechts* (1895) (= Barraclough, ii. 35–70), also his article *Eigenkirche, Eigenkloster* in Herzog-Hauck's *Realencyclopädie*, xxiii. (1913) 364 sqq.

by the original owner in fee; but if not, though the revenues from the church were lost, its power to form or consolidate a community persisted. This effect was the greater in proportion as it was possible to secure privileges for the church—tithes, baptismal and burial rights, or even full parochial rights.[1]

The objects of landlords who built churches differed widely. Piety no doubt led many to desire to have in the neighbourhood a church and a priest whom they trusted, for the benefit of themselves and their families, or only for their tenants if they themselves lived elsewhere; this was the same motive from which the heathen domestic priest-hood of the Germanic peoples had originated, and shows how deep lay the roots of the proprietary church system. Others again were more attracted by the prospect of material gain through tithes, the gifts of the faithful and church dues. In any case, however, the foundation of *Eigenkirchen* had the effect of decentralising the Church, loosening the ties which had hitherto bound it together and creating smaller, local units of organisation. Bishoprics and large parishes were gradually broken up. There were complaints that private churches had been built but that the lord paid no further heed either to bishop or parish priest. Not only did the proprietary system largely break up the old ecclesiastical organisation, but in France, for example, it was even prejudicial to the close relations of Church and State, since many laymen succeeded in turning cathedrals into private churches and controlling bishoprics.[2]

However, the proprietary system was not only destruc-tive. It carried ecclesiastical organisation everywhere, into the most important, if also the. smallest, strata of society; its general prevalence was directly responsible for

---

[1] On the influence of the idea of lordship on the proprietary system, see Stutz, *Eigenkirche*, p. 28 (= Barraclough, p. 54) and Böhmer, *Eigenkir-chentum in England*, p. 337.

[2] Stutz, *Eigenkirche*, p. 25 (= Barraclough, ii. 51) shows how the origins of the consolidated bishopric of modern times can nevertheless be found in the proprietary period. On the decentralising effect of the proprietary system, see Agobard of Lyons, *De privilegio et iure sacerdotii*, c. xi. (MPL. 104 col. 139): " putant ex hoc, quod maioris ordinis sacerdotes non eis sint necessarii et derelinquunt frequenter publica officia et predicamenta."

bringing the Germanic peoples of western Europe into the Church, and thereby laid the foundation for the gradual spread of the Catholic faith.

Attention has rightly been called, on the other hand, to the disadvantages of the proprietary system. It was the owner's sense of responsibility alone which determined whether he would pay heed to the spiritual objects of his church or his monastery, or whether he would rather use it to extend and strengthen his domain and to increase his revenues. It happened often enough that church services were neglected, churches and monasteries remained unoccupied, or that clerics were appointed who were quite unsuited to their spiritual duties but very useful as estate-managers or in conducting other purely secular business. Tithes were frequently pocketed without the priest seeing a penny of them, the church fell into ruins and the poor remained hungry; church lands might be used for private purposes or even sold. Often enough lords built churches but did not endow them, and then finally sold them after procuring or usurping on their behalf a number of profitable rights. Many churches became in this way the objects of economic speculation.

The evils of the royal theocracy and the proprietary church system were no doubt very great, but it would be wrong to lay all responsibility for the ills of the Church in the ninth and tenth centuries on the laity. Since Carolingian times the proprietary system had ceased to be predominantly in the hands of the laity, and bishoprics and monasteries had gradually become the principal owners of land and churches. Apart from this, however, there is as much evidence in contemporary sources—which often exaggerate and generalise—about moral imperfection or sheer depravity among the clergy as there is about the wickedness of the laity. The accusation that they were ignorant, avaricious and too much concerned with secular affairs can be sustained; bishops and clergy bought and sold the gifts of the Holy Ghost to enrich themselves, neglected their spiritual duties, used consecrated ground for storing grain or stacking hay, wasted Church property in dissipation with women, and kept dogs to gratify a purely worldly pleasure in the chase; monks, we are told, had no thought of living according to their rule. Yet such complaints are unjust when applied too generally. If from the second half of the tenth century a large number of churches were restored after having fallen into decay while in the hands of bishops or secular lords, the latter had by no means always been responsible for their ruined state. The hundred years between 850 and 950 were a time of wars, and there was presumably a sharp decline in the population. In all probability there were often no people for the churches to serve with their Masses and sermons, and when monasteries were being laid waste by Normans and Hungarians it was no time for prayer, but it was better to take sword in hand and defend one's own skin. These were frequently the reasons why churches and monasteries stood empty, why their lands lay untilled or were turned by the lord to his own private use, and why the monks wandered about homeless.

At all times, however, attempts were made to repair as far as possible the damage which the Church suffered through becoming involved in worldly affairs, through the domination of laymen and the turbulence of the times. There was never any lack of men, whether laity or ecclesiastics, who set out to fulfil the Church's religious purpose; even the owners of proprietary churches were not all entirely influenced by considerations of financial profit, but many of them were ready to see their devotion cost them something. In their capitularies the Frankish kings and emperors prepared the way for the most comprehensive reforms, and this work was continued by the rulers in the succession-states and by local councils, which repeated the phrases of the Frankish laws. They renewed the old canonical rules about simony, clerical morality and the alienation of Church property; they attempted to impose legal limits upon the proprietary system and to protect spiritual interests; and they instituted the tithe, managed on the whole to preserve it, and gave the Church thereby considerable material assistance. Further, we must not forget the gifts which poured in upon the Church from all sides, and at least partly compensated for the losses occasioned by secularisation.[1]

The reform of monasticism was urged on with particular zeal, since the spiritual force of the whole Church seemed to be dependent upon it. As king in Aquitaine, Louis the Pious had already shown favour to abbot Benedict of Aniane, and as emperor he called upon him to introduce reforms into all the monasteries of his land. Abbot Wala of Corbie, a member of the Carolingian house, was responsible for considerable reforms, and later on, under Charles the Bald, great efforts were again made to raise the standard of monastic life. At the beginning of the tenth century there occurred the foundation, epoch-making in its effects, of the Burgundian reform at Cluny; it had no particularly striking features at first, but later, through its connection with the papacy, and still more through its energetic reform of the Benedictine rule and the strong personalities of its long-lived abbots, it rose to a position of unparalleled importance. From Cluny reformers went to hundreds of monasteries in Burgundy, France, Italy, Spain and England; among its daughter-houses three in particular— Fleury, Saint-Bénigne-de-Dijon and San Benigno di Fruttuaria—themselves became centres of reform. Three other such centres came into being during the second half of the tenth century: Gorze in the diocese of Metz, Brogne in that of Liège, and Einsiedeln. Gorze and Brogne directed their efforts towards eastern France and western Germany, while Einsiedeln was enabled to spread its influence to Bavaria through the saintly Wolfgang of Regensburg, and later to other parts of Germany as well. A few decades later came St Vannes at Verdun, from which reform reached many parts of Germany by way of Stablo. In Italy St Romuald founded the congregation of Camaldoli, and later Johannes Gualbertus founded that of Vallombrosa; both were closely related to the hermit-tradition, which had always been particularly lively in Italy.[2]

---

[1] See Appendix II.

[2] See E. Sackur, *Die Cluniacenser in ihrer kirchlichen und allgemeingeschichtlichen Wirksamkeit bis zur Mitte des elften Jahrhunderts*, 2 vols., 1892–4, and L. M. Smith, *Cluny in the eleventh and twelfth centuries* (1930).

III

It was the intention of all the monastic reformers to make possible a life of service before God which should be really ascetic and should involve a real flight from the world. The assurance of a sufficient income was therefore one of the essential pre-requisites for reform. In the case of new foundations this demand was satisfied by rich endowments, but in the case of existing houses it often happened that either the proprietor of the *Eigenkloster* or some other layman held the title and the rights of the abbot in place of a religious, turned the monastic property to his own uses and left the monks to starve. Such a situation was avoided by setting aside certain estates to provide for the needs of the inmates of the cloister, or by making a division between the property of the abbot and that of the convent, and freeing the latter from all burdens. This separation was a particularly common measure of reform in the ninth century. The most important thing, however, about all monastic reforms is the establishment of life according to a fixed rule, and here the Benedictine rule was usually the model. Benedict of Aniane collected all the rules to which he had access, and on this basis drew up his own rule, which had an enduring influence, especially at Cluny. The reformers were not satisfied with a return to the original strictness of the Benedictine rule, but they also laid down minute provisions for carrying it into effect. The order of precedence in the cloister was exactly precribed, strict obedience was enjoined upon the lower ranks, and the duties of each official were carefully defined. Regulations were made governing food, drink and fasts, the colour and quality of the habit, and a restriction set upon the permitted number of articles of clothing. Above all, however, the zeal of the reformers was directed towards fixing the liturgical order of the day and the year.

The ultimate purpose of all these measures was to secure freedom for contemplation through the renunciation of the private will and bodily enjoyment. At the same time everything, especially the sacrifice of the Mass and meditation in prayer, was designed to secure a heavenly reward and after death a place for the soul near the Creator. In monastic religion the Last Things and the doctrine of justification by works exercised an influence second only to that of the doctrine of grace. Monastic piety became the piety of all classes in the middle ages because of its strong feeling of the unity of all creatures and its sense of common responsibility with the whole Church before God. The belief that merit could also be acquired on behalf of others was the factor which allowed European monasticism to play a decisive part in the history of religion. The Mass stands out above all other good works, for it is celebrated by Christ and the whole Church, and its fruits bring comfort to all Christians, living and dead. In a secondary sense, however, it increases in value if it is celebrated by a devout congregation and by a priest acceptable to God. It is permissible here to recall once again the legend according to which more souls were freed from purgatory by the Masses celebrated at Cluny than by any other kind of good works; and it became known through a vision that pope Benedict VIII had been received into Heaven through the prayers of the Cluniacs. By good works penance could not only be done vicariously—which resulted in the remission of punishments for sin and the cancellation of minor sins—but the grace of God could even be effectively supplicated for the living and the dead, the just and the unjust.[1]

Care for the dead was recognised as the special task of monks, and is in conformity with their predominant interest in the next world. Monasteries kept lists of obits, in which the anniversaries of the deaths of members of other monasteries, bishops, priests and layfolk were entered, besides those of their own monks, and with the help of these lists Masses were said for the souls of the departed. The intro-

---

[1] Cf. Harnack, DG. iii. 9: " The history of piety in the middle ages is the history of monasticism." On the application of the *fructus speciales* of the Mass for the benefit of others, see Scheeben-Atzberger, p. 664, Abschn. 536, C. Pesch, *Praelectiones dogmaticae*, vi. (1914) 450 sqq. ; on the application of good works, *ibid.* v. (1916) 266 sqq. On the effectiveness of Masses at Cluny, cf. *supra*, pp. 46-7; on Benedict VIII, *Jotsaldi vita Odilonis*, ii. 14 (MPL. 742 cols. 927 sq.).

duction of the feast of All Souls by Odilo of Cluny (d. 1048) shows to what an extent the monastic reformers regarded prayers for the dead as their special duty; this feast spread rapidly through the monastic world and was adopted by the secular Church. The monks' prayers were offered not only to God the Father and to Christ, but they also entreated the powerful assistance of the Virgin and the saints, among whom those held to be most efficacious were the patron saint of the monastery, who was the real protector and advocate of the monks, and those saints whose relics were preserved in the Church.[1]

Monastic life and monastic prayers, however, could obtain benefits on earth as well as treasures in Heaven. Prayers were often offered for enlightenment before some important decision; and the imperial monasteries of Germany were often privileged or endowed on the ground that the servants of Christ were praying there day and night for the prosperity of the empire. So, too, victory and peace were always the object of specially solemn prayers.

The respect paid to the life of monks and nuns, because they brought salvation to the whole Church, shows how highly contemporaries regarded their vocation. People tended more and more to adopt the monastic outlook upon life and to attempt to copy it. The foundation of monasteries can always be regarded as an act of piety; for if the possession of an existing monastery was ordinarily a profitable investment, a new foundation was always an economic sacrifice, for there could be no hope, as in the case of a proprietary church, of gain through tithes and fees. The religious motive is often clearly expressed in wills or in foundation charters; very frequently the wording is to the effect that " though I cannot myself despise all earthly things, yet I hope to share in the reward of those who do, if I give them shelter;" [2] and similar phrases are to be found in deeds of gift. Great confidence was placed in the prayers

---

[1] *Orationis suffragium* is often asked for at the beginning of letters, e.g. Fulbert of Chartres, *Epp.* 11, 12, 14, 23 (MPL. 141 cols. 206 sqq.). On Odilo's decree introducing All Souls' Day, of. Sackur, *Cluniacenser*, ii. 231.
[2] See, for instance, *Gallia Christiana*, ii. 168 no. 6; Bruel, iii. 562, no. 2484; Bouquet, ix. 667, no. 6.

of monks, and the more devout they were and the more closely they followed their rule, the greater was the confidence; prayers were often the only return that a lord demanded from his *Eigenkloster*. If such a lord wished himself and his family to be buried in the monastery-church, this was yet another reason why he should desire to have devout monks. Even in the catacombs, men had desired to be buried next to a martyr, hoping to receive help from him on the Last Day, when all flesh rose from the dead; and similar considerations subsequently led them to desire to be buried under the feet of men who had a claim that their requests should be heard by God on the Day of Judgement. This, too, was the reason why the bodies or relics of saints were so anxiously sought after. A gift was made to the church of Saint-André-de-Rosans in the following terms: " I know that he [i.e. St Andrew] sits at God's right hand in glory, and so I give him my earthly goods, that he may entreat God to forgive me my sins, and may stand by me on the day when I leave this evil world and save me from the powers of darkness." Charles Martel, who was buried in St Denis, was said to have been carried off by the Devil to Hell, and this fate was regarded as a punishment for the secularisations by which he had robbed the Church. This story, however, did not only have the intended effect of frightening his successors from committing similar crimes, for King Philip I of France declared that he would not be buried in St Denis, meaning that if the saint had not been able to help Martel, he would rather not run the same risk himself.[1]

Those who founded monasteries took many precautions to ensure the effectiveness of their foundations. In order to protect the house from danger, they put it under the control of the pope, a bishop or some other powerful monastery, sometimes with the provision that it could be bought back if the church under whose protection it was put failed to perform its appointed duties. If they retained it for themselves and their heirs, they often set strict limits to their rights, so that their heirs should not have power to

[1].Ordericus Vitalis, *Hist. eccl.*, xi. 18 (MPL. 188 col. 838).

harm it. They might obtain exemption from episcopal jurisdiction; but above all else they laid it down that the monks were bound to follow their rule. Such measures were a bitter necessity, since zeal for the rule tended gradually to cool and there were many external dangers, so that the pious founders had continually to fear that all their efforts to save their souls would be brought to nothing.

The preoccupation of secular society with monastic religion is not only shown in the respect and support given to asceticism and in the use which was made of it. Of greater historical importance was the fact that laymen and secular clergy strove as far as possible to imitate the monks. The renunciation of property was regarded as an act of asceticism worthy of reward; what was given up on earth, it was believed, would be returned a hundredfold in Heaven. Apart from this, many sought to flee the world, and it is often recorded of a layman that he was a true monk though in worldly dress. Most noteworthy of all is the frequency with which, in this reforming period, laymen show the characteristic monastic feeling of responsibility for their fellow-men; gifts are often made for the salvation of the souls of certain named relations or servants, or, in more general terms, for the welfare of the whole Church and of all believers, living and dead.[1]

Good relations, based on a similarity of religious interests, soon grew up between the reformed monasteries and all classes of the population. Though many individual bishops showed themselves the friends of reform, relations with the episcopacy as a whole were strained, for the bishops naturally wished to preserve the integrity of their dioceses in

[1] For texts frequently quoted on the occasion of donations, see *supra*, p. 45, note 1 ; also *Matth.* vi. 19 sqq., *Tob.* iv. 11, *Luke* xi. 41, xxi. 33, *Prov.* xiii. 8. Cf. also the following examples: " quibusque consulit ditibus, ut ex propriis rebus, quas transitorie possident, centuplicatum valeant adquirere foenus, si modo eisdem bene utendo rebus ea quae habent studeant erogare pauperibus" (Bruel, iii. 562, no. 2484); " cogitabat qualiter ea quae temporaliter possidebat, ita disponeret ut ei perpetualiter profuissent " (*Odonis vita Geraldi*, ii. 1, in MPL. 133 col. 670). On the idea of the unity of all Christian people, cf. Bruel, *ut sup.*: " Postremo, sicut omnes christiani unius compage caritatis ac fidei tenemur, ita pro cunctis preteritorum sc. ac futurorum seu presencium orthodoxis hec donacio fiat." Gifts *pro statu et integritate catholicae religionis* are to be found, e.g., in Bouquet, ix. 667, no. 6, and Bruel, i. 358, no. 379.

face of the monks' efforts to obtain exemption from diocesan control. No such questions of principle, however, arose to mar the friendship of the reformed monasteries with the laity; the latter were entirely on the side of the monks in their demands for exemption, and until the third quarter of the eleventh century no monastic reformer thought of attacking the secular power or the proprietary system.

The monastic reformers made relatively little use of their relations with kings, princes and bishops in order to secure political influence, and did not as a rule take a very active part in the general movement for a reform of the Church. If they had done so, the fact would have been mentioned in the voluminous literature which grew up around them. The chief characteristic of monasticism was its flight from the world, and thus it was not likely to take a leading part in a movement to improve earthly institutions; but we know nevertheless that the reformers thought the same about simony and priestly marriage as did the princes and councils which had for centuries been combating these two evils. In this connection the Italian ascetics and monks were the most prominent, and this was no doubt due to the particularly unsavoury condition of the Italian Church and to the more active Latin character. Apart from this, however, the Italians placed great faith in administrative changes as a means of eradicating moral failings, whereas in the north more was expected from a spiritual reformation. Be this as it may, the strictness of a Guido of Pomposa and the burning zeal of a Peter Damian were everywhere turned against transactions that suggested simony. The French Cluniacs played an active part in politics by working energetically with the bishops to promote the Truce of God, but their actions were at least in large part guided by their special monastic interests, in particular the protection of their lands from the growing perils of private warfare. It must not be forgotten that the monks were usually good economists, and showed a consciousness of purpose and a knowledge of the ways of the world in this field as well as in the dissemination of their reforming ideas and the establishment of monastic congregations.

Yet there can be no suggestion that reform was a purely monastic affair. On the contrary, we have already seen that without engendering any completely new ideas, it was responsible for a great religious revival. The ascetics set out to be the first-line troops of the Church in the battle for Christ and against evil ; and by their merits they hoped to save not only themselves but also their fellow-men from damnation. This purpose determined the nature of their relations with the great ones of the world. They became their spiritual advisers, and kings and emperors, bishops and popes, princes and nobles listened to their words. We have only to recall the close friendship that bound Majolus of Cluny to the Ottonian house, how he reconciled Otto II with his mother Adelaide, how he interceded for all who had something to request of the emperor, and with what difficulty he dissuaded the emperor from making him pope. The influence which great ascetics like Nilus and Romuald exercised over the sensitive spirit of Otto III is equally well-known, and so too is the friendship between Otto and the visionary martyr Adalbert of Prague.   Odilo, Majolus' successor, was the honoured counsellor of many kings of his time—Henry II, Conrad II, Henry III and the French king Robert, by whom Abbo of Fleury was also held in great respect.   Hugh of Cluny was the god-father of Henry III's son, and during the Investiture Contest was the confidant of both parties, besides being closely bound to Alfonso VI of Castile.   Richard of St Vannes and Poppo of Stablo had great influence with Henry II.   Poppo, for instance, is said once to have gone to Henry's court and seen how much of his time the king devoted to the company of fools and to frivolous exhibitions.   A naked man was covered with honey, and allowed himself to be licked clean by a bear. Poppo rebuked Henry for risking the life of a Christian for the sake of a game, and received the promise that such a thing should not happen again.[1] Poppo, who

---

[1] *Vita Popponis*, c. 12 (MGH. SS. xi. 301).   At the beginning of the *Vita* of Richard of St Vannes (MGH. SS. xi. 280 sq.) there is related the well-known but rather improbable story that Henry II wished to take the habit at St Vannes, but that the first command the abbot gave him was to retain the throne.   On the relations of Hugo to Alfonso VI, see the *Statuta s.*

went so far in mortifying the flesh that he beat his breast with a stone in an attempt to draw forth tears, was the wonder of the worldly emperor Conrad II and his wife Gisela. Conrad was also influenced by abbot Guido of Pomposa, who later became the friend of Henry III, and gave Henry more encouragement in his fight against simony than anyone save Peter Damian. There is in the *Vita Guidonis* another story which is valuable for the light it sheds on the history of Christian ethics. A dying monk regained consciousness for the last time, and related that demons had afflicted him because of one single sin: while still a layman he had learnt a certain lewd song, and though he had not sung it, he had kept it in his memory. Such stories were widely repeated and helped to bring about a greater sensitiveness of conscience.

The possibility of personal influence by monastic leaders was increased by the relations of abbeys to kings, nobles and bishops under the prevailing system of royal theocracy and proprietary churches. During the eleventh century, the monastic attitude to religion penetrated these circles deeply, and managed progressively to christianise them. Though the majority of monks seem to have held themselves aloof from direct participation in the work of reforming the Church and getting rid of the manifold abuses of the time, yet by accustoming people to think of the Day of Judgement they made clergy and nobility take up the work of reform with greater attention and energy. The increased piety and interest in the welfare of the soul which the monks had awakened brought many to penance and to a better way of life. The chief result, however, was to increase reverence for the means of grace which the Church provided, since men felt themselves dependent upon them; and from this arose an occasionally fanatical desire to get rid of everything that could threaten.the effectiveness of the sacraments. This provides the reason why demands that spiritual offices should no longer be

---

Hugonis abbatis pro Alfonso rege in J. L. d'Achéry, *Veterum aliquot scriptorum spicilegium*, iii. (1723) 408.   Cf. also *Vita s. Guidonis*, c. 7 (Mabillon, AA. SS. vi. 1, 450).

bought and sold, that the life of the priesthood should
reach a higher moral standard, that the anti-clerical activity
of laymen should cease and greater attention be paid to the
precepts of the canon law, were raised more frequently and
put forward with more energy and force from the beginning
of the eleventh century onwards. This, too, was the reason
why there was so much dispute about the validity of sacraments received at the hands of a priest tainted with
simony or heresy.[1]

IV

The religious sentiments of his time affected the emperor
Henry III more deeply than any other contemporary
ruler, and determined his ecclesiastical policy. Henry
seems to have been an earnest, almost melancholy man,
strong in spite of his religious sensitivity, for whom government was a divine vocation. This mixture of humility and
consciousness of power can be psychologically explained by
the hierarchical conceptions that were so notable a part of
his character. It was a spiritual dualism, comparable to
that of the great popes: a feeling of utter subjection to God,
coupled with the firm conviction that his own will was
divinely inspired, and that his commands should be obeyed
without question. He shaped his own life in strict accordance with the teaching of Christ as he understood it. After
his marriage with Agnes of Poitou he allowed the vagrants
who had appeared for the occasion to depart unrewarded,
and thus made improbable their return. In 1043 he made
a famous speech at Constance, in which he forgave all his
enemies and demanded that they should do the same, and
it is clear that he was not thereby pursuing a purely political
object—the strengthening of the Land-peace—because he
repeated his action more than once thereafter, on one
occasion in the middle of the thanksgivings for a victory
over the Hungarians. Further, we are expressly told that
on his death-bed the emperor forgave all his enemies, and
we know that he showed a fervent veneration for relics.
At the dedication of the new church at Stablo he assisted

[1] Cf. the remarks of A. Dempf, *Sacrum imperium*, (1929) p. 172.

personally to carry the shrine that held the body of St Remaclus. He was on terms of intimacy with the great monastic leaders of his time, men like Odo and Majolus of Cluny, Poppo of Stablo, Halinard of Dijon, Guido of Pomposa and Peter Damian of Fonte Avellana, and honoured them highly. When Halinard, whom he had appointed archbishop of Lyons, refused to take the oath of fealty because he was a monk, Henry accepted the refusal after some deliberation, although Halinard's attitude was most unusual. He bore no grudge against Halinard, travelled in his company, listened to his advice after as before, and was even prepared to make him pope. He issued a constitution which forbade clerics to swear oaths in the law-courts; and when he had appointed bishop Bruno of Toul to the papacy, and Bruno wished to make his acceptance dependent upon the approbation of the clergy and people of Rome, the emperor unhesitatingly agreed. It must be remarked here that Henry neither had, nor could have had, any idea that his theocratic position was in danger, and would have revenged himself on anyone who offended against the prevailing system as effectively as he did on purely political enemies like Godfrey of Lorraine or Gebhard of Regensburg, or on the heretics whom he hanged out of hand at Goslar. It would be a mistake to look for defensive tendencies in Henry's ecclesiastical policy.[1] Secular control of the Church had been an accepted fact for generations, and in this respect Henry was purely conservative, although he took a leading part in the introduction of reforms. The contemporary Cluniac, Ralf Glaber, reports a speech of Henry's against simony, the substance of which seems credible ; in it Henry is said to have called the bishops " the representatives of Christ in His Church," " the Church which was His Bride, and which he redeemed with His Blood." Dogmatically, Henry was fully aware of the sin of simony, and treated it as sacrilege that endangered the soul; according to Glaber, his speech ended with the solemn promise: " For as God freely gave me the crown out of the fulness of His mercy, so will I freely give what

---

[1] See Appendix I.

belongs to His religion. And I will, if it pleases you, that you do likewise."[1]

In these words Henry is made to utter his belief in the divine right by which he ruled, and we have other evidence that he attributed a sacramental character to himself.[2] Replying to bishop Wazo of Liège, who, more than anyone else, impressed upon Henry the sacred character of the priesthood, the emperor explained that he also had been anointed with holy oil. Glaber, again, tells a story of Henry which is so unusual that it seems to have a core of truth in it: the emperor had been given a horse by a certain abbot; one day he was riding it when a knight met him and recognised it as his own, saying that it had been stolen from him. The emperor compelled the knight, according to the customary process of seizure, to lay his hand upon the horse and upon himself, and to lead him into his house; then he sent for the abbot, who was innocent, for he had bought the horse from the thief in good faith. At this point the chronicler loses the thread of his story and begins another, more important than the first, which is simply designed to illustrate Henry's strict sense of justice. The emperor said to the abbot: " Lay down your pastoral staff, which you believe should not be held at the gift of a mortal man." The abbot obeyed ; then the king put the staff into the hand of a figure of Christ, and commanded the abbot : " Go and receive this at the hand of the King Almighty, and be no more indebted for it to a mortal, but use it freely, as becomes the majesty of His name."[3] If we believe this story, Henry must have felt, whenever he bestowed the staff on a bishop or abbot, that Christ was working through him just as through the priest at the celebration of the Mass.

In the same way, Henry must have felt himself to be the representative of Christ when he called the synod of Sutri to give a worthy head to the Church on earth. His behaviour throughout was in conformity with contemporary

---

[1] Glaber, *Hist.* v. 5 (ed. Prou, p. 134).
[2] See Anselm, *Gesta ep. Leod.*, c. 67 (MGH. SS. vii. 230).
[3] Glaber, *Hist.* v. 4 (ed. Prou, pp. 132 sq.).

ideas, and he was careful to carry out the deposition and the new election without offending against the law, though naturally his will was the deciding factor.   It was one of his objects to revive the purity of the Roman Church and to protect the papacy and papal elections from the Roman factions, which were responsible for the weakness and demoralization of the Mother of Churches.   The ruler of the Roman Empire acted as the God-given head of Christendom. There can be no clearer sign than this, that the world had been completely conquered by Catholic Christianity.   He, the strongest and most pious of all princes, had, with the approval of the best minds of his time, reformed the Roman Church.   At this moment there begins a new epoch in the history of western Europe.

CHAPTER IV

THE STRUGGLE AGAINST LAY DOMINATION OF THE CHURCH: THE INVESTITURE CONTEST

I

DURING the ninth century, powerful voices had been raised to deny the laity an active part in the work of the Church; but they fell on deaf ears, and had not been able to arrest the development of a new body of ecclesiastical law, consonant with the ideas of the age. Nicholas I had been the last to attempt to ignore the new law and recognise only the old. He wrote in a tone of rebuke to the Eastern Emperor, who had summoned a council, saying that he had taken upon himself the duties of the priestly office; he must be content with the empire, and not usurp what belonged to the servants of the Lord. Again, Nicholas mockingly corrected archbishop Ado of Vienne, who, in one of his letters, had quite innocently referred to the priest of a certain count Gerhard: " This, dearest brother, sounds ridiculous. . . . As if count Gerhard had ordained the priest, or as if the priest belonged to the count's diocese!"[1]

Since the ninth century, however, the sacred power of the king had been revered by all. It was accepted as natural that the ruler should lead the people in Church affairs as much as in matters of politics. He summoned synods and councils, fixed their agenda, and presided over them either in person or by deputy. Things had already gone so far in the days of Nicholas I that archbishops Gunther of Cologne and Theutgaud of Trier, whom the pope had deposed, appealed to the emperor, explaining that injustice had been done them, for no one had ever heard or read that a metropolitan had been deposed without the knowledge of the ruler. When, under Henry I, the archbishop of

---

[1] Nicholas I, *Epp.* 88 and 39 (MGH. *Epp.* vi. 469, 313).

Cologne on his own authority ordained a bishop of Liège, it was regarded as an unusual innovation that this should be done without the consent of the king and the magnates, and pope John X himself rebuked the archbishop, for it was a firmly established custom that a bishopric might only be obtained at the hands of the king. Saints like Ulrich of Augsburg, Gerhard of Toul, Wolfgang of Regensburg and Adalbert of Prague, in common with all other bishops, accepted their bishoprics from the king through investiture with the pastoral staff. The words which St Gerhard of Toul uses are characteristic: " We received the care and the government of the church of Toul by divine decree and at the command of the emperor Otto and his noble brother, the archbishop Bruno." The German and Italian bishops felt themselves to be officials of the emperor, and were bound to him on oath to render ecclesiastical and secular services of many kinds; so close was this tie that they even had to ask leave of the emperor when they wished to go to Rome. In France, England and Spain the position was similar. Fulbert of Chartres, a man learned in the canon law, discussing the appointment of a bishop by a count, writes that he would have had no complaint if the appointment had been made in a regular way, but the bishop had intruded himself without the royal command and the consent of the neighbouring bishops; once again, installation by the king is regarded as the will of God.[1]

Most bishops and popes, then, accepted the royal domination of the Church as of divine institution. The monastic reformers of the tenth and early eleventh centuries had equally little thought of raising objections to it, and were on the contrary full of praise for devout princes, entered into close relations with them, and gave enthusiastic approval to their intervention in the most intimate ecclesiastical affairs. The *Vita* of one of the greatest benefactors

---

[1] Gerhard of Toul, in Calmet, *Preuves*, i. 389; Fulbert of Chartres, *Ep.* 70 (MPL. 141 col. 235). The completeness with which some kings dominated the Church in their lands is shown with extraordinary clarity in the acts of the synod of Grateley (928: *Mansi*, xviii. 354), where king Athelstan speaks of ' his ' archbishop and ' his ' bishops.

of monastic reform, count Burchard of Melun, relates with sympathy that the king gave him the abbey of St Maur-des-Fossés so that he might reform it, but retained proprietary rights in his own hands;[1] for if Burchard's successors were to ruin the monastery, this would seriously endanger the well-being of the king's soul. When reformers like Majolus of Cluny, Richard of St Vannes, Poppo of Stablo and Halinard of Dijon were reluctant to accept bishoprics, this was not because they had any objection in principle to the prevailing system, but because as monks they shrank from returning to the life of the world and taking upon themselves a diocesan's political obligations. This is also one of the reasons why few Cluniacs are found ruling imperial abbeys, though apart from this such houses hardly corresponded to their ascetic ideals, even if the noble monks who filled them were as a rule not entirely without some feeling for the devotional side of the life they had professed.

As little exception was taken to the proprietary system as to the theocratic powers of the king. The popes themselves possessed large numbers of *Eigenkirchen* and *Eigenklöster*—though the degree of their dependence on the Holy See varied very widely—and papal privileges for bishoprics, monasteries and laymen confirmed property of this kind as willingly as any other. Ulrich of Augsburg was praised because he never enfeoffed laymen with *Eigenklöster* belonging to his see, but the fact was only used as an example of his administrative foresight, not to suggest that he objected to lay proprietorship as such; both pope and bishops regarded this as absolutely normal.

Both lay and ecclesiastical circles, however, tried to define and limit proprietary rights. To this end, Carolingian capitularies and councils laid down regulations, which with slight variations were repeated for centuries. A glance at them is the best way of showing how strongly rooted the proprietary system was.

1. It was first of all laid down, in accordance with the

---

[1] *Vita Burchardi*, c. 2 (ed. Bourel de la Roncière, *Coll. de Textes*, xiii. 7 sqq.).

old law, that all churches were to be subject to the bishop and that no church should be dedicated if the founder still laid claim to its endowments. Yet side by side with this there stood an express recognition of the founder's right, and in our period this must naturally be understood as being proprietary in character.

2. No layman is to install a priest in his church without the permission of the bishop, but must first send him to the bishop or his representative for it to be ascertained whether his age, knowledge and morals fit him to be given the cure of souls. Laymen must not remove priests from the churches which have been canonically handed over to them, without the assent of the bishop.

3. On the death of a priest, no one shall attempt by gift or petition to detain the vacant church from the lord in order to hold it with his own; even in the case of a mere chapel, pluralism shall be illegal except on the bishop's recommendation. Each church shall have its own priest.

4. Many lords are so covetous that they oppress the priests of their churches with demands for dues, customary payments, gifts, food, services or fodder for their horses. Spiritual services alone may be acquired in return for the endowment and the gifts of the faithful.

5. No layman shall beat or in any way mishandle his priest.

6. Bishops shall see that the priests pay due honour to their lords and fulfil their duties to them. In cases of ingratitude or disobedience the priest may be accused before the bishop and, if he was originally a villein, may once again be reduced to unfree status.

7. In churches which belong to more than one person, proprietary rights shall be exercised in common and in an orderly fashion.

8. Each church shall have one hide of land free of all dues and services.[1]

These ordinances show what dangers and encroachments on its rights the Church had to foresee and prevent, and

[1] See Appendix II.

they demonstrate equally clearly that the most conscientious and determined of churchmen had no thought of seriously questioning the proprietary system. This is just as true of the monastic reformers. We have already seen that the best monks of the tenth and eleventh centuries were only moderately interested in church organisation, that they accepted the state's theocratic point of view, and that they were scarcely more zealous in attacking simony and clerical marriage than other classes. In the same way, they found nothing wrong in the system of proprietary churches—provided that it was regulated and defined—whether proprietary rights were in the hands of bishops, monks or laymen. Cluny itself was the pope's *Eigenkloster*, though his rights were of a purely formal nature. No objection was raised if a church was handed over to Cluny or one of its dependents, and attention was expressly paid to the benefits which derived from the property that went with it. It made no difference to the reformers whether a monastery were given to Cluny itself or to the pope, or whether it remained in the possession of a bishop, the king or any other layman. Even if the lord made use of the monastic lands, there was no objection. Thus archbishop Sewin of Sens, who restored the monastery of St Peter at Sens and filled it with Cluniac monks, retained half its property for himself, and it was remarked that he did this from necessity, not from gre [1] The lord

---

[1] Clarius of Sens, *Chron. S. Petri vivi Senon.* (St Pierre-le-Vif), ed. L. M. Duru, *Bibl. hist. de l'Yonne*, ii. (1863) 491 : " medietatem ipsius abbatiae illi reddens, aliam in proprios usus retinens. Fecit autem hoc non cupiditate sed causa necessitatis." On the reform of St Maur and Robert I's appointment of an abbot, cf. *Vita Burchardi*, c. 5 (ed. Bourel de la Roncière, p. 13); on Odilo's reform of St Denis, Sackur, *Cluniacenser*, ii. 32 sqq.; Fleury, Johannes, *Vita s. Odonis*, iii. 8 (MPL. 133 cols. 80 sqq.), and JL. 3606 (Bouquet, ix. 220): " in ordinando autem abbate tam rex quam episcopi vel boni principes vel laici hanc potestatem iuxta b. Benedicti praeceptum habeant, ut pravorum non permittant praevalere consensum, sed talem constituant, qui. . . .:" so even the Benedictine rule itself could be twisted to cover the nomination of an abbot to a proprietary monastery! For the " ordination " (i.e.—at that time—" appointment ") of Gauzlin, the successor of Abbo of Fleury, by king Robert, see Ademar of Chabannes, c. 39 (ed. Chavanon, p. 162). Cluny's policy towards the houses it had reformed changed at the end of the eleventh century: see P. Kehr, *Das Papsttum und die Königreiche Navarra und Aragon*, in *Abh. d. Berl. Ak.*, 1928, no. 3, p. 9.

regularly retained an interest in the appointment of the abbot; next to the right of alienation, this is, in fact, the best criterion of the contemporary legal position. As long as it is admitted that laymen have the right to give their churches away and to impose clergy or abbots upon them, it is impossible to speak of opposition to the existence of lay rights in the Church. Cluny reformed royal abbeys like St Maur-des-Fossés, St Denis and Fleury, but the king did not surrender the smallest fraction of his rights in them. Fleury became one of the chief daughter-houses of Cluny, and was itself an important centre of reform. Towards the end of the tenth century it was ruled by the famous Abbo, whose historical, canonistic and dogmatic studies had roused in him some suspicion of the existing order: " Let him who wishes the health of his soul beware of believing that the Church belongs to any other than God alone. For He said to Peter, the Prince of the Apostles, ' I will give thee My Church:' 'Mine,' not 'thine.' Therefore the Church is not the Church of Peter. And if it is not the Church of Peter, to whom does it then belong? Can the successors of Peter claim that which Peter himself did not possess? In truth, dearest princes, we neither live nor speak as Catholics when I say that this church is mine, or some other says that church is his." Such an outlook appears to sap the foundations of the proprietary system. Yet, if we examine his views more closely, we see that Abbo is more concerned to protest against its legal implications, and to show the impossibility of introducing it into the body of accepted doctrine. In his collection of canons we find important sentences quoted from the Carolingian legislation which we have just discussed, and their acceptance of the proprietary system repeated without question. The importance of Abbo's criticism lies in the fact that it shows that the old canon law was not entirely forgotten. Abbo was himself not the man to draw revolutionary practical consequences from his deep insight; rather he shared the common beliefs of his time. And how could the abbot of a monastery which itself possessed many *Eigenkirchen* and was itself the property of the king, think of the abolition of the system?[1]

St Bénigne-de-Dijon, where St William was abbot, was another important centre of reform and came under Cluniac influence. William reformed the monasteries of secular lords both in France and Italy. In one of his charters he mentions the fact that the houses of which he himself had the care were happy in their owners and protectors.[2]

Conditions in Normandy, Lorraine and Germany were similar to those in France. Waulsort, the oldest reformed house in Lorraine, where the Scot St Cadroe was abbot, was the property of a noble lady. Zealous episcopal reformers like Gerhard, Gauzlin and Bruno of Toul, or Adalbero and Dietrich of Metz, naturally retained possession of their monasteries after, as before, their reformation. Gorze belonged to Metz, and so did St Trond in the diocese of Liège. Bishop Gauzlin of Toul went so far as to demand certain dues and services from his reformed house at St Èvre on the occasion of royal campaigns. Gerhard of Brogne, a reforming abbot of lower Lorraine, undertook the reformation of several *Eigenklöster* belonging to the counts of Flanders, among them names as famous as St Vaast, St Bertin, and Mont St Blandin. Later on, the West German reformers, Richard of St Vannes and Poppo of Stablo, were also active on behalf of the Flemish counts. In Germany the introduction of measures of reform again

---

[1] Abbo, *Apologeticus*, (MPL. 139 col. 465); positive expressions of *Eigenkirchenrecht*, in *Coll. can.*, c. 19 (*ibid.* 487): *De abbate ad regem pertinente* (following can. 20 of the council of Ver in 755, MGH. LL. i. 27), and c. 38 (*ibid.* col. 495), where Eugenius II's decree of 826—" monasterium vel oratorium constructum canonice, a dominio constructoris eo invito non auferatur " (MGH. *Capit.* i. 374, no. 180 c. 21)—is quoted. Sackur, *Cluniacenser*, ii. 62, tells how a pupil of Abbo, Bernard of Cahors, received two abbacies, Solignac and Beaulieu, from his father, while the father retained a controlling interest in them.

[2] HPM. i. 414, no. 244, for Fruttuaria, which was a papal *Eigenkloster*: " Verumtamen quoniam singula loca, in quibus cura nostra vigilabat, se gaudebant et gaudent habere proprium possessorem et defensorem et hic, de quo fit specialis mentio, quia gratia libertatis nullum videbatur habere protectorem, licet diversi inde contenderent." The reform of lay *Eigenklöster* by William is recorded, for example, in HPM. i. 466, no. 272; the founders lay it down that God shall be their heir, but add: " ut si filio masculino ex nostro coniugio fuerit relicto, fiat ipsum monasterium in eius ordinamentum, non ad minandum nec ad praemium propter ordinationem abbatissae recipiendum vel (*sic*: ? sed) ad gubernandum et defensandum et gratis abbatissae ordinandum."

frequently occurred without affecting questions of ownership. A typical example from Normandy will serve to close our examination of the attitude of the reformers to the proprietary system. St Evroul, where the historian Ordericus Vitalis lived in later years, was given by its founders to duke William. They received permission from him to select an abbot, chose a monk from the reformed house at Jumièges, and presented him to the duke, who approved him and installed him as abbot by investing him with the pastoral staff.[1]

The connection between a monastery and the centre from which it had been reformed varied widely in different cases. Often it was only a moral bond that remained, or one of friendship, as happened when the daughter-house acquired an independent abbot; sometimes, however, the abbot of the mother-house would merely put a prior in charge, retaining final authority in his own hands. In either case, the daughter-monastery remained both under diocesan control and in the possession of whoever had owned it up till that time. But there were also many ways of establishing closer relations. Privileges of exemption might be obtained which would give partial or complete exemption from episcopal authority, or the mother-house might seek to make the daughter its *Eigenkloster*. The regulations which later established congregations, the election of an abbot-general whom all the others had to obey, the assemblies of all the abbots at fixed times and the appointment of a committee to carry out the visitation of the parent-house, were all still unknown in the tenth and eleventh centuries. The congregations which existed at this time were looser, and the legal relationships of the members less systematised. The strongest bond was established when one monastery became the owner of another, put a prior in to rule it, and obtained exemption from the bishop's authority. Reformed monasteries were, indeed, always glad to be presented with *Eigenklöster*, and from the

---

[1] Leo VII, in JL. 3609 (Pflugk-Härttung, *Acta*, i. b., no. 8), and MGH. DO. I. 70; Bishop Gauzlin of Toul's charter for St Èvre is in Calmet, i. 132; on St Evroul, see Ordericus Vitalis, iii. 4 (MPL. 188 cols. 235 sqq.).

eleventh century onwards frequently exercised pressure upon lay owners to surrender their proprietary rights. But there was at first no far-reaching principle behind this policy. It resulted rather from the energy with which reformed houses pursued their taste for creating new congregations; and it was in the formation of new congregations, it must be remembered, that the monastic reform movement began seriously to develop its political activity.[1]

II

It has been argued that Henry III's ecclesiastical reforms were a political mistake, on the ground that they strengthened the Church and so helped to endanger and weaken the power of the German state. This argument is, however, incorrect. The emperor, whose statesmanlike talents were as great as those of the rest of the Salian house, was acting in accordance with the ideas of his time. Royal theocracy and the proprietary system had existed almost unquestioned for centuries. It is one of the most surprising events in world-history that in the space of a few years the morally-purified papacy, which had hitherto been happy to regard its authority as complementary to that of the monarchy, should suddenly, unerringly and instinctively put the finishing touch to a thousand years of speculation about the nature of the Christian hierarchy and draw the conclusion that the existing order of the Church and of Christian society must be set aside as contrary to God's will. A more than earthly wisdom would have been necessary to foresee this revolution. The popes whom Henry III chose fulfilled Henry's expectations. After the synod of Sutri he seems to have taken a less prominent part than hitherto in

---

[1] A bishop disliked it when a house in his diocese was under the control of the abbot of a monastery in another diocese, since the abbot could too easily escape from his influence. It cannot be denied that mother-houses often sought to draw more close the dependence of their daughter-houses upon them: e.g. *Vita Burchardi*, c. 5 (ed. Bourel de la Roncière, p. 13): " Robertus rex . . . consilio et hortatu comitis [Burchardi] eidem Teutoni [whom Majolus had installed in the abbey as prior], donum abbatie idem rex dedit, eumque abbatem ordinare praecepit. Quod cum ad aures Cluniacensium pervenisset, valde tristes effecti sunt, quia cupiebant sibi ipsum locum ad cellam redigere."

ecclesiastical affairs, and perhaps he felt the true relations of king and pope to be those which had subsisted between the Saxon emperors and popes like Leo VIII, Gregory V, Sylvester II and Benedict VIII. He is not likely to have considered which of the two would have to give way in a case of conflict; the age believed in the existence and force of objective Right, and consequently whoever made his own policy coincide with the demands of Right would carry the day against the other. We have no reason to assume that the emperor refused to grant the pope independence in the usual sense. A few weeks after he ascended the papal throne, Clement II held a synod,[1] in which he pursued the same reforming objects as Henry. He thought highly of the papal dignity—which did not in any way diminish his opinion of the majesty of the empire—but died before he could develop any of his ideas.

After the three weeks' pontificate of the second German pope, Damasus II, Bruno of Toul ascended the papal throne as Leo IX; his pontificate marks an important stage in the rise of the eleventh-century Church to maturity. It was Leo who collected round himself many of the great personalities who, a little later, were to develop new and epoch-making ideas, and to work forcefully for their realisation: Hildebrand, Frederick of Lorraine, Humbert of Silva-Candida, Hugh the White and Boniface of Albano. They found a bond of union in their common service of Rome, and through them the curia under Leo IX changed its character completely. They were the pope's assistants. The pope listened to their advice, and questions of papal policy were discussed among them, in particular measures of reform. Thus we know, for instance, that they hotly disputed the question whether the orders of a priest who had been ordained by a simoniac were valid. Humbert maintained that they were not, but Peter Damian took the opposite view; Leo himself inclined towards Humbert's opinion, but left the matter undecided, urging all to pray for enlightenment from God.

The object of curial policy under Leo was to restore and

---

[1] Synod of January 1047, in MGH. *Const.* i. 95, no. 49.

develop the primacy of the Roman bishop within the Church, in face of the pretensions of Byzantium. The ideas of pseudo-Isidore on the authority of the pope were more current in Rome than ever before, and the main purpose of the first great collection of canons composed in Rome was to set forth the legal position of the Successor of Peter; two hundred and fifty of its sections are taken from pseudo-Isidore. An increase in the esteem in which the papacy was held and in its own self-reliance, and an effort to secure a position of real leadership in the Church: such were the innovations due to the pontificate of Leo IX.[1]

What did Leo and his fellow-workers think of the contemporary constitution of the Church? Were they disturbed by the position which laymen, and especially kings, held within it?

Bruno of Toul was a relation of the emperor, and though his personal piety exceeded that of his equals in rank, his political opinions did not differ seriously from theirs. He had, in accordance with the usual practice, received investiture with ring and staff from the king, and had sworn him the feudal oath; as bishop he was the proprietor of several churches, and as pope he showed a lively interest in the Roman *Eigenklöster*. He had been a friend of the emperor the whole of his life, and had great influence with him, spending many months of his five years' pontificate travelling about with him. His reforming activity was a natural continuation of what Henry had begun, and in it he showed tirelessness and a high sense of responsibility, but in his work no alterations or important additions to the original objects of reform are to be noticed. There were occasional conflicts of interest between emperor and pope, but the

---

[1] See P. Fournier, *Mélanges d'arch. et d'hist.*, 'xiv. (1894) esp. pp. 187 and 196. When Fournier writes on p. 195: " Les idées fondamentales qui inspirent la collection en 74 titres sont à coup sûr les idées fondamentales de la réforme ecclésiastique qui marque la seconde moitié du xie. siècle . . .," this must only be accepted with reserve; the collection still shows no tendency to attack the rights of the laity, and there is no prohibition of lay investiture. The main interest of this compilation is the question of the Roman primacy, as is clearly seen from a comparison of it with Burchard's collection, where the papacy receives little notice; cf. P. Fournier and G. Le Bras, *Histoire des collections canoniques en occident depuis les fausses décrétales jusqu'au décret de Gratien*, ii. (1932) 16 sqq.

spiritual and ecclesiastico-political ideas of both remained fundamentally the same. It has, indeed, been remarked that Bruno, while bishop of Toul, had supported abbot Halinard of Dijon against the emperor, when Halinard, as archbishop of Lyons, had refused to swear the feudal oath; but there was in reality no political background to Halinard's refusal to be untrue to his monastic rule, and the emperor was in no way annoyed. It would therefore be quite wrong to draw conclusions from the incident suggesting that Bruno's attitude was critical of the imperial power. There has been an even stronger attempt to construe as opposition Bruno's demand at Worms—after the emperor, in agreement with a Roman delegation, had made him pope—that his acceptance of the dignity should be dependent upon canonical election by the clergy and people of Rome. It has, however, long been recognised, and it has recently become clearer, that at that time " canonical election " had a special meaning; an election was held to be " canonical " if clergy and people gave their approval to an already nominated candidate. It also sometimes happened that clergy and people, or even a convent, would suggest a likely man, and thus anticipate the public election, or that a small section of the population would make the proposal and general agreement only be given after the office had actually been conferred. Such without doubt was the " election " which Leo demanded, and it consisted of the usual applause of the people as he entered the papal city. It is, nevertheless, a sign of his reforming ideas that he attached some importance to it, for at the great reforming synod which he held for the French clergy at Reims he caused it to be laid down, in the first canon, that no one should accept an ecclesiastical office without election, though, of course, he only intended the words to bear the meaning we have suggested above. Leo's insistence that what he understood by a canonical election should be observed, was due to his respect for the canon law in the contemporary sense only, and was at the same time a measure against simony; for it happened only too often that a pastor was sent to a congregation to whom he was both repugnant and unqualified to minister, because he had bought the office for a large sum.[1]

It can scarcely be deduced, from the fact that Leo had drawn so many of the leading figures of the next decades to his court, that he himself was inspired by the new and anti-monarchical ideas of reform. We know little of what these men thought about 1050, and have no right to assume that, hiding their true purposes, they were awaiting a favourable moment to launch an already matured and completed programme, however much historians old and new may credit them with such plans and read back later ideas into these early years. It has been said, for instance, that Hildebrand greatly blamed Leo for recognising the tyrannical authority of Henry by accepting the papacy from him. Leo is even supposed, when reproached by Hildebrand, to have cast off the papal robes and clothed himself in the simple garb of a pilgrim, in order to make clear that he wished to owe his position solely to canonical election in Rome. But the two accounts which we have of this incident are unreliable and of much later date, and there is no reason to suppose that they have any foundation in truth. We are only entitled to say that Gregory VI's chaplain, who had followed the deposed pope into exile, regarded with deep suspicion the novel arrangements of Henry III's patriciate and the legalisation of the imperial influence over papal elections. Hildebrand's opposition to Henry III was only concerned with his power over the papacy, and we have no right to assume that he was already applying some of the principles of a carefully-prepared reform programme.

A further suggestion is that Bruno of Toul and many of his associates had learnt a new conception of ecclesiastical order in the " Lotharingian schools of law." But what exactly are these schools, which are supposed to have taught so new a doctrine? We hear that bishop Notker of Liège (972–1008), who was a Swabian by birth, did much to raise the extremely low level of education in his diocese, and

---

[1] On this paragraph, cf. in particular, P. Schmid, *Der Begriff der kanonischen Wahl in den Anfängen des Investiturstreites*, (1926), and criticism of contrary opinions in my review of A. Michel, *Papstwahl und Königsrecht*, (1936) in HZ. 156 (1937) 123 sqq.

that he was assisted in this work by his friend, abbot
Heriger of Laubach. Laubach, where the learned bishop
Ratherius of Verona and Liège may have created some
tradition of scholarship and study, was one of the most
famous schools of the age, with a sphere of influence cover-
ing Germany, France and England. Prominent among its
scholars were abbot Olbert of Gembloux and bishops
Burchard of Worms, Adalbold of Utrecht and Wazo of
Liège. From what we know of these men we can deduce
that canon law could certainly be learnt in the diocese of
Liège, and so the supposition may be correct that the
Lorrainers in Leo's circle—especially the archdeacon
Frederick and Hildebrand, who spent some years in Cologne
—had absorbed something of this knowledge. But it must
not be assumed that a knowledge of the canons and a
recognition of the value of canon law would necessarily
lead to protests against the prevailing state of ecclesiastical
institutions. The most important early eleventh century
collection of canons was made by two products of the
Liège schools, Olbert of Gembloux and Burchard of Worms,
but the work was written in full accord with the spirit of the
age—the spirit of royal theocracy—and Burchard was as
loyal to the emperor and as little interested in papal authority as any other German bishop of the period. Canon law
could, in fact, be interpreted in a number of ways—we have
only to recall the different meanings given to " canonical
election "—and right into the time of the Investiture
Contest the anti-papalists felt themselves to be the champions of the true canon law. We cannot therefore simply
say that the study of canon law produced a new outlook
in the eleventh century; it was rather the other way round:
when the new outlook had arisen, the study of canon law
revived. Its maxims may be likened to rocks on the sea-
shore, which are covered at high tide; when the waters fell,
they stood out sharp and straight once more, and broke the
force of the waves.[1]

[1] The " Lotharingian law-schools " play a great part in recent literature.
It has been usual to rate their influence very highly, but there has rarely
been any attempt to bring forward evidence of their existence. Thorough
examination suggests the need for great caution in discussing them.

There was, however, one man in Lorraine whose ecclesiastical ideas fitted in but ill with the era of royal theocracy, and who can rightly be regarded as a forerunner of Gregory VII: Olbert's fellow-student Wazo, who taught at the Liège cathedral school before becoming bishop of Liège in 1042. Expressions like those he is reported to have used, but still more radical in tone, are only to be found in the writings of one of his contemporaries, the so-called Auctor Gallicus, and he was a Lotharingian or a Frenchman. If we examine Wazo's personality more closely, however, we can see that even he was far from taking up a definitely revolutionary attitude and from attacking the position of the laity in the Church in the way that was later the fashion among the men who surrounded Gregory VII. He was for a short time chaplain at the court of Conrad II, and grew grey in the service of the church of Liège as dean and provost. Once before the emperor had wished to make him a bishop, but Wazo persuaded him that another and younger man, whom he put forward, was more suited for the imperial service. When he did later become bishop, he accepted lay investiture, took the oath of fealty and felt it to be incumbent upon his honour to be an active and dutiful servant of the emperor. In spite of this, Wazo opposed the emperor on several occasions. Asked by Henry III to suggest a worthy successor for pope Clement II, he did not give the required information, but said that he had consulted the law-books and had found that no one could judge a pope. Wazo, then, had the personal courage to criticize what had been done at Sutri, and it is this which has drawn attention to him. Yet his thesis is not so extraordinary, even at the time at which it was advanced; Thietmar of Merseburg himself records with disapproval that Otto I deposed Benedict V and sent him into exile at Hamburg. Neither Wazo, therefore, nor the Auctor Gallicus—who protested with equal warmth against the deposition of Gregory VI—were adopting new legal standards. Nor was Wazo's attitude any more novel on the other occasion on which he found himself in opposition to the emperor—when he criticized Henry for wishing to depose an Italian bishop, Widger of Ravenna, on the judgment of a German synod over which the emperor himself had presided. The principles upon which Wazo took up his stand concerning the deposition of bishops, far from being unheard-of in his time, were plainly set out in Burchard of Worms' widely-read *Liber Decretorum*. Many could recall the famous conflict between Gerbert and archbishop Arnulf of Reims, when Abbo of Fleury, with the help of quotations from pseudo-Isidore, had defended the supreme judicial authority of the pope; and even a courtier like Wipo remarks how unpopular Conrad II became by his action in deposing without trial the archbishop of Milan and several Italian bishops, " priests of the Lord." As far as the ecclesiastical constitution is concerned, Wazo's distinction between the obligations of a bishop towards the emperor as his temporal superior and towards the pope as his spiritual superior is more important than his protests against the deposition of a pope and a bishop, for it foreshadows the division between temporalities and spiritualities which came to the front during the eleventh century. It had become more and more common for a cleric to receive the cure of souls from the bishop, and the church and its lands from the lord who owned them. Was it the belief that such was the right relationship of spiritual and temporal which led Wazo to condemn the existing conditions in the imperial Church and to wish for the secular authority to be more restrained in its intervention in purely spiritual affairs?[1]

---

[1] On Wazo, see *Anselmi Gesta ep. Leod.*, in MGH. SS. vii. 210 sqq., ed. Koepke, and *ibid*. xiv. 111 sqq., ed. Waitz; cf. G. Waitz, *Über Anselms Gesta ep. Leod.*, in NA. vii. (1882) pp. 75 sqq., R. Gorgas, *Über den kürzeren Text von Anselms Gesta pontif. Leod.*, Diss. Halle 1890, and R. Huysmans, *Wazo van Luik in den ideenstrijd zijner dagen*, (1932) pp. 3 sqq. The origin and date of the *Gesta episcoporum Leodiensium* is obscure, and presents problems which, I feel, are not yet fully cleared up.—Wazo's remarks quoted above are taken from Anselm: c. 43 (MGH. SS. vii. 215), Wazo as chaplain of Conrad II; c. 49 (p. 218), recommendation of Nithard; c. 50 (p. 219), he is sent with *virgae et litterae* [*commendatoriae*] to the court of Henry III; c. 60 (p. 225), Wazo's loyalty to the empire; c. 65 (p. 228), opinion on Clement II's successor; c. 58 (p. 224), Widger of Ravenna; c. 66 (pp. 229 sq.), comparison of the priestly with the imperial consecration. The *De ordinando pontifice* of the so-called Auctor Gallicus is edited by Dümmler in MGH. *Lib. de lite*, i. 8 sqq.

The real importance of Wazo and the Auctor Gallicus rests on their clear perception of the dignity of the ecclesiastical hierarchy—above all, of the papal dignity—and of the essential difference between the spiritual and the temporal powers. In practice, however, as we have seen, they only drew local and special consequences from their principles, and were far from contesting, in a general sense, the active share of the laity in the direction of the Church. A century earlier, Atto of Vercelli and Ratherius of Verona, two men who were perhaps still more strongly influenced by the traditions of ancient canon-law, had gone even farther in this direction. They were fully aware that it ran counter to the spirit of the Church's organisation for the emperor to nominate bishops and abbots, but they were not consistent in their personal and political life; Ratherius welcomed Otto the Great's efforts to reform the papacy, and his opinions did not prevent him from buying an abbey from the French king, after he had been driven out of his Italian and German bishoprics in turn.

When all is said therefore, we are not in a position to assert that the men who came to the court of Leo IX from Lorraine and the lower Rhine—even if they were personally influenced by Wazo of Liège—brought more with them than a wide knowledge of canon law and a burning zeal for reform. In Leo's time, as we have seen, they were inspired above all by the desire to maintain and strengthen the renewed importance which the emperor had given to the papal office. On that account it was intolerable, in the eyes of the new curia and of the regenerated Church as a whole, that the papacy should be dependent upon party struggles in the city of Rome. It was these struggles which had put the leadership of the Church into the hands of evil men, and which were continually preventing the popes' actions from being of benefit to Christendom. If the pope must always live in a fortress surrounded by armed men, and if the few estates which had not been mortgaged or stolen from him scarcely brought in enough to support him, then he could not lead the movement for reform in the way that all demanded of him. When Henry III set out for Rome, the situation there had already to some extent improved under Gregory VI; but even this pope was a Roman and the dependent of a Roman party, in addition to being compromised by simony, which could be forgiven in a bishop but scarcely in the pope. Moreover, he had two rivals, who were always in a position to rise against him. It was impossible, just as it was later impossible at the time of the Great Schism, to recognise any of the existing popes without running the risk of new disturbances. Gregory had to give way, and Henry III gave the Romans rich presents in order to secure from them the patriciate and thereby the decisive influence over papal elections. Henry freed the papacy from the purely local and Roman chains which were binding it, and the defence of the Roman Church against the city of Rome was one of the principal political objects which the reformed papacy took over from Henry III; perhaps more political skill was directed to this object than to any other, for everything depended upon the possession of an assured income and military power in Italy. Henry promoted this policy during his lifetime. Later its scope became continually wider, and the aim was to make the states of the Church able to protect the Mother of Churches not only against the Romans, but against the German king himself and against the Norman dukes. It was in the very nature of such a policy of territorial expansion that, the more the secular connexions of the Church grew, the more they laid claim to attention; the more widely the frontiers were extended, the greater was the number of neighbours with whom the papacy came in contact.[1]

The main importance of the local territorial policy of the Church lies in the effect it had on the main lines of eccle-

---

[1] See Appendix I. There is a close connection between the liberation of the papacy from purely local influences, the introduction of foreigners into the college of cardinals, and, to some extent, the changes in the organization of the papal chancery: cf. P. Kehr, *Scrinium und Palatium*, in MJÖG., *Erg.-Bd.* vi. (1901) in especial p. 81. On the disorganization of papal finance, see K. Jordan, *Zur päpstlichen Finanzgeschichte im xi und xii Jhdt.*, in QF. xxv. (1933–34) pp. 64 sq. On the origin of the college of cardinals, cf. H. W. Klewitz, *Die Entstehung des Kardinalkollegiums*, in ZRG. *kanon. Abt.*, xxv. (1936) pp. 115 sqq.

siastical development. Leo IX exchanged Bamberg and
Fulda for Benevento, a clear proof that Henry III was
prepared to give a loyal pope freedom of action in southern
Italy. Leo dared to give battle to the Normans, and papal
policy collapsed entirely as a result of a crushing defeat at
Civitate. The emperor, advised by his chancellor, bishop
Gebhard of Eichstätt, had given Leo no active support in
his Norman campaign; he was clearly not ready to risk
German forces in southern Italy after giving up Benevento,
and it is quite likely that the campaign appeared to him a
fantastic piece of universalist policy. On Leo's death a
Roman embassy is said to have asked Henry for the bishop
of Eichstätt as pope. There is much probability in this
report of initiative on the part of the Romans. They were
asking for the leader of the opposition to Leo IX's anti-
Norman policy, a man who at the same time possessed the
greatest influence with the emperor; perhaps they hoped
that he would find other ways of advancing the Church's
secular policy, or would give up his opposition. It is not
certain whether Hildebrand was a member of the delegation, though the attitude it adopted almost suggests the
fact. The importance then accorded to the recovery of
the papal states is clearly seen in the demand of the new
pope, Victor II, that the emperor should return certain
lands and castles. Henry granted Victor's request, and
even enfeoffed the pope with the duchy of Spoleto and the
mark of Fermo. Admittedly, the main reasons for this
transaction were reasons of state. The emperor's most
dangerous opponent, Godfrey of Lorraine, who had just
been defeated after a great deal of trouble, had become the
strongest power in central Italy through his marriage with
countess Beatrice of Tuscany. He had been driven out of
Italy, but the situation remained insecure; it was therefore
to Henry's advantage to make his friend Victor as strong
as possible, and the pope accepted the emperor's proposals.
Yet he continued unchanged the policy of internal reform,
though with less energy, at least as far as the monasteries
were concerned, than either his predecessor or his successor.
Hildebrand, Humbert and all the other leaders of the reform

party remained with him; only Godfrey of Lorraine's brother, archdeacon Frederick, withdrew for political reasons to Monte Cassino, though his personal relations with Victor remained undisturbed.

The events which hastened the development of the Investiture Contest were insignificant from the standpoint of the contemporary Church and fortuitous from that of the modern historian. Henry III and Victor II died within two years of each other. The Romans wished to free themselves from the weakened German kingship and to recover their former share in papal elections; they disavowed the promises they had made to Henry III, and proceeded to an election on their own account. It was cleverly done; Frederick of Lorraine, from whose brother help was expected and who was himself sure of curial support, was elected as Stephen IX. After some hesitation the confirmation of the German court was asked and received, but for the first time since the revival of the papacy there was open discussion of the right of the king to participate in papal elections and in Church government as a whole, and eventually of the general position of laymen within the Church. These discussions received a new impetus when, after Stephen's premature death, the Roman nobility made an election against the will of the cardinals, in an attempt to regain their ancient hold over the papacy. What could Humbert, Hildebrand and their circle, who had just secured the predominant influence in the curia, do in such circumstances? Their only course was to play off the authority of the German king against the Romans, and a petition was sent to the German court, asking for approval of the choice of bishop Gerhard of Florence. The curia can scarcely have done this with much readiness, and it is not to be expected that all the cardinals were in agreement with this diplomatic step; some of them were certainly very keenly aware of the divergence between what was politically expedient and what they held to be right.

The theories which cardinal Humbert evolved in the third book of his epoch-making work, the *Libri adversus*

simoniacos, are one of the fruits of the debates provoked by
the political situation during the years 1057 and 1058, and
they amount to the first frontal attack on the whole position of laymen within the Church, especially the ideas of
royal theocracy which had held the field for centuries. The
sacred character of the kingship was ignored, and for
Humbert the king was a layman pure and simple. Each
class of society, he says, should have its rights and fulfil its
obligations; but the secular princes are not content with
what is rightly theirs: they grasp what belongs to the
Church, preside over and dominate synods, and their power
is so terrifying that everything is discussed and settled
according to their arbitrary will. Yet the Church has her
own laws and her own judges, by whom the transgressions
of her officers and her servants can be punished. Bishops
should be first of all elected by the clergy, then acclaimed
by the people, and finally, should be consecrated, after
examination, by the metropolitan and the neighbouring
bishops.[1] But now, says Humbert, the true order is
reversed; the king, a layman, elects, the metropolitan
consecrates, and last of all the clergy and people have to
give their approval, whether they like it or not. What does
it mean, when kings give investiture with the sacred
symbols of ring and staff?—It means that they, though
only laymen, are presuming to celebrate a sacrament by
conferring the grace of the episcopal office. If the *electus*
subsequently brings the episcopal insignia to the metropolitan and receives them a second time at his hand, this is
merely an empty form. This evil custom has taken such
deep root that it is even held to be canonical, and men no
longer know what the Church's commands really are, nor
do they observe them. No metropolitan, no prince of the
Church, dares to raise his voice against these practices;
the Bride of the priests, the Church, is continually violated
by others, since it is ruled and governed by laymen, who
have no business to interfere in it.

[1] Even for Humbert, it has recently been shown, the king had a canonical
right to participate in elections, provided the right order was maintained:
cf. A. Michel, *Papstwahl und Königsrecht,* p. 122.

It is astonishing with what suddenness the basic ideas of
the Investiture Contest appear in Humbert's writings, and
with what force he demands that they shall be put into
practice. If we look back from the year 1058, we can
perceive connections with the ecclesiastical outlook of an
earlier age, and we can see that in recent times there has
been a certain tension in the spiritual atmosphere, but the
practical conclusions which Humbert draws were to all
intents and purposes without parallel. The Auctor Gallicus comes nearer to him than any other in his attacks on
secular participation in church government, but we have
no evidence that his works were commonly known in
Rome. When was the idea first conceived in Rome that
the Church needed something more than a moral reformation—a thorough-going overhaul of its organisation?
When were radical criticisms of the prevailing order first
made, and when was opposition to unconnected details of
the system replaced by something wider and more comprehensive? Humbert's was a speculative mind, and he had a
great gift for theology. It is manifest that he had long
before this penetrated to the heart of Catholic thought, and
that he had done so rationally and not, like Hildebrand,
merely intuitively: we possess early writings of his which
show this as clearly as the *Libri adversus simoniacos*. Yet in
spite of his emphasis on action—he was always making use,
in political argument, of the forged Donation of Constantine,
and was the only writer of his age to do so—we find no trace
in these early writings of what were later to be his main
political objects. His interest was concentrated on reform
and the realisation of the claim to primacy. He was sympa-
thetic towards Henry III, and he had devotedly served the
German popes who had unquestioningly accepted royal theocracy and the proprietary system. Apart from the revival
and strengthening of the Church, the question which most
disturbed men's minds during Henry III's last years was
simony in its narrowest sense; and it was at this time,
probably as early as the pontificate of Leo IX, when the
question of the validity of ordinations made by simoniacs
was being vehemently argued, that the first book of the

Adversus simoniacos was written or at least conceived. Of the other leading reformers, only Peter Damian was active in the literary field, and he took less interest than most of them in questions of organisation; later on, when the movement against lay investiture was well under way, he still held it to be a false step which had diverted attention from the main task, the moral regeneration of the Church and its servants. It is, therefore, extremely unlikely that others had anticipated Humbert in realising whither the movement would eventually lead, and had cunningly kept themselves in the background; it is far more reasonable to suppose that in 1058 a great revolution in world-history took place, which even those most closely concerned had only dimly foreseen.

The reason why events moved so fast after the publication of the *Adversus simoniacos* was that Humbert's ideas had not come to birth in the mind of a philosopher remote from the world, and so did not have to wait till they were accepted by men of action. On the contrary, Humbert himself was a man of action, in close touch, intellectually and practically, with other men of action; and in consequence it was only one year before decisive political steps were taken and far-reaching official pronouncements made. Encouraged by the success with which they had resisted the German court and the Roman nobility at the last two papal elections, the curia dared to issue an election decree, the aim of which was the abolition of all lay interference. The share of the Roman people was reduced to a mere formality, and Henry IV's patrician rights were so skilfully formulated that in a favourable political situation they could be interpreted as practically meaningless. The same synod—it was the Easter synod, which met at Rome on 13 April 1059—took a step of even more general importance. Its sixth canon runs: " In no circumstances shall any priest or cleric be invested with a church by a layman, whether gratis or for payment." The intention, in other words, was to force the laity once again to be content with the position which was properly theirs in the ecclesiastical order, and this, as previously, was to be the passive position of a minor who cannot act for himself.[1] The stage was thereby set for the gigantic struggle which now ensued.

III

The sixth canon of the Easter synod of 1059 had laid down the programme of the reformers; its terms—in all probability like their object itself at that time—were general and unconcrete. With the march of events, however, the final object grew larger and nearer, the different aspects of the dispute were revealed and became more definite and more readily apparent. The instructions which went out from Rome became more definite and more detailed with every pontificate after that of Nicholas II. The old reforming decrees, which aimed at a moral regeneration of the Church, continued, but in addition to them, and going far beyond them, there was now the ever-increasing bias against the laity. As early as the Easter synod of 1059, Louis the Pious' statutes defining the rule of the cathedral clergy were repealed at Hildebrand's suggestion, on the significant ground that Louis had no power to alter the true rule without the consent of the Holy See, since, although emperor by divine right, he was still only a layman. Under Alexander II, not only was the canon of 1059 re-enacted, but there was also a cautious attempt to limit the royal right of investiture, though without actually promulgating any new legislation. Bishop Peter of Florence, who had requested the king to approve his election, was sternly rebuked with the words: " Since no emperor or king is permitted to meddle with the Church's affairs, it is plain that you did this out of contempt for the Holy See."

Under Nicholas II and Alexander II, and in the early years of Gregory VII, the chief measures taken towards the realization of the programme of 1059 aimed at keeping papal elections free from secular influence and at attempting

---

[1] C. 6 of the Easter synod at Rome in 1059 runs: " Ut per laicos nullo modo quilibet clericus aut presbyter obtineat ecclesiam, nec gratis, nec pretio" (MGH. *Const.* i. 548).—See my criticism of A. Michel's contrary view (in his *Papstwahl und Königsrecht*), in HZ. 156 (1937) 123 sqq.

to secure free canonical election everywhere. According to the new ideas, it was no true election if the bishop was chosen by someone other than the electors and then received the electors' approval; the electors themselves, it was held, must make the choice. Success was at first not very considerable; a hundred years had still to pass before the new conception of canonical election was everywhere understood and accepted. Failure brought about no weakening of the papacy, however; it merely stimulated the angry impetuosity of a Gregory VII. Far from shaking his resolution, defeat only awoke the innate qualities from which he derived the strength and the clearness of thought that made him so great. Had he gained an easy victory, it may be doubted whether Gregory would ever have established the principles on which the position of the papacy and the whole Christian world-order were to be based for centuries.

It was probably at the Easter synod of 1075 that Gregory repeated the prohibition on receiving investiture at the hands of laymen, but in a decisively more concrete form. The king was forbidden to invest with bishoprics or abbacies, and both the person investing and the person invested were threatened with the severest ecclesiastical penalties. This amounted to nothing less than the annulment of the existing ecclesiastical law of the empire. It was an act of unparalleled boldness, more so than even Gregory supposed, and is only to be explained by the fact that he grossly underestimated his chief opponent, Henry IV. His omission to publish the new decree as binding everywhere, and his readiness to accept modifications, were only diplomatic moves, which were abandoned, at any rate as far as Germany was concerned, the moment the inevitable struggle actually broke out. A little later, the prohibition of lay investiture was published with implacable rigour in France by the legate, bishop Hugh of Die. Gregory did, in the event, show himself more moderate than his representative; but if as an act of pure grace he allowed the French bishops who had been deposed for accepting investiture from the king to retain their bishoprics, this none the less clearly emphasised his position. Archbishop Manasses of Reims, the primate of France, who had consecrated a royally-invested bishop, was forced to give way after a struggle lasting many years. The age-old practice of lay investiture was now suddenly to be abolished as " an ancient and very evil custom." After election, consecration, investiture with ring and staff by the metropolitan and enthronement —only after all this should the king give the bishop whatever rights there remained for the crown to confer. Just how much this left to the king was allowed to remain undecided, and did not particularly interest the papalists, so long as it did not adversely affect the freedom of the Church. The reformers of this period were, at any rate, quite convinced that office and endowment formed an indivisible unity like body and soul, and the attempts of the other side to arrive at a compromise, by which only the lands should be conferred by the investiture, met with sharp, even scornful rejection. The sacred character of the lands, as the possession of Christ and the saints, was strongly emphasised; the laity were not permitted to rule them, and any attempt to do so counted as an usurpation of spiritual power.[1]

Lay domination of minor churches was attacked as bitterly as that of bishoprics and abbacies. The old rules governing the dedication of churches were revived; no church was to be dedicated until the founder had set it completely free. The very basis of the proprietary system was called in question when the alienation—even to monasteries—of churches which up till that time had been proprietary, was made dependent on the consent of the diocesan bishop. The council of Clermont proclaimed in 1095 that henceforth it was prohibited for all laymen to

[1] In spite of Schmid's arguments, *Kanonische Wahl*, pp. 207 sqq., it must still be maintained that Gregory VII issued his first prohibition of lay investiture at the Lenten synod of 1075. Gregory's offer of modifications to Henry IV is in *Reg.* iii. 10 (ed. Caspar, p. 263): with this, cf. J. Haller, *Das Papsttum*, ii. 2 (1938) pp. 520 sq.; on *Reg.* iv. 22 (p. 330), to Hugh of Die, cf. W. Schwarz, *Der Investiturstreit in Frankreich*, in ZKG. 42 (1923) 292: " With this letter of 12 May 1077 the quarrel about lay investiture was transplanted to France." Synod of Autun, Mansi, xx. 491; *Reg.* iv. 13 (p. 313) ("antiqua et pessima consuetudo ") and vi. 3 (p. 394), for example, are significant of the new condemnation of lay investiture.

retain control of churches, and laymen were even forbidden
to have domestic chaplains without the bishop's consent.
These were, of course, only theoretical prohibitions; in
practice the curia was disposed to be much more concilia-
tory towards the possession of ordinary churches by laymen
than towards their control over bishoprics and abbacies.
War had been declared, however, along the whole front.

The Investiture Contest was the first medieval crisis to
call forth a considerable propagandist literature, in which
the aims of the two parties were reflected. It provided a
running commentary on practical politics, and in it the
theoretical principles are often formulated more clearly and
at greater length than they are in the actions of the great
men of the time. The reason for the struggle was everywhere appreciated. Even an opponent of the pope like
Wenrich of Trier could write: " That which is done
concerning clerical benefices, namely the freeing of them
from secular authority, and concerning bishops, who ought
not to receive their bishoprics at the hands of a lay prince,
all this creates bad blood at first through its very novelty,
but there seems none the less to be a certain semblance of
justice in it." Lively discussion centred round the part to
be assigned to the laity in the Church, and both sides
appealed to the authority of canon law. The Investiture
Contest gave a definite impulse to the study of canon law.
Three important collections of canons were made at Gregory VII's instigation alone—those of cardinals Atto and
Deusdedit and that of bishop Anselm of Lucca. The evolution through which the Church had in the meantime passed
is well shown by a comparison between the selection made
by these canonists from the writings of the Fathers, the
decretals of the popes and the decrees of synods, and the
selection made by Burchard of Worms at the beginning of
the century or even that of the anonymous author of the
Diversorum sententiae patrum, the " compilation in 74
titles," made in the time of Leo IX. Burchard, though
fully conscious of his priestly dignity, in no way criticises
lay activity in the Church, and the author of the *Sententiae
patrum* is only interested in the primacy of Rome; this, it

is true, the Gregorians still emphasised strongly, but they were primarily concerned to provide arguments for the struggle to enforce the withdrawal of the laity.[1]

Urban II continued the work of Gregory VII with skill and greater diplomatic adroitness. If at first the weakness of his position compelled him to exercise self-restraint, his legislation shows no relaxation of the old demands, and he condemns secular control of the Church as vigorously as his great predecessor. In a charter for the bishopric of Maguelonne in the south of France, which had been given to Gregory VII by count Peter of Substantion, we find the words: " The whole body of Holy Church was endowed, through the mercy of God and the Blood of His only Son, our Saviour, with His own eternal freedom; but through the cunning of evil men and the neglect of the pastors, many churches have fallen into the hands of earthly rulers."[2] As he gained more power, Urban tightened up his legislation against the laity. At the council of Clermont, where

[1] Cf. Wenrich of Trier, *Ep.* c. 8 (MGH. *Lib. de lite*, i. 297); on Gregory's side, see, for instance, *Manegoldi ad Gebehardum liber*, c. 53 (MGH. *Lib. de lite*, i. 405), or Deusdedit, *Libellus contra invasores et symoniacos*, c. 1, 4 (MGH. *Lib. de lite*, ii. 303). On the collections mentioned, P. Fournier, *Les collections canoniques romaines de l'époque de Grégoire VII*, in *Mém. de l'Acad. des Inscr. et des Belles Lettres*, xli. (1918) pp. 271 sqq., and Fournier-Le Bras, *Histoire des collections canoniques*, ii. 20 sqq., and 139 sqq. The following provides an admirable example of the way in which the canonists of the later eleventh century made their material suit the new tendencies against the laity: Peter Damian, in his famous *De privilegio Romanae ecclesiae ad Hildebrandum*, *Opusc.* v (MPL. 145 col. 91) bases the supreme rights of Rome on the fact that the church at Rome was the only one founded by Christ Himself, whereas all the others were founded by emperors, kings and the like; these passages were taken over by Deusdedit (*Coll. can.* i. 167, ed. Wolf von Glanvell, p. 106), Anselm (*Coll. can.* i. 63, ed. Thaner, pp. 31 sqq.) and Bonizo (*Liber de vita christiana*, iv. 82, ed. Perels, p. 146), but they no longer ascribe the merit of founding the other churches to princes, etc.—i.e. to laymen—but to the Roman Church!

[2] JL. 5377 (MPL. 151 col. 293, no. 10). Peter of Substantion's gift to Gregory VII, April 1085, is in *Gallia Christiana*, vi. 349, no. 11 and *Hist. gén. de Languedoc*, v. 695. Canon 17 of the council of Clermont (Mansi, xx. 817) contains the prohibition of the vassal's oath, and canon 18 prescribes that clerics are only to become the chaplains of laymen with the bishop's permission (cf. *supra*, p. 115). The earliest of the later prohibitions on the taking of oaths are: can. 8 of the synod of Rouen, 1096, in Mansi, xx. 925; can. 3 of the synod of Poitiers, 1100, *ibid.* p. 1123, and the council of Troyes, 1107, in Jaffé, *Bibl.* iii. 384, no. 38. This question too found a place in contemporary polemics after 1095: see, for instance, Rangerius of Lucca, *De anulo et baculo*, v. 879 sqq. (MGH. *Lib. de lite*, vii. 527): " An non eripitur libertas pontificalis,/Quando iuratur, regibus et dominis?/Quando manus dantur et per sacra iura ligantur,/ Et ius et ratio subditur imperio."

he proclaimed the Crusade, he forbade clergy to become the vassals of laymen and to take feudal oaths. It is possible that this had already been discountenanced under Gregory VII; but now, in order to complete the freedom of the Church, it was expressly laid down by law that even that part of the old process of investiture which was based on secular law was to be attacked. The new ordinance was repeatedly re-issued at reforming synods, and Paschal II desired to advance still farther. He made a violent attempt to exclude lay influence from the Church, but took so little account of existing facts that he was bound to fail. His abortive treaty with Henry V, by which the emperor, in return for the surrender of the *regalia*, was to set the Church entirely free, is so well-known that a bare mention of it will suffice.

The object of the so-called Investiture Contest was to drive the laity from the position which several hundred years of royal theocracy and of the proprietary system had given them. There was, however, no thought of attacking proprietary rights as such; so far as they lay in the hands of popes and bishops, monasteries and parish churches, they remained substantially unmolested. We must remember, moreover, that by the eleventh century the majority of *Eigenkirchen* were in fact owned by ecclesiastical bodies. On the other hand, the reforming spirit did much to promote legislation with the object of reorganising and consolidating the unity of the diocese; and in the course of the next century and a half this legislation was completely successful in grafting private ownership on to the main trunk of the canon law.[1]

---

[1] It is worth pointing out that Fliche, describing the eleventh century reform movement, neglects the proprietary system, in spite of the evidence brought forward by Stutz in the works quoted, *supra*, pp. 71-2 n. It is only in the second volume of his *Réforme Grégorienne* that he raises the question whether Gregory wished to abolish *Eigenkirchenrecht*, answering it in the negative; cf. p. 118 sq., n. 5 and p. 182 sq., n. 2. He is right in doubting whether Gregory intended to abolish the proprietary system entirely; but Stutz had already shown that clerical ownership of churches and monasteries persisted (e.g. *Eigenkirche*, pp. 23, 25 [= Barraclough, pp. 49, 51] and, in particular, the article *Eigenkirche, Eigenkloster*, in Herzog-Hauck, *Realencyclopädie*, xxiii. 374-6). The difference between the reformers' attitude towards lay and clerical proprietorship must not be overlooked, since only through an understanding of it can the true meaning of the Investiture Contest be grasped.

This legislation is in no way a discovery of the reforming period, but is simply the old proprietary church legislation specially adapted to the needs of the clerical *Eigenkirchen*. Earlier it had been stated generally that each proprietor must appoint his priest in co-operation with the bishop, to whom the priest would be responsible for the spiritual side of his office. A similar demand was now made on clerical proprietors. If a church is given to a monastery, it was ordered, the priest should remain in possession and receive the same income as before the gift; on his death, the abbot is to seek another and present him to the bishop: if he is suitable, the bishop must accept him; he must be subject to the bishop and pay him the customary dues; he may live with the monks if he so desires: if not, then he is to have as much of the revenues from the endowments of the church as will enable him to live in reasonable comfort and to perform the church services, and the remainder may be applied to the general purposes of the monastery; he is to render account to the bishop for his clerical functions, and to the abbot for the temporalities belonging to the monastery. To some extent, then, the separation of temporalities and spiritualities was recognised in the settlement of the problem of clerical *Eigenkirchen* at a time when it was still being attacked in the case of churches owned by laymen; it prevailed finally in both spheres, and contributed largely towards the transformation of proprietary rights into patronage, both lay and ecclesiastical.

Clerical proprietary rights were not molested, then, but put under the strict control of the appropriate Church official. Many reforming synods even forbade monasteries to acquire churches without the consent of the diocesan bishop. Abbot Frotard of Saint-Pons-de-Thomières, in spite of the fact that he was one of the most outstanding representatives of curial policy in southern France and northern Spain, was deprived of a monastery which he had illegally received from a layman. Devout laymen who wished to make gifts, and the monasteries which were to receive the churches were, however, recommended to seek help from Rome if the bishop refused the necessary permission out of mere avarice. Paschal II seems to have attempted a further step in the limitation of clerical proprietorship, though without success. He wrote to Anselm of Canterbury: " A bishop should not receive churches at the hand of a layman if they lie in a diocese other than his own; in all other cases he may accept them with a clear conscience, for this is no gift, but a restoration. All the churches in the diocese should be in the bishop's power, and abbots should receive them at his hand." Paschal thus wished to prevent bishops possessing *Eigenkirchen* in other bishops' dioceses; had it been possible to carry this measure into effect, the proprietary system would have ceased to act as a force which broke up the unity of the diocese.[1]

The only man whom we know to have contemplated a complete and absolute liberation of the Church from the proprietary system is a Swabian chronicler, supposed to have been Berthold of Reichenau. Recording the Lenten synod of 1078 in his Annals, he writes that anathema was proclaimed not merely against all laymen but even against clerics and all persons who, contrary to the canonical decrees, should give bishoprics, abbacies, priories, churches, tithes or ecclesiastical dignities of any kind to a cleric or any other person as a benefice, if this was done as a result of ancient usurpation. Such a law would have destroyed royal theocracy and the proprietary system at one blow, and this, it seems, is what the chronicler imagined the object of the reformers to be. His description of the legal standing of the monastery of Hirsau is also very remarkable. Hirsau was among the most highly-privileged of the papal *Eigenklöster*, but the Swabian monk, it is plain, intentionally ignored its dependence on the papacy, and regarded it

---

[1] For limitation on the acquisition of churches, cf. can. 6 of the synod held at Poitiers in 1078 by Hugh of Die (Mansi, xx. 498; on the date, Schwarz, in ZKG. 43 [1924] 143); can. 5 of the synod of Melfi, 1086 (Mansi, xx. 723); can. 15 of the synod of Rome, 1099 (Mansi, xx. 963 sqq.); can. 21 of a council of London in the time of Paschal II (Mansi, xx. 1152). On Frotard and St Cugat de las Vallés, cf. P. Kehr, *Papsturkunden in Spanien*, i. (1926) 277, no. 17, and the same author's *Das Papsttum und der Katalanische Prinzipat*, in *Abh. d. Preuss. Ak.*, (1926) no. i., 40 and 45 sqq. Paschal's letter to Anselm is in JL. 5909 (MPL. 163 col. 91).

as absolutely free, subject only to the dominion of God and saints Peter, Aurelius and Benedict. Influential leaders of the Church did not draw such conclusions, and indeed would have felt them pointless, for it was only the laity whose rights they wished to limit.[1]

We have seen how this task was ever more clearly perceived, and how the growing consciousness of purpose led to the formulation of more definite demands, which the reformers strove to realize. But the secular powers rapidly collected their forces to resist the onslaught. From the time of William the Conqueror onwards, for instance, the English kings did not allow themselves to be seriously disturbed by the reform programme. Spain was less open to attack, since there the old system was not only deeply rooted, but was used in the Church's interests. In France the king was not in a position to offer serious resistance, but the bishops presented a more difficult problem, and used the revived study of the canon law to find new means of saving many important elements of the existing system. The strongest resistance, however, was met with where the attack had been strongest, in the imperial lands. The last two Salians defended themselves and the foundations of their power against the new ideas with astonishing tactical skill; the retention of control over the German Church was for them a matter of the most urgent political necessity, needing no circumstantial proof, while from the moral point of view, the opponents of the new ideas could comfort themselves with the thought that the existing state of affairs and their existing rights were sanctified by ancient usage.

The power of tradition and the strength of their opponents compelled the leaders of reform to proceed with care, to avoid formulating their principles too bluntly, and occasionally to give way in order to be able to advance elsewhere. It is often difficult to decide whether, in any given case, reform measures had long been planned, but had been held back out of prudence, or whether they arose

---

[1] Cf. Berthold, *Annales*, ad ann. 1078 (MGH. SS. v. 308 sqq.); on Hirsau, *ibid.*, ad ann. 1075 (*ibid.* p. 281).

directly out of the struggle itself. Both suggestions are true; it would be wrong to believe that the reformers already had their programme in their pockets at the accession of Leo IX or at the Easter synod of 1059, and that they proceeded at favourable moments to hold its various points up before an astonished world, but it is certain that political events sometimes promoted and sometimes hindered the cause of reform. The emergence of the fundamental idea of the Gregorian movement in 1058 was caused, as we have seen, almost solely by political events. Alexander II, seriously embarrassed by the setting-up of the anti-pope Honorius II, was forced to make concessions and could not proceed so boldly as his predecessor. He, the pope, who was responsible to no man, had to clear himself of the charge of simony before a synod, and to negotiate with the German court about the regularity of his election. It had been no departure from the new principles, on the other hand, when Gregory VII informed the German king that he had been elected, for this announcement was not different in character from that which he sent to other princes, to bishops and to abbots. Yet even Gregory's measures against the laity were sometimes influenced by what were really extraneous incidents. In 1074, for example, he planned a great crusade against the Saracens, intending to bring aid to the Greek empire and so to recover the influence over the Eastern Church which Rome had lost as a result of the schism.[1] When, about the end of the year, he had to drop this plan, he was free to turn to other things, and in the following February he issued the prohibition on lay investitures. Again, the open breach with Henry IV, and the confusion in Germany, by removing any temptation to compromise, led him to pursue his ends with increasing bluntness. The short pontificate of the monastically-inclined Victor III brought a temporary modification into Roman practice, but after his success against the anti-pope Guibert, Urban II returned to the lines of Gregory's policy, and even increased the strictness of the latter's rules;

[1] Cf. W. Holtzmann, *Studien zur Orientpolitik des Reformpapsttums*, in *Hist. Vierteljahrschr.* xxii. (1924–25) 175.

though his crusading plans soon forced him to give way on several points. This is perhaps a sufficient indication of the close connection between the reform movement and the general current of politics.

It is more important to observe in detail that the curia was often driven to abandon principles which had already been proclaimed as canonical, and to determine precisely how much had been attained by the time the struggle ended and how much had had to be given up. A year after the Easter synod of 1059, the cardinal-priest Stephen held a synod in Tours, in which the old legislation favouring the proprietary system was still maintained intact. A synod held at Gerona in 1078 in the presence of Gregory VII's legate, bishop Amatus of Oléron, declared that the laity had, properly speaking, no right to churches; but, recognising that churches could not everywhere be entirely removed from lay ownership, the assembly was content to enact that the laity should at least be prevented from having the offerings. In fact, the ordinary method of procedure was not to deny in principle the right of the laity to own churches, but gradually to annul the rights that flowed from ownership, attempting at the same time by persuasion and threats to move lay owners to a voluntary surrender: Richard of Capua, for example, had to renounce all the churches in his land when he received it in fee from the pope. At the autumn synod of 1078 in Rome, Gregory ordained that the laity should be informed how much they endangered their souls by retaining possession of churches and tithes. Under Urban II a synod laid it down that anyone who possessed a church or its lands by hereditary right should lose his clerical fiefs until he surrendered the church. On the whole, however, the struggle centred round the bishoprics and large abbacies until the concordat of Worms, although the first investiture decrees had not applied to them alone. Even at Calixtus II's general synod at Reims in 1119 a proposed canon had to be significantly altered in deference to stormy protests. In its first form it ran: " We forbid all lay investiture with churches and clerical estates," but it was modified to read: " We forbid all lay investiture with bishoprics and abbacies;" the prohibition had, in short, to be limited to the higher offices.[1]

The laity did not give up even these, however, without a struggle. When monasteries were voluntarily given to the Holy See, the pope was willing to make concessions to the donors. He might allow them to retain jurisdiction over the lands, or even grant them a share in the choice of the abbot; examples are the concessions made by Nicholas II to viscount Arnald of Ager for San Pedro de Ager, and by Alexander II to the count of Nellenburg for All Saints at Schaffhausen, and Urban II's command that count Bernard of Besalú's consent was to be held necessary to the election of the abbot of San Juan de las Abadesas.[2]

In the same way, the popes were far from insisting rigidly on " canonical election " in strict conformity with the new decrees. It was impossible for them to draw upon themselves the enmity of the whole world, and royal investiture was frequently tolerated both before and after Gregory VII's general prohibition. Alexander II wrote in 1068 to an archbishop of Rouen who had been appointed by William the Conqueror, telling him to accept the election and not attempt to go against what divine providence had ordained for him.[3]

The relations of the curia with England are typical of the way in which the popes had to concentrate their efforts on the most dangerous opponents, and in consequence to modify or even temporarily to abandon their demands in other directions. They refrained at first from attacking royal theocracy and the proprietary system in England, not only because the Conqueror did at least combat simony

---

[1] Scholasticus Hesso, in MGH. *Lib. de lite*, iii. 27.

[2] Cf. JL. 4432 (MPL. 143 col. 1337, no. 19) on S. Pedro de Ager: " et liceat eis ordinare abbatem in supradicta ecclesia secundum suam voluntatem, quem congruum et idoneum et servitio Dei aptum ipse cum clericis ecclesiae S. Petri canonice elegerint," and Kehr, *Papsturkunden in Spanien*, i. 267, no. 11 (repetition by Alexander II) and pp. 178 sqq. Alexander II's concessions to the count of Nellenburg can be deduced from Gregory VII's withdrawal of them, *Germania Pontificia*, ii. 2, 11, no. 3 (*Quellen z. Schweizer Gesch.*, iiia. 20, no. 8). Urban II's grant for S. Juan de las Abadesas, JL. 5395 (J. Villanueva, *Viage literario á las Iglesias de España*, viii. (1821) 242, no. 15).

[3] Cf. JL. 4643 (MPL. 146 col. 1339, no. 56).

and priestly marriage with energy, but also because Gregory hoped that the king would hold England from him as a fief, and in consequence did not wish to arouse his antagonism. During the confusion of the period of schism there was the danger of driving William into the camp of Henry IV's antipope, and behind this there was always the risk that England might abandon the papacy altogether. As a result, Rome was prepared to put up with a good deal of laxity. Archbishop Anselm wrote to Paschal II, for instance: "It is sometimes necessary to make certain compromises which depart from apostolic and canonical precept, especially in a kingdom where nearly everything is confused and corrupted, so that very little can be done according to the laws of the Church. I beg for your permission to moderate some things as God shall direct me. I asked the Lord Pope Urban for the same permission, and he put it within my discretion." Paschal granted the request.[1]

The Investiture Contest was settled by compromise in England, France and Germany. The first agreement was reached with France, though no formal treaty was drawn up. There it became the custom for bishops and abbots to be freely elected, and thereupon to request the king's consent, swear the feudal oath to him and be put in possession of the church lands, and finally to receive ordination. The London concordat of 1107 was strongly influenced by the French solution, and set up a similar legal position in England. The concordat of Worms was similar in principle, but its terms were a little more definite; the king obtained only a strictly limited influence over elections, and investiture remained essentially the same, though he was denied the use of the ancient symbols. In Burgundy and Italy, however, he had to be content with far less.

The Church had been compelled to abandon many of its demands, and had been unable entirely to set aside the rights of the laity. No other course had been left to it than to give up the theory—maintained with so much force—of

[1] Cf. Böhmer, *Kirche und Staat*, pp. 94 sqq., 127 sqq., 144 sqq., and Schwarz, ZKG. 42 (1923) 326 sqq. Anselm's agreement with Urban II and Paschal II can be seen in JL. 5909 (MPL. 163 col. 93, no. 74).

the spiritual character of clerical property and its insepar-
ability from the spiritual office, and to accept the standpoint
of its opponents on these matters.   In some cases, the
Church had been forced to grant the laity a considerable
share in elections, and it had failed to win acceptance for
its principle that a cleric could not be the feudal vassal of a
layman nor swear the feudal oath.   The ordinary parish
churches and chapels were left entirely outside the scope of
the agreements which were drawn up both before and after
the turn of the century, and so far as they were concerned
success was very modest: laymen long continued to possess
churches and monasteries.   As a result of all this, it might
seem as if the reformed papacy had been defeated and
forced to be content with purely formal concessions.   But
such a conclusion would be false.   The main intention had
been to deprive the laity of their spiritual functions, and
this object had very nearly been attained so far as bishoprics and abbacies were concerned, at least in the agreements
made with Germany, France and England.   In future, free
canonical election made it possible for the Church to
choose suitable pastors, and the sacred symbols of spiritual
authority, the ring and the staff, were only given at consecration.   The lay princes were driven out of the ecclesiastical sphere, and from now on their power was purely
secular.

CHAPTER V

LIBERTAS ECCLESIAE

THE STRUGGLE FOR RIGHT ORDER IN THE CHRISTIAN WORLD

" Erat enim catholicae religionis ferventissimus institutor, et ecclesiasticae libertatis strenuissimus defensor. Noluit sane, ut ecclesiasticus ordo manibus laicorum subiaceret; sed eisdem et morum sanctitate et ordinis dignitate praemineret." (Bernold of St Blasien.)

I

IN moments of considered solemnity, when their tone was passionate and their religious feeling at its deepest, Gregory VII and his contemporaries called the object towards which they were striving the " freedom " of the Church. Freedom has always been regarded as at bottom something indefinite and relative, and this was particularly so during the middle ages: it is both dignity and humility, possibility and bondage, lordship and dependence. One freedom alone has no limitations, is endless and absolute: the freedom of God. " Protect, O freest of all, God and Lord, Thine incomparable freedom," prays cardinal Humbert in the preface to his work against the simoniacs.[1] Freedom of this highest order is, of course, as much a possession of Christ and the Holy Ghost as of God the Father. But what is the real meaning of an appeal to the One God to defend His own freedom? Can this freedom be violated in any way? The answer to this question will explain in a very significant sense what is meant by the freedom of the Church. At the same time it is necessary to bear in mind the ancient symbolical descriptions of the nature of the Church, for only then will it become quite clear how the Church's freedom could be endangered and how protected, and only then will the expressions used by our authorities reveal their true meaning.

In Christ, the Son of God took human nature upon Him-

---

[1] Humbert, *Adv. sim.*, praef. (MGH. *Lib. de Lite*, i. 102); cf. also Rangerius of Lucca, *De anulo et baculo*, v. 895 (*ibid.* ii. 527): " Sed Christus liber, et nulli subditur unquam. . . ."

self, and so united Himself with humanity. As one of us, as the perfect man, the representative of mankind, He propitiated God the Father by His life and His sacrificial death, and won back the grace which was lost by the Fall of Adam. He left behind Him the sacraments, in which He is always present and is eternally becoming man again within the community of believers, who are united with Him in their belief and in the sacraments in order to become sharers with Him in grace and co-heirs of the Heavenly Kingdom. The visible Church and all its institutions, as founded by Christ, is His earthly community. Just as once He put on an earthly body, so now the Church is His mystical body which He fills with His Spirit; He is its head, and all believers are its members. The Church is the heir of Christ and His kingdom; He appeared in order to found it, and it represents the eternal presence of Christ on earth. It is bound to Him as the body is to the head, and shares in all that is His; hence His freedom is its freedom. It follows, therefore, that the freedom of the Church in its deepest and most universal sense is thought of in absolute terms like the freedom of God; and furthermore: if the freedom of the Church can be injured by corrupt and avaricious clergy or by infidel and violent laymen, God Himself and Christ are touched thereby, and it no longer appears remarkable that prayers are offered to them to protect the Church's rights.

The image of bride and bridegroom was used in these medieval centuries even more frequently than that of head and body, to describe the relation of Christ to the Church. Christ made mankind into His Church through His faith-bringing union with it; it is the Bride, to whom He is mystically married.[1] It is filled with His spirit, and as the " Mother of heavenly grace " it has the means of awakening men to a new spiritual life. Hence the Christian is said to have spiritual parents—Christ and the Church—as well as fleshly. " Mother " Church is the third of the symbols which were living and vital to every medieval Christian;

[1] Cf. John Scotus, *Comm. in ev. Joh.*, (MPL. 122 col. 326): " Qui propter ecclesiam venit, ut haberet sponsam, venit."

she is his Mother because she is the Bride of Christ. It is shameful to oppose her, and it is the Christian's highest duty to fight for the freedom, chastity and catholicity of the Church, since on it depends the salvation and the freedom from eternal death which Christ won for men. It was thoughts like these which gave the medieval struggle against simony so extremely violent a character.

According to the Acts (viii. 9 sqq.), a man named Simon Magus went to Peter and offered him a sum of money in return for the gift of the Holy Ghost; Peter dismissed him with angry words. Simon gave his name to the sin which consists in acquiring for money the gifts of the Holy Ghost, which can in reality only be gained as a result of its own free action. Simoniacs are held to be heretics, worse than the Macedonians, whose sole error was to believe that the Holy Ghost was subject to the Father and the Son, whereas the simoniacs think they can control it as they would a slave whom they have bought. Simony occurs not only when spiritual gifts are purchased for money (*simonia a manu*), but every time a spiritual office is given in such a way that the free working of the Holy Ghost is interfered with, especially in cases where an attempt is made to influence the choice of the donor by word (*simonia a lingua*) or deed (*simonia ab obsequio*). Giver and receiver are both guilty, for both have acted contrary to the freedom of the Holy Ghost. At the height of the struggle between *sacerdotium* and *regnum* men were very quick to make accusations of simony. If popes or bishops received their offices not by the prescribed election but at the word of emperors, kings or other laymen, even though no money may have passed between them, or if other clergy were appointed in this way rather than by their duly-ordained superiors, then simony was seen in the transaction, and a gift (*munus*) spoken of, though perhaps only in the sense of *simonia a lingua* or *ab obsequio*; it all counted as a violation of the freedom of the Holy Ghost.[1]

[1] Humbert, *Adv. sim.* i. 3 (MGH. *Lib. de lite,* i. 106) declares that the simoniacs are worse heretics than the Arians, but seems to confuse Arians with Macedonians. Simony has never been properly discussed from the dogmatic point of view.

We can only see how much simony and lay investiture injured the dignity of the Church if we first of all make it clear what these things meant for the Church in the sense of the Body or the Bride of the Lord. Pope, bishop and priest are each the representative of Christ, the earthly head or earthly Bridegroom of the Church; consequently, if they are appointed in any way contrary to the will of God, both the nature and the mission of the Church are endangered, and thereby the salvation of mankind jeopardised. " The Church lives through faith, chastity and purity. When she no longer has these, she droops and dies. She loses the charter of freedom which Christ gained for her on the Cross and left behind for her, His Bride, so that she, being free, might make men, who had become slaves through sin, free and the children of God." So wrote Godfrey, abbot of the French monastery of Vendôme; long before his time Gregory VII had sounded the call to battle for the chastity, purity and freedom of the Church, and given a warning against restricting the freedom of the Church, with which Christ deigns to link Himself in heavenly marriage.[1]

When simple priests are called the vicars of God or of Christ, this usually means that they are regarded as divine instruments in the dispensation of the sacraments; it even occasionally happens that they, in place of Christ, are called head or husband of the Church, and so on. Bishops, on the other hand, are regularly called husbands of the Church: " each bishop, as the bridegroom of his own see, shows the likeness of the Saviour," writes Ralf Glaber. In the same way Clement II addresses the church of Bamberg, over which he had ruled as bishop, as his dearest bride and as the most chaste of virgins; and Anselm, the historian of Liège, finds nothing absurd in recording that Wazo became bishop, and was thereby changed from the true son of the church of Liège into its husband. A ring was given to the bishop after consecration, as well as the staff, in token of the mystical marriage which had been

---

[1] Godfrey of Vendôme, *Libellus*, i. (MGH. *Lib. de lite*, ii. 682) and vi. (*ibid.* p. 694); Gregory VII, *Reg.* iii. 10 (ed. Caspar, p. 267).

made between him and his church, " so that he may know,"
writes Rangerius in his poem *De anulo et baculo*, " that he
is a bridegroom, and must love the church which is committed to him, or rather, not to him, but to Christ;" the
last phrase is intended to bring out his position as merely
the deputy of Christ.[1]

The idea of the marriage-bond between the bishop and
his church—i.e., the particular church over which he ruled
—does not mean that it was not realised that individual
churches could only come into the question in so far as in
them, together with all other churches, the one universal
Church lived and had its being. Only in this sense is
Christ the Bridegroom of the churches, and so too are His
servants, with whom He is united. Cyprian's words,
" There is but one episcopate," were not forgotten. About
the middle of the eleventh century a French cleric wrote:
" The Church is the Bride of Christ, and the bishops
exercise their authority in His place. Yet these are not the
husbands of the Church, but the husband. The number of
bishops makes no difference; unanimity must make them
into one." All the bishops together, then, represent Christ
in His union with the virgin Church, which lives in all the
individual churches.[2]

Christ Himself alone, working through the Holy Ghost,
has power to confer on men the authority to represent
Him.[3] First of all He makes His choice, and then makes
His will visibly known by means of the inspired choice of
clergy and people in canonical election; finally He provides
the grace necessary for the exercise of the office through the
instrumentality of the consecrators at the ceremony of
ordination. In addition, we find the idea that the church
gives its own assent through the assent of clergy and people,
and the canonical rule which decrees that no bishop shall
be imposed on an unwilling community thus preserves the

[1] Glaber, v. 25 (ed. Prou. p. 133): Clement II, JL. 4149 (MPL. 142 col.
588); Anselm, *Gesta ep. Leod.*, c. 52 (MGH. SS. vii. 220); Rangerius of
Lucca, *De anulo et baculo*, v. 860 sqq. (MGH. *Lib. de lite*, ii. 527).

[2] Auct. Gall. (MGH. *Lib. de lite*, i. 9); cf. Humbert, *Adv. sim.* iii. 23
(*ibid.* p. 228): " Individui quippe sunt Christus et eius ministri."

[3] Christ was the only door into the fold of the Lord, according to *John* x.
1, a passage which is quoted numberless times in this connexion.

church's own right of assent.   When a simoniac usurps the
rights of Christ, when against His will a church is married
to an evil man, through whom the Saviour scorns to become
mystically present, then the connection between Christ and
the church ceases.   The church is no longer His Bride, but
becomes a harlot, loses the freedom of Christ and is no
more the church of Christ; and this is to deceive the souls
who hope to obtain grace through it, and to prepare a
dreadful fate for them.   The struggle against simony and
the domination of the laity was never more full of hatred
nor expressed in more unrestrained terms than when the
leading thought was the fate of the Bride of Christ and the
low and vulgar crimes that were being committed on her
body.   Here it must be emphasised that these ideas were
more than symbols in our sense of the word; for medieval
man there was more truth and greater clarity in them than
in abstract expressions of the relation of Christ to the
Church, and in involved discussions of the disturbances to
which this relation was subject.   In contemporary phrase,
the free woman became a slave, the chaste virgin a whore.
The simoniacs were overwhelmed with abuse, and reformers
did not shrink from calling them adulterers and fornicators;
it goes without saying that they were wicked heretics.

Another evil, the neglect of celibacy by the higher clergy,
nicolaitism as it was called, was sharply criticised in similar
terms.   What could be worse, it was said, than for those
who were affianced to the most holy, the most chaste virgin,
to devote themselves to fleshly women?   It was an insult
and an outrage to the noble lady whom it was their duty to
serve on behalf of her heavenly Bridegroom.

It is particularly common to find simony compared with
rape, and here the part played by the laity, especially the
emperor, becomes very clear.   The act of simony is compared to the act of a criminal in stealing the intended bride
of another man with the connivance of her evil and covetous guardian, to whom in return he pays a sum of money.
The Church, said the papalists, was regarded by the world
as so base and abandoned that no one defended her chastity,
and no one lifted a hand to save her from the ravisher.   The

emperor himself, they said, who after God should be her chief protector, is a party to the crime, and surrenders her to prostitution. He, who as a dutiful son ought to honour and defend his noble mother, scorns her and spits in her very face. Above all, it is laughable and *monstruosum* for a layman to appoint a priest or a bishop, his spiritual father; it is as if a son should beget his father, or a man should dare to think he could create God. In the wickedness of his heresy the simoniac places himself above God. This is all the Devil's work. " It is nobler to strive persistently for the freedom of Holy Church than to bend beneath the miserable yoke of Satan. For those wretched men who are the limbs of Satan labour in his hateful service, while the members of Christ strive to lead them back to the freedom of Christ." In these words Gregory VII calls the faithful to battle and exhorts them to care lovingly for the Church, so that hereafter they may pass from the transitory kingdom of bondage to the eternal kingdom of freedom.[1]

In comparison with the everlasting kingdom of God, the world was called the kingdom of bondage. Only in the Church could some part of the supernatural freedom of Christ be seen pushing its way into terrestrial affairs. In what way, then, and to what extent, did the holders of ecclesiastical office, the representatives of Christ on earth, share in His freedom, His omnipotence and His other qualities? We have already seen what the sources have to

---

[1] Ratherius, *Prael.* iv. 34 (MPL. 136. col. 284): " Noveris autem ecclesiae dei te advocatum esse institutum, non dominum (non enim matri dominari quis nisi absurde valet);" Lambert, *Annales*, ad ann. 1071 (ed. Holder-Egger, p. 128): " introducta est consuetudo, ut abbatiae publice venales prostituantur in palacio." On the comparison with rape, see in particular Auct. Gall. (MGH. *Lib. de lite*, i. 11) and Humbert, *Adv. sim.* iii. 5 and 11 (*ibid*. pp. 203 and 211); among Gregory VII's remarks, it is sufficient to refer to *Reg.* iv. 3 (p. 298): " non ultra putet sanctam ecclesiam sibi subiectam ut ancillam, sed prelatam ut dominam. Non inflatus spiritu elationis consuetudines superbia contra libertatem sanctae ecclesiae inventas defendat. . . .;" Cf. also *Disput. vel def. Paschalis papae* (MGH. *Lib. de lite*, ii. 665): the emperor insults the Church; Paschal II uses the word *monstruosum* in JL. 5868 (MPL. 163 col. 70); Godfrey of Vendôme, *Libellus*, iv. (MGH. *Lib. de lite*, ii. 691) talks of men who set themselves above God. The sentences of Gregory VII quoted at the end of the paragraph are from *Reg*. ix. 3 (p. 575) and viii. 21 (p. 562; this is the last sentence of the second letter to Hermann of Metz).

say about the vicarship of the bishops; if now we turn to consider the current conceptions of the rank and functions of the successors of Peter, we might almost get the impression that the bishops, and in especial the pope, completely embodied the presence of the Lord on earth. There are, however, powerful voices on the other side, emphasising the purely representative and instrumental character of the earthly hierarchy. Peter Damian prefaces one of his chief works with the remark that " the fulness of all grace remains with Christ himself, although He distributes His gifts to many." Cardinal Humbert avoids equating the reigning pope with Peter. There is no need here to cite the anti-papalist writers of the period; it is sufficient to bear in mind what a clear distinction even Gregory VII makes between himself and the prince of the Apostles. Like many of his predecessors, he began his summonses to emperors, kings, priests and princes with the words: " In the name of the prince of the Apostles we command, in our own name we beg. . . ." He styled himself the servant of Peter more frequently than other popes had done. The two excommunications of Henry IV take the form of prayers of supplication to St Peter, and there is a note of despondency over his personal insufficiency in his prayer to Christ in a letter to Hugh of Cluny: " I am weak. One thing alone remains, that Thou Thyself, together with Thy Peter, shouldst protect the papal office, otherwise Thou wilt see me perish and the papacy suffer terrible defeat." It is plain, then, that Gregory—who believed, perhaps more strongly than any other pope, that his Lord, the Apostle Peter, was mystically working through him—felt quite clearly the distance that separated him from the heavenly rulers of the Church; and this in spite of the fact that at one time he felt so sure of the supernatural influence at work in him that he felt himself able to prophesy the death of his most hated adversary, Henry IV.

We can see, then, how many-sided were the doctrines concerning the position of the earthly rulers of the Church, and how numerous were the conceptions of their nature and their power. Consequently, although it must, as

Harnack says, be left to dogmatists to decide exactly the measure of Christ's presence in the earthly hierarchy, a consideration of the attitude of contemporaries will at least serve to show the historian in how far-reaching a sense he must regard the purely human officials of the Church as being none the less the servants of Christ, to whom their Lord distributes His gifts in incomprehensible wise. Their share in the freedom of Christ and their peculiar service-relationship with Him were the two facts which formed the roots of their " freedom " and the cause of all their victories.[1]

The service of a noble lord is itself ennobling. Earthly nobility is often the result of serving the ruler, and the more trusted the servants and the more important the duties committed to them, the greater their distinction and the respect in which they are held, and the wider their claims to authority. The same is true of the servants of God. By the mystery of ordination they are set apart from the people, so that through them may work the divine grace that alone brings salvation to men; the dignity of their service raises them far above ordinary humanity. Lay authority in the Church was in consequence attacked not only as an interference with the freedom of Christ and of the Church, but as a gross disturbance of the right order of the kingdom of God and a wicked oppression of the class which is called to leadership and authorised to exercise it. The presumption of the laity in not being content with their due rank was responsible for the fact that " they who ought to be freer than all, whose inheritance is God Himself, and who therefore are the property of God, are less valued than any others. The lowest serf is subject to his own lord, but the clergy are expected to serve strange

---

[1] On the papal primacy and the plenitude of the Petrine authority see below pp. 138–142 and 160–1; Peter Damian, *Liber gratissimus*, c. 1 (MGH. *Lib. de lite*, i. 19), with which should be compared the passage from Rangerius quoted above, p. 130, n. 1; Humbert, JL. 4302 (MPL. 143 col. 766); the two excommunications of Henry IV, *Reg.* iii. 6*, 10a and vii. 14a (ed. Caspar, pp. 253, 270 and 483); the prayer for help, *ibid.* v. 21 (p. 385), and cf. ii. 9 (p. 138): " cum per Petrum servus et Petrus in servo diligitur;" iv. 2 (p. 293): " utinam beatus Petrus per me respondeat qui sepe in me qualicunque suo famulo honoratur vel iniuriam patitur." The first express identification of the pope with Peter was made by Leo the Great; cf. Caspar, *Papsttum*, i. 429.

masters." This was Humbert's opinion, and in one of his poems Rangerius of Lucca demands that the clergy shall serve God alone, since Christ is free and subject to no man, and has given control of his anointed into no man's hand. Everyone who assumes the power of punishing clergy may be answered in the words of the Apostle: " Who art thou that judgest another man's servant? " It is wrong that a cleric who, being so closely bound up with God, stands high above the layman in dignity, should be compelled to take a subordinate position. If the lay power presumes to appoint the bishops to their office, in so doing it is contradicting the rightful order of the world and making the bishops subject to itself.[1]

In attacking the rights of the laity, those who defended the freedom of the Church and its servants had the strongest arguments on their side, since their claims were in exact conformity with the catholic idea of the Church, the belief in the sacraments and the manner of their operation, and to this fact they owed their greatest victories in the battle against lay investiture and against the *Eigenkirchenrecht* of the laity in general. From the moral point of view, their opponents had a bad case. What arguments were there against the elevation of free Mother Church, against the purification and deepening of belief in the sacraments, and the consequent reverence for the episcopal and priestly functions? What shelter was there from the storm of wrath over simony and the secularisation of the Church? The strongest bulwark was still the medieval respect for the " good old law." The traditionalists continually appealed to the fact that the rights of the laity were not only of immemorial antiquity, but that they had been willingly accepted by earlier popes and by many holy men. The importance which this argument assumed in the eyes of the anti-papalists can be seen in the fact that several

---

[1] Humbert, *Adv. sim.* iii. 10 (MGH. *Lib. de lite*, i. 210), and cf. iii. 20 and 23 (pp. 223 and 227); Rangerius, v. 895 (*ibid.* ii. 527); Paschal II, JL. 5909 (MPL. 163 col. 91, no. 74); Godfrey of Vendôme, *Libellus*, ii. (MGH. *Lib. de lite*, ii. 685): " Nam quae secularis potestas sibi vindicare nititur investituram, nisi ut per hoc aut pecuniam extorqueat aut, quod est gravius, sibi *inordinate* subiectam efficiat pontificis personam? "

papal bulls giving solemn papal sanction to the royal right
of investiture were forged at Ravenna. In these fabrica-
tions the forgers were in no way guilty of falsifying the
law, but were merely constructing impressive documents
which would be of great use for polemical purposes. The
rights of the laity in the Church were maintained in the
eleventh and twelfth centuries with a tenacity which was in
inverse proportion to the real depth of their religious justification. A readiness to deny their spiritual character was
soon apparent, and indeed, as is well known, lay investiture
was most successfully defended when its defenders fell back
on the argument that it was a purely secular act.[1]

It would be expected that at least the king's right of
investiture would be defended with all the means at the
disposal of those who upheld the monarchical conception
of the hierarchy, and there were in fact very effective
attempts to do this. The king is no layman, asserted the
imperialists, but the anointed of the Lord, the head of the
Church, and he must therefore not be denied his place in
the establishment and control of the office and duties of the
members of the Church. Henry III's idea that Christ
Himself works through the king at the ceremony of investiture is carried to a more logical conclusion by the Anonymous of York than by any other writer. If the spiritual
shepherd enters the fold through the king, he enters by the
right door. The right door, according to a much-quoted
passage from St John (x. 7), is Christ: but through the
deifying grace (deificans gratia) given him at his consecration the king partakes of the nature and grace of Christ.
Yet the very men who held so firmly to the monarchical
conception of the hierarchy surprisingly enough surrendered
royal investiture in the older and fuller sense, and contented themselves with defending it as an act of secular
law, proceeding from the plenitude of earthly authority,
and with using the old theory of the two powers to restrict
their opponents' claims to the spiritual jurisdiction which

---

[1] On the conservative attitude of anti-papal literature see Mirbt, *Pub-
lizistik*, pp. 478 sqq. The most recent study of the Ravenna forgeries is K.
Jordan, *Der Kaisergedanke in Ravenna zur Zeit Heinrichs IV*, in *Deutsches
Archiv*, ii. (1938) 85 sqq.

they were prepared to surrender on the king's behalf. Thus the result of a long period of development was that everything concerned with investiture by laymen, including the king, which conflicted with the ecclesiastical conception of freedom, was set aside. The clerical and monarchical schools of thought sharpened their historic weapons and came to grips with each other on another battlefield, this time more seriously and more irreconcilably.[1]

II

In the final analysis, the aim of the Gregorians was to realise the true, the God-ordained order of the Christian world, and to give its true value to the maxim that each man should receive his own and be preserved in the enjoyment of it—his freedom, his rights, his position before God and man. The attempt to attain this object not only called forth a desire fundamentally to change the relationship of clergy and laity, and in particular that of the leaders of the Church with the head of the state, which had predomin. ted in the period then coming to an end, but it also produced a series of changes designed to re-define and make precise the relations of the various ranks within the Church itself. Here, too, it was felt, the true order must prevail. Gregory VII often expressed his wish to observe and protect the freedom of every other church, as well as the Roman. But in his eyes Rome's true place was at the head of the universal Church, and the true order could only exist if Rome

---

[1] Cf. *infra*, p. 149, n. 1. Gregory of Catino, *Defensio orthodoxa*, c. 2 (MGH. *Lib. de lite*, ii. 536) on the king as *caput ecclesiae*; on Henry III, cf. *supra*, pp. 85-8; Anon. of York, *Tract.* iv (MGH. *Lib. de lite*, iii. 672): "Ac per hoc denique, dum per reges intrant in ovile ovium, id est in potestatem regiminis, per hostium, id est per Christum, intrant, et pastores sunt ovium. Rex enim per potestatem Christus est et Christus hostium. Quicumque igitur per regis potestatem intrant, per Christum intrant;" (p. 664): " virtus deificans;" (p. 667): " Verum si sacerdos per regem instituitur, non per potestatem hominis instituitur, sed per potestatem dei. Potestas enim regis potestas dei est, dei quidem est per naturam, regis per gratiam," and *Tract.* v (p. 680). On the attitude of the Anonymous towards the question of investiture itself, cf. Böhmer, *Kirche und Staat*, pp. 232 sqq.; cf. also Gregory of Catino, c. 5 and 6 (MGH. *Lib. de lite*, ii. 538 sq.); Hugh of Fleury, *De regia potestate*, c. 5 (*ibid.* p. 472); *De investitura*, (*ibid.* p. 501).

ruled. Among his contemporaries, however, there was no
general agreement whether the visible Church was a
monarchy or an aristocracy, whether all bishops were
subordinate to the pope or whether they were his equals,
holding their jurisdictional authority direct from God.
From this difference of opinion arose the second historic
struggle which Gregory VII, his supporters and successors,
had to wage.[1]

The idea of the primacy of Rome was of great antiquity,
had long ago found its classical formulation, and had
already been in a sense completed by Leo the Great. The
starting-point of every discussion of the nature of the
papacy was always Christ's words as recorded by St
Matthew (xvi. 18, 19); the two other famous passages in
the Gospels about the plenitude of the Petrine authority
(Luke xxii. 31 sq. and John xxi. 15 sq.), were often quoted,
though less frequently. Leo the Great had called the
Roman Church " the mother of the priestly dignity," and
had written a sentence which magnified the distinction
between the Roman pope and the other bishops; they all
have the same dignity, he says, but they are not equal in
rank: for, despite their common honour, there had existed
a difference of authority between the holy Apostles, and
although they were equal by election, yet one was given
pre-eminence over the others. Still more serious in its
implications was his assertion that Christ had wished that
His gifts should be transmitted to the whole body of the
Church through Peter, as its head; and similar conclusions
can be drawn from a prayer in the Roman sacramentary
named after Leo. Later generations paid equally careful
heed to the additions which Felix II, Gelasius I, Gregory I
and other popes made to his doctrine. These theories,

---

[1] Gregory's principle of order, corresponding to the *pax* of the ancient and
early Christian world, can be seen, for example, in *Reg.* iii. 7 (p. 257):
" Sed quia desideramus non solum vobiscum, quem deus in summo rerum
posuit culmine, sed etiam cum omnibus hominibus pacem, que in Christo
est habere, iusque suum unicuique observare. . . .;" on the idea that every
church has its own right, see *Reg.* iv. 16, vi. 34 (pp. 321 and 448) and elsewhere, and Urban II's privilege for Maguelonne in JL. 5375 (MPL. 151 col.
293, no. 10): " quatenus debeamus omnibus modis quae ad earum spectant
salutem et gloriam providere, ut, ab omni servitutis vinculo liberae sua
semper libertate gaudeant."

however—apart altogether from the prevailing practice—
were still far distant from the idea of the pope as "universal
Ordinary." The first notable approach to this idea was
the legend of pope Sylvester, which grew up towards the
end of the fifth century, according to which the first
Christian emperor ordained that all priests should recognise
the pope as their head, just as all judges were subject to
their master, the emperor. This legend had nothing like so
strong an influence, however, as the pseudo-Isidorian
forgeries, which transmitted almost the whole of the earlier
doctrine of the Roman primacy, and enriched it with
fruitful and productive phrases. Not only is the Apostolic
See the head, the mother and the corner-stone of all the
churches, but, in a surprising misinterpretation and extension of an expression of Leo the Great's, the Roman church
is said to have made the other churches its representatives in such a way that they were only called upon to
undertake a part of its activity, and were not in possession
of plenary authority. Such phrases suggest a completed
form of the idea of the pope as "universal Ordinary;"
other remarks, however, show that even the forgers did not
feel sure of themselves in this respect, and were still hesitat-
ing between episcopalism and papalism. In the succeeding
period, during the decline and eclipse of the Roman
church, papalist theories were faithfully preserved by the
curia, though they were seldom realised in practice. If on
occasion the primacy was claimed in distant parts for the
pope, the episcopal church was the prevalent form in all
the countries of Europe. On the one hand Abbo of Fleury
wrote that the Roman church imparts authority to all
other churches; others firmly maintained the episcopal
standpoint and rejected papal interference: since each
bishop of a faithful community stands, as the husband of
his church, in the place of the Saviour, they argued, it is
therefore no one's business to cause mischief in another's
diocese. A well-known example is provided by the per-
sistent opposition of the German bishops to pope Benedict
VIII when the pope accepted the appeal of the count and
countess of Hammerstein, who had been condemned in

Germany for marrying within the prohibited degrees.[1]

From the time of Leo IX onwards, the idea of the primacy of Rome and the pope's claim to be " universal Ordinary," though at first weakened by the historic conflict with Byzantium, advances from strength to strength. The importance of the Roman church is emphasised with ever more passionate enthusiasm. Hildebrand went to the trouble of collecting, or causing to be collected, all the legal weapons of the Holy See; Peter Damian composed a widely-read work on the privileges of the Roman church; Humbert showed that the whole Church was dependent for its merits on the Throne of Peter: the members of the whole of Christendom, he wrote, are unharmed when the head is unharmed, and when it is weak they too begin to fail. More important still was the fact that Leo IX and his successors really ruled the Church and exercised to the full rights which had hitherto been largely theoretical. They made their presence felt everywhere by sending legates, armed with full powers, into distant parts, and through them they kept a finger on all important ecclesiastical affairs. Yet although the popes and their fellow-workers could rest their claims in large part upon ancient laws, these were in many cases unknown to the world at large, to which the commands of Rome appeared new-fangled

---

[1] On the Sylvester legend see W. Levison, *Konstantinische Schenkung und Silvesterlegende*, in *Studi e Testi*, xxxviii. (1924) 166 sq., and pseudo-Vigilius c. 7 (ed. Hinschius, p. 712); on the origin of the formula *in partem vocatus sollicitudinis, non in plenitudinem potestatis*, cf. Caspar, *Papsttum*, i. 455 sq. The importance of pseudo-Isidore in the history of the papal primacy, especially in the tenth and eleventh centuries, has not yet been sufficiently investigated. G. Hartmann, *Der Primat des römischen Bischofs bei Pseudo-Isidor* (1930), offers some very valuable suggestions, and feels able to assert the predominance of episcopalism (pp. 74 sqq.). On Abbo of Fleury, see *Ep.* v (MPL. 139 col. 423) and *Can. coll.* v (*ibid.* col. 479), Sackur, *Cluniacenser*, i. 281 and Brackmann in HZ. 139 (1929) 39. Glaber ii. 5-7 (ed. Prou, pp. 32 sqq.) relates how John XVIII interfered in the dedication of the monastic church of Beaulieu-près-de-Loches in the juris-diction of the archbishop of Tours, by sending a legate; during the service a storm of wind arose and destroyed the church roof, thereby making known God's wrath at the infraction of archiepiscopal rights.—In his voluminous work on the papacy (*Das Papsttum*, 2 vols., 1933-8), J. Haller sets out a theory according to which the papal idea only originated through the contact of the Roman Church with the Germanic peoples. Though his ideas are interesting and of much use in detail, they are on the whole unacceptable.

and contrary to established custom. Nothing could be more marked than the different tone in which the papacy now asserted its rights, as compared with times past. In earlier days the papal claim to intervene in the ecclesiastical life of other dioceses had been cautiously phrased, and modified with explanations and ambiguities. Now the claim rang out categorically, in proud and dominating tones. In order to see the change we have only to compare the language of the *Dictatus Papae*, the letters of Gregory VII or of the somewhat later law-books with the passages in the writings of Nicholas I or in pseudo-Isidore upon which they are founded. The Hildebrandine period, moreover, did not remain bound by tradition, but by extending and forcing the old laws created entirely new ones. The old command that every Catholic church must be in harmony with Rome was no longer restricted to matters of belief alone, but was made to include liturgical uses and external organisation; the Mozarabic rite, for instance, was replaced by the Roman in Spain, and from this time bishoprics were only to be created and divided, or monasteries and other foundations reformed, with the pope's permission, whereas hitherto the king and the lay owners had had the chief voice in these matters. Similarly, in Gregory's time the principle of the devolution of ecclesiastical appointments to the pope was first asserted : when elections were contested the nomination to the vacant church was to fall to the pope. Where earlier Roman doctrine had merely asserted that bishops could only be deposed with the consent of the pope, Gregory VII laid down briefly and concisely that the pope or his legates could depose bishops without the co-operation of a synod, and in certain circumstances even without hearing the accused. Another ordinance which had a far-reaching effect was that which, contrary to existing custom, allowed clerical superiors to be accused by their subordinates, if the latter secured papal consent. On the basis of the old law which ordained that important matters were to be reported to Rome, the pope now felt himself justified in interfering in the life of individual churches and in exercising the functions of the local dignitaries either in person or through legates. This is, in fact, the real meaning of the universal episcopacy claimed by the pope: the pope is bishop everywhere, the bishops are merely his representatives in their own particular dioceses.[1]

An idea of the far-reaching changes which the internal Church policy of the reforming curia sought to introduce into the old Church constitution, and of the novel and revolutionary appearance which these changes presented to contemporary eyes, is best conveyed by a glance at the strength of the forces which resisted innovation. Under Leo IX, a certain measure of discontent among the bishops were already noticeable. The French prelates, summoned by the pope to a national council at Reims, were, like their king, on the whole disinclined to obey. Energetic resistance to one detail of papal policy, so strong that it can only be explained by a deep and embittered feeling of opposition, gave importance to the well-known scene between Leo IX and archbishop Liutpold at the Christmas service of 1052 in Mainz. The point in dispute was a difference between the German and the Roman liturgies; the archbishop took upon himself the ruthless and forcible defence of the German use against the pope. Even in later times similar Roman attempts to introduce uniformity were resisted, among others by the Anonymous of York, who rather surprisingly appeals to a tolerant phrase of Gregory the Great's about diversity in works and unity in belief.[2]

The opposition between papacy and episcopate ceased on the death of Leo IX. Victor II's relations with the bishops were good, Stephen IX and Nicholas II reigned only for short periods, and Alexander II was at first hindered by the schism. A few years before Gregory VII's election, however, Roman control again became stricter. The bishops

---

[1] Peter Damian, *Opusc.* v (MPL. 145 col. 89); Humbert, *De sancta Romana ecclesia*, Fragment A (ed. Schramm, *Kaiser, Rom und Renovatio*, ii. 128).—The novelty of the tone in Gregory's proclamations is brought out by a comparison of the *Dictatus Papae* with the texts collected by Caspar in his edition (pp. 202 sqq.).

[2] Cf. Steindorff, *Jahrbücher*, ii. 85 sqq. and 188 sqq.; Hauck, *Kirchengeschichte*, iii. 612 sq.; Anon. of York, *Tract.* xi (ed. Böhmer, *Kirche und Staat*, p. 456), and cf. Gregory I, *Reg.* i. 41 (MGH. *Epp.* i. 57) and Caspar, *Papsttum*, ii. 150.

first attempted to continue silently in their accustomed ways, were deaf to papal wishes, or had recourse to explanations and excuses. Soon, however, protests were raised against individual measures of Gregory's, which were felt to be encroachments. Udo of Trier, otherwise loyal, asks the pope to spare him commands which cannot be carried out. Siegfried of Mainz complains of the treatment of his suffragan, the bishop of Prague, whom Alexander II had suspended and deprived of his revenues without a hearing, contrary to canon law. He is ready, he says, to refer to the pope cases which are so difficult that he and his suffragans cannot decide them, but the Prague affair should first of all have been brought before a provincial synod. Siegfried uses hard words on this occasion, saying that the name and office of bishop, which are holy before God and man, are suffering unbearable outrage. About the same time, in conjunction with the archbishop of Bremen, he bluntly refused obedience to the papal legates, and hindered the assembly of a German council which the legates wished to hold on the pope's behalf. This opposition to disturbances of the customary process of law and to the intervention of papal legates continued, but until 1076 the pope himself was in general respectfully addressed. Nevertheless, the extent to which passions were already roused, especially in Germany, is shown by a letter from archbishop Liemar of Bremen to bishop Hezilo of Hildesheim: " This dangerous man," he writes of Gregory, " wants to order the bishops about as if they were servants on his estates; and if they do not do all that he commands, they have to go to Rome or else they are suspended without legal process."[1]

In the fateful days of January 1076, when Henry IV had assembled a large number of German bishops around him at Worms, the consistently rising feeling led to a violent outbreak. The letters in which king and bishops at this

---

[1] Cf. Meyer von Knonau, *Jahrbücher*, ii. 447 sq.; Siegfried of Mainz to Gregory VII, in *Cod. Udalrici*, no. 40 (Jaffé, *Bibl. rer. Germ.*, v. 84 sqq.), and cf. no. 42 (*ibid.*, pp. 88 sqq.) and Gregory VII, *Reg.* i. 60 (pp. 87 sqq.) and ii. 29 (pp. 161 sqq.); Liemar of Bremen's letter to Hezilo of Hildesheim is printed in E. Bernheim, *Quellen zur Gesch. des Investiturstreites*, i. 3 (1930) 58 sqq.

time withdrew obedience from Gregory VII deal as much with the pope's evil deeds against the bishops and with his infringements of episcopal rights as with the injuries he had done to Henry IV. Among points of detail, the disturbance of episcopal jurisdiction by the reservation of all appeals is mentioned—a proof that it was felt to be a considerable grievance. So too, the prestige of the diocesan bishop and the obedience of the parochial clergy must have been severely shaken by the discovery that it was relatively easy for the latter to get judgments against the former from pope or legate. With great emphasis the accusation is made: " So far as lay in your power, you have torn from the bishops' hands all the authority given them through the grace of the Holy Spirit, who takes part in their ordination." The pope, they say, has reduced the noble order, which used to exist among the members of Christ, into a lamentable confusion, and through his glorious decrees (*gloriosa decreta*) has humbled the name of Christ into the dust. It is clear from this that the anti-Gregorians were as insistent as the reformers on a " right order " in the Church; it was because of this that they defended the rights of the bishops. In this connection, they put a striking emphasis upon the value of episcopal consecraticn, which, they say, is not to take second place to any other; in other words, the chief point of their polemic is a conviction—that of the independence of . episcopal authority—which has been decisive in all conflicts between episcopalism and papalism.[1]

It is easy to understand why the question of the primacy seems to drop into the background in the time of the anti-pope Guibert. The opponents of Gregory and his successors had no longer so much need to combat papal claims so fundamentally, since they could range themselves behind the

[1] Cf. the letters of king and bishops from the Worms synod of 24 Jan. 1076, MGH. *Const.* i. 106 sqq., no. 58 sqq., K. Hampe, *Heinrichs IV Absagebrief an Gregor VII*, in HZ. 138 (1928) 315 sqq., and C. Erdmann, *Die Anfänge der staatlichen Propaganda im Investiturstreit, ibid.* 154 (1936) 491 sqq. Henry IV accuses Gregory in the following terms: " Rectores sanctae ecclesiae, videlicet archiepiscopos, episcopos, presbyteros, non modo non tangere, sicut christos domini, timuisti, quin sicut servos, nescientes quid faciat dominus eorum, sub pedibus tuis calcasti. Quos omnes nihil scire, te autem solum omnia nosse iudicasti."

anti-pope, whose internal church policy followed other lines. But the quarrel becomes more lively again shortly after Guibert's death; the defence of the rights of the particular churches against too great an increase in papal power continues, and the traditional gradations of the clerical hierarchy are stoutly maintained. A defiant note is sounded in Cologne, for instance: " As the Roman bishop claims due obedience from the archbishop of Cologne, so the archbishop demands that the bishop of Rome refrain from interfering in canonical discipline within the archiepiscopal territory." This was defence; but there were attacks also, which sometimes even called in question the foundation of the papal rights and plenitude of power. At a synod at Quedlinburg in 1085 a cleric of Bamberg had contested the assertion that cases which the pope had decided could not be further discussed. This protest was occasionally repeated later on, and was even turned against the doctrine of the judicial irresponsibility of the pope. So considerable a representative of the moderate ecclesiastical party as Ivo of Chartres wished to see the pope's power of legislation carefully restricted; and ardent Gregorians like Placidus of Nonantula and Godfrey of Vendôme would hear no more of the pope's *plenitudo potestatis* after Paschal II had used it, as they said, to hand over the Church to the emperor. The memorandum on investitures which was probably intended to serve as instructions for the imperial ambassadors who waited on Paschal in 1109 even dares to doubt whether the power of binding and loosing possessed by the representative of Peter really coincides with the will of God: " Let the pope beware lest God loose in Heaven what he binds on earth, and bind in Heaven what he looses on earth." To hold this possible is to reject the core of the idea of primacy.[1]

[1] Cf. E. Bernheim, *Artikel gegen Eingriffe des Papstes Paschalis II in die Kölner Metropolitanrechte*, in *Westdeutsche Ztschr.* i. (1882) 324 sqq.; on similar complaints in France, see Schwarz, ZKG. 43 (1924) 99; on the synod of Quedlinburg (1085), MGH. *Const.* i. 652 no. 443, and Hauck, iii. 844, n. 1; Ivo to Hugh of Lyons, MGH. *Lib. de lite,* ii. 642; Placidus of Nonantula, *De honore ecclesiae,* c. 142 (MGH. *Lib. de lite,* ii. 631) and c. 70 (p. 597); Godfrey, *Libellus,* i. (*ibid.* pp. 680 sqq.) ; *Epistola de vitanda missa uxuratorum sacerdotum,* c. 2 (MGH. *Lib. de lite,* iii. 7): " quod, etiamsi

The pope's primacy was rejected on deeper theological grounds and much more radical grounds of Church policy by the so-called Anonymous of York. His astonishing doctrine stands quite alone throughout the whole period. He boldly denies the authority of tradition, and explains that the Roman church received its position by the decrees of the Fathers and on account of the pre-eminence of Rome as the capital of the world. According to him, there was no such thing as primacy in the primitive Church, and Christ had said nothing of it. Christ gave all the Apostles equal power; the bishop of Rome can claim no more control over the archbishop of Rouen than Peter possessed over the other Apostles—indeed, he can really only claim the authority Peter exercised over himself. For each bishop is the successor of Peter, the archbishop of Rouen as much as the bishop of Rome; no church is higher than another—here again the basic argument of episcopalism is brought forward —for all have the same sacraments. Or are they nobler in Lyons, for instance, than in Rouen? The assertion that one church is superior to another makes two churches out of one, that is to say, divides the one indivisible Church. The bishops are the representatives of Christ, and can therefore, like Christ, be judged by none save God. The direct dependence of the bishops on God, in opposition to the papal theory, cannot be more ruthlessly set out than this.[1]

The idea of the episcopal church and of episcopal independence was once more to play an important part in ecclesiastical history. It could never be altogether set

Romana auctoritas circumveniatur aliqua hereticorum fraudulentia eisque reddi iubeat indebitam communionem vel dignitatem, magis nos sequi debere cognitam veritatem quam deceptam auctoritatem." With this may be compared, for instance, the threatening letter of the synod of Vienne, 1112: cf. Meyer von Knonau, *Jahrbücher*, vi. 243 sqq. and *De investitura* (MGH. *Lib. de lite*, ii. 500), where it is also pointed out that he who sits in Peter's seat is not necessarily Peter.

[1] Anon. of York, *Tract.* iii. and v. (MGH. *Lib. de lite*, iii. 656 sqq. and 680 sqq.), ii. (Böhmer, *Kirche und Staat*, pp. 437 sqq.) and xii. (*ibid.* pp. 457 sqq.). For the importance of these treatises, see in particular Böhmer, pp. 256 sqq., Dempf, *Sacrum Imperium*, pp. 199 sqq., A. Brackmann, *Die Ursachen der geistigen und politischen Wandlung Europas im xi und xii Jhdt.*, in HZ. 149 (1933) 233 sqq.—" The most independent writing of the early middle ages;" Funk, HJ. 55 (1935) 261 sqq., writes: " Plainly, we have here one of the most radical expressions of the opposition to the canonistic and dogmatic extension of the idea of primacy."

aside by the rise of the papacy, whose victory was never complete. The restlessness of the older powers which were being repressed made itself apparent in the eleventh and the early twelfth centuries, and yet their counter-activity is a clear indication of the irresistible force with which the idea of Roman primacy was being developed at this time. The internal organisation of the Church was formed in the spirit of Gregory VII; it was he who made the papal monarchy a reality and opened the way for the age of papal domination.

III

While the old episcopal constitution of the Church prevailed, any attempt to make the spiritual power predominate in the political, as distinct from the moral sphere, was without prospects of success; it was the rapid advance of the papacy within the Church in the narrower sense which gave the attempt its real chance. The Roman bishop became in very fact the priest of priests, and united in himself, according to the opinion of the times, the power and dignity of the priesthood. Only as a consequence of this did it become possible to solve the wider problem: namely, how to give to the Church in its widest sense, that is, to the whole of Christendom, the order which corresponded to the will of God, for only now was there a tribunal capable of undertaking the heaviest of tasks—that of restraining king or prince in accordance with ecclesiastical principles of world-order. The bitterest and most hotly-contested battles were fought round the position of the king., The Gregorians had little patience with the now traditional belief in the supernatural sanctity of the king, or in his spiritual capacity as the directly-ordained representative of Christ on earth, and felt little of the old reverent fear of the secret magic of kingship, the joyful faith in the prince's grace-bestowing powers, which had ruled past ages, and they opposed an exaggerated respect for the secular office of kingship. For this purpose they made industrious use of the old arguments in favour of priestly

claims. Spiritual and secular authority were compared
with soul and body, heaven and earth, gold and lead, sun
and moon, and by means of such comparisons the inferiority
of the kingly office was suggested. But this was not sufficient, and violent attacks were made on the sacramental
character of kingship, which had always formed the basis
of the king's domination of Church and State. " Where is
it written that the emperors are the representatives of
Christ? " is the question already put by one of Henry III's
few serious opponents, and the historian of Liège takes a
very critical view of Henry's Church government; the
emperor, he says, in the weakness of the flesh and in vanity,
has sought to assume control of the bishops, and, appealing
to the sanctity of his ordination, received a severe defeat at
the hands of bishop Wazo, who forced him to admit that
the orders of a subdeacon were superior to his, the
emperor's. Even more uncomplimentary to the imperial
consecration was the comparison which Gregory VII drew
between the exorcist (one of the minor orders) and the
emperor: the exorcist is a spiritual emperor, having power
over demons, and therefore even more power over secular
rulers, who are bound in wretched servitude to the demons,
and are consequently their instruments. If even exorcists
possess this superiority, writes Gregory, how much more
do the priests? Placidus of Nonantula ironically asks those
who defend imperial control of bishops by appealing to the
divine ordination of the emperor, why then God did not
give the emperor the keys of Heaven, and with them the
authority to bind and loose.[1]

The attacks of the Gregorians gave rise to equally determined counter-attacks from the imperialist side, and indeed
the monarchical conception of the hierarchy is set out during these troubled years in terms of unusual clarity and
ruthlessness. The thirteenth chapter of Romans served the
imperialists well as a defence of their contention that the
emperor was the representative of God. If the king is
indeed a layman, which many deny—so runs this argument

---

[1] Auct. Gall. (MGH. *Lib. de lite*, i. 12 sqq.), *Gesta ep. Leod.*, c. 66 (MGH.
SS. vii. 229 sq.), Gregory VII, *Reg.* viii. 21 (pp. 555 sq.).

—yet by his consecration he is mystically elevated above other laymen, and shares in the priestly office. Gregory of Catino accepts the emperor's right to take part in papal elections, on the ground that the holy oil has made him the anointed of the Lord; and even Hugh of Fleury, though a man of moderate views, declares: " Within the boundaries of his land the king seems to take the place of God the Father, and the bishops that of Christ," and goes on to explain that in consequence it seems reasonable that all the bishops of his realm should be subordinate to the king, as the Son is to the Father. This same explanation of the relationship of king and priest, which Hugh of Fleury had taken over from earlier writers, is also to be found in the Anonymous of York, who very definitely ascribes a higher spiritual rank to the king. For him the king embodies the divine, the priests the human nature of Christ. Christ was both king and priest, but the king in him was the higher; the Church is the Bride not of Christ as priest, but of Christ as king; and he even dares to point out that the Church is called Queen not Priestess.[1]

Belief in the sanctity of kingship was obstinately maintained by many, and in spite of repeated victories the Church never succeeded in exterminating it. The Church did manage, however, to drive it out of its own official life into the realms which were from the ecclesiastical point of view illegitimate, where it was at a later date once more to be extremely dangerous to the system founded by Gregory VII. The clearest picture of the Church's success in

---

[1] Cf. Petrus Crassus, *Defensio Heinrici IV imperatoris*, c. 7 (MGH. *Lib. de lite*, i. 450), on *Romans* xiii; Wido of Osnabrück, *De controversia Hildebrandi et Heinrici* (*ibid.* p. 467): " Unde dicunt nulli laico unquam aliquid de ecclesiasticis disponendi facultatem esse concessam, quamvis rex a numero laicorum merito in huiusmodi separetur, cum oleo consecrationis inunctus sacerdotalis ministerii particeps esse cognoscitur " (cf. also Mirbt, pp. 150 sqq. and 481); Gregory of Catino, *Orthodoxa defensio*, c. 6 (*ibid.* ii. 538): " Nam reges et imperatores propter sacram unctionem christi nuncupantur et sic suorum ministerio vel officio sive prelatione sacramentis ecclesiae sunt uniti, ut in nullo debeant separari;" on Hugh of Fleury, see *supra*, p. 60, n. 1; on the Anon. of York, see the same note and *Tract.* ii. and iv., MGH. *Lib. de lite*, iii., esp. p. 666: "Sacerdos quippe aliam praefigurabat in Christo naturam, id est hominis, rex aliam, id est Dei," p. 667 and pp. 662 sq.: " Sancta ecclesia sponsa Christi est, qui est verus rex et sacerdos, sed non secundum hoc quod sacerdos est, sponsa eius dicitur, sed secundum hoc quod rex est; haec sponsa regina dicitur, non sacerdotissa."

depriving the princely office of its spiritual character is
given by the changes in the ceremony of consecration and
by the elimination of royal consecration from the sacraments
of the Church. During the twelfth century " the boundary
between spiritual and secular was more sharply drawn
both in fact and in ceremonial."[1]

It was only by weakening the belief in the priesthood of
the king that kings could be assigned their " right " place
in the world-order. The supporters of the kingship were
accused, on the basis of St John xix. 15, of thinking that
they had no pope other than the emperor,[2] and that the
emperor had the power of judging the bishops and issuing
commands to them. Though there had in fact been no such
theory, governmental practice in the various European
countries had been along these lines. To the reformers,
however, this system implied that the higher was judged by
the lower, " the head by the tail," and that kings, moved by
a sinful lust for power, usurped what did not belong to
them. In the reformers' view, an end had to be put to this;
but the princes should nevertheless have " their primacy "
in the Church—should, that is to say, be its protectors and
enjoy its support; kings and priests should each have what
was rightly theirs.[3]

But the papal party could not stop at the mere rejection
of royal usurpation. Their idea of the right order of the
Christian world was bound to unfold itself as soon as the
kingship refused friendly co-operation, and as soon as it
came to a conflict. At that point it had to be decided
whether the pope was really supreme on earth. At the
beginning of his pontificate, Gregory VII had already
drawn the logical conclusion from his principles when in the

---

[1] Cf. Kern, pp. 85 and 88 (Chrimes, pp. 39–40), notes 115 and 155;
Eichmann, *Königsweihe und Bischofsweihe*, pp. 55 sqq.; Mayer-Pfannholz,
Wende von Canossa, in *Hochland*, xxx. (1930) p. 404.

[2] According to Manegold, *Contra Wolfhelmum liber*, c. 23 (MGH. *Lib. de
lite*, i. 306), the Germans are supposed to have said: " Non habemus pontificem nisi Caesarem."

[3] Paschal II, in JL. 6050 (Jaffé, *Bibl*. iii. 379, no. 33): " Sacerdotii ac
regni grave iam diu scandalum fuit, quia, usurpantibus non sua regibus,
ecclesia quod suae est libertatis amisit. . . . Habeant in ecclesia primatum
suum, ut sint ecclesiae defensores et ecclesiae subsidiis perfruantur. Habeant reges, quod regum est; quod sacerdotum est, habeant sacerdotes."

Dictatus Papae he claimed for the representative of Peter the right of deposing emperors; and he acted in conformity with this conviction when in 1074 and 1075 he threatened the French and German kings with the loss of their thrones. In the conflict with Germany the pope advanced from theory to practice. The German king was the strongest, the least open to conciliation, and the most inclined to base his actions on first principles.[1] A combination of audacity, force and an underestimate of his enemy's strength led Henry IV to condemn the pope and to contest the legality of his position, and the papacy was thereby compelled either to surrender or to take up a struggle in which everything was at stake. Gregory VII did not hesitate to put the theories of the *Dictatus Papae* into practical application and acted with unheard-of severity: he excommunicated Henry, deprived him of his throne and released his subjects from their oaths of fealty.

Excommunication is a purely spiritual penalty, and earlier popes had several times imposed it on sovereign princes. Some of Henry's supporters wrongly denied the pope the right to punish the king at all, and many regarded the sentence as so null and void that it did not even need to be raised. In excommunicating Henry, however, Gregory still remained within the limits of the Church's spiritual jurisdiction as it had long been exercised. Gregory and his party sought to explain even the deposition as in no way an innovation. The pope himself asserted that Gregory the Great had threatened kings with deposition, but it has been made clear that on this occasion he was misinterpreting an adjuration as an order, and " converting the threat of (divine) punishment into a (papal) command."[2] It is in fact undeniable that Gregory was the first

[1] Recent attempts to suggest that action according to a principle is a peculiarly German characteristic are on the whole to be rejected: see the interesting discussions in A. Reinke, *Die Schuldialektik im Investiturstreit* (1937), and G. Kallen, *Der Investiturstreit als Kampf zwischen germanischem und romanischem Denken* (1937), which, however, lead to rash and unsatisfactory conclusions. I have deliberately avoided any attempt to distinguish the attitudes of the different nations during the Investiture Contest: this is at present impossible, since a continuous comparison of their attitudes in other centuries as well would be necessary.

[2] Cf. Caspar, in HZ. 130 (1924) pp. 15 sqq.

pope to depose a king, and this action was at once the most decisive and most disputed act of his life. In the conflict that raged around it both his supporters and his opponents became involved in discussions of the most fundamental nature. Gregory himself took great pains to justify it; in this connexion the historical arguments just described were in his eyes of secondary importance, and the real grounds for his actions are to be found in the depth of his belief.

Here he appealed to two principles: the nature of the spiritual power in general, and the special authority of the successor of Peter. But his explanation moves so readily from one to the other, and the two are so closely bound up together in his mind that it is hardly possible to reproduce his thought and at the same time keep these two ideas clearly distinguished. The spiritual power, he says, was created by God in His own honour, and was vouchsafed to the world by His mercy. The priests of Christ are the fathers and teachers of all kings and princes. The priest baptises men, drawing them out of the Devil's power and strengthening them in their belief by the holy chrism. It is the priest who prepares the Body and Blood of the Lord, and who grants absolution from the bondage of sin; to him is given the power to bind and loose on earth and in Heaven. If, therefore, kings have, on account of their sins, to be judged by priests, by whom can they more rightly be condemned than by the highest of all priests, the Roman bishop?[1]

The priestly power to bind and loose draws its greatest strength from the power to give absolution, which is transmitted by the sacrament of ordination. The jurisdiction of the pastoral office is added, in order to lead men to salvation in this life. The highest jurisdiction is that of the pope, which draws its strength and its peculiar character from the unerring orthodoxy of the Roman church. The power thus given by God is one and undivided, and the distinctions which later ages made between primacy in jurisdiction and primacy in belief are foreign to the eleventh

[1] Cf. the two letters to Hermann of Metz, *Reg.* iv. 2 and viii. 21 (pp. 293 sqq. and 544 sqq.). This paragraph is taken almost verbally from viii. 21.

century; the close relationship of the two has indeed always been emphasised in Catholic dogma. The highest claim ever made on behalf of the judicial authority of Peter and his successors is clearly expressed in Gregory's programme, the *Dictatus Papae*, where clause 25 reserves the deposition of bishops, absentees and emperors to the pope. Before Gregory's time excommunication was the limit of the power of priests, bishops and popes to punish kings. Gregory boldly connected the power to open and close the gates of Heaven—the core of which is the power of absolution—with the right to judge on earth: " cui ergo aperiendi claudendique coeli data potestas est, de terra iudicare non licet? Absit." The Son of God had given Peter and his successors the power to bind and loose souls, a power, that is to say, which is spiritual and heavenly; how much the more, then, can Peter dispose of what is purely earthly and secular? This phrase " how much the more " is the crucial point in all Gregory's arguments, and reappears under many forms in his letters and in Gregorian literature; by means of it the chains which had hitherto bound the spiritual power were forcibly broken. The pope's power of binding and loosing now extended over every phase of human life. The view of Gregory and his supporters that the limitation of the power of the keys to the soul alone was unreasonable, seems even to have found an echo in the liturgy. A significant alteration was made in a prayer for the feast of Petri Cathedra (February 22); the original form was: " Deus qui beato Petro apostolo tuo, collatis clavibus regni caelestis, animas ligandi et solvendi pontificium tradidisti," etc., but in the contemporary sacramentaries of the Roman church the word *animas* was left out.[1]

In exactly the same way as he developed the power of binding and loosing, Gregory VII extended and amplified the doctrine of the infallibility of the Roman church. In

---

[1] Cf. *Dictatus Papae* xxii, in *Reg.* ii. 55a (p. 207). Apart from the sentence quoted (from viii. 21, p. 550), the directness with which Gregory derives his jurisdiction from the power to give absolution is shown by iv. 2 (p. 295): " Nam qui se negat non posse ecclesiae vinculo alligari, restat, ut neget se non posse ab huius potestate absolvi, et qui hoc impudenter negat, se a Christo omnino sequestrat."

the theory, if not always in the practice, of earlier times, this doctrine had only been asserted in matters of belief, but Gregory ignored this reservation. Clause 22 of the *Dictatus Papae* bluntly and unhesitatingly claims " that the Roman church has never erred, and according to the witness of Holy Writ shall not err throughout eternity."

In thus extending the sphere of priestly and papal activity, Gregory VII was acting in full accordance with the sacramental conception of the hierarchy; the clergy exist in order that through them the world may be raised to the Kingdom of God. Gregory drew the conclusions of this theory, and brought the world unreservedly into the sphere of the Church. Secular government thus becomes an ecclesiastical office, and the pope can set up and put down princes as he can bishops. His claim that all important matters (*causae maiores*) must be brought before him is no longer limited to Church affairs, but covers everything that may happen on earth. But it is his position with regard to the king which most concerns him. As he judges bishops, so can he impose penalties on princes, if the welfare of the Church demands them. The punishment of secular rulers may even be a spiritual necessity: for " he who disregards the privileges of St Peter and refuses as a Christian to obey him, is unworthy to rule over a single Christian. He who leaves the duties of a Christian king unfulfilled, must lose his office. A prince who is ensnared by the Devil, and who therefore does not hold even the lowest place in Christendom, is not fit to govern Christians." Since the pope can depose princes, he can also release their subjects from an oath of obedience—otherwise the deposition is pointless—and in so doing he does no more than when, as was customary, he absolves the vassals of deposed bishops from their oaths of fealty. On the other hand, the obedience which the subject owes to the pope takes precedence over the oath which he has sworn to his prince, for the pope is the higher and stands in the place of God, and God must be obeyed rather than man.[1]

[1] Cf. Kern, pp. 233 sqq. (= Chrimes, pp. 108 sqq.), and see also *Reg.* iii. 10 (p. 267), ix. 2 and 9 (pp. 572, 586), and i. 22 (p. 38): " Cum ergo mundanis

This claim by the representative of Peter to obedience is just as unlimited as his disciplinary power. All are subject to him: " Are kings excepted therefrom? Are they not among the sheep whom the Son of God has entrusted to St Peter? Who, I ask, in view of this power to bind and to loose, can think himself free from the power of Peter, unless it be the wretch who will not bear the yoke of the Lord, but takes upon himself the burden of the Devil, and refuses to count himself among the sheep of Christ? To shake the power of Peter, which was given him by God, from off his wicked neck, in no way helps him to obtain his miserable freedom, for the more a man struggles to throw it off in pride, the more surely is he led to damnation at the Judgment."[1]

The general duty of obedience to his spiritual superior, incumbent upon every Christian, was the foundation of all papal claims to rule; Gregory appeals to it again and again. He wrote to William the Conqueror, for instance: " If I therefore have to represent you at the dread tribunal before the Just Judge who is not deceived, the Creator of every living being, pay heed and consider whether it is right or possible for me not to be greatly concerned for your salvation, and whether it is right or possible for you not to obey me promptly, in order that you may secure your own salvation and possess the land of the living."[2] The pope's duty to warn, to amend and to intervene arises from this responsibility for the person of the prince and the people subject to him, and hence it became necessary to undertake far-reaching political activity, to depose kings, to influence their election and enthronement, even to make alliances with revolutionaries like the Patarini of Milan, and to claim to be judge between contending parties.

Down to our own time, Gregory VII has been defended against the charge of interfering in political affairs. It is,

potestatibus obedire predicavit apostolus, quanto magis spiritualibus et vicem Christi inter christianos habentibus; ?" Bernold, *Libellus*, xii (MGH. *Lib. de lite*, ii. 147): " Sicut autem Romani pontifices summos patriarchos deponere possunt, ita et inferiores utpote mundi principes."
[1] *Reg.* viii. 21 (p. 548); cf. also iii. 10, iv. 2, iv. 11 (pp. 270 sqq., 295, 311). Paraphrases and commentaries are in Bernold, *Libellus*, v (MGH. *Lib. de lite*, ii. 97) and Hugh of Flavigny, *Chron.* ii (MGH. SS. viii. 437).
[2] *Reg.* vii. 25 (p. 506).

however, wrong to suppose that, because his aims were purely religious, he must as a result have withdrawn from worldly affairs; for there was, in the eyes of the Gregorians, no antinomy between the religious and the secular life. On the contrary, their fundamental conviction was that the world is the testing-ground of religion.

It cannot be doubted that political power possessed attractions for a nature like Gregory's, but, quite apart from this, he needed such power for the purely material reason that without it the pope's commands would pass unheeded. The reforming popes were clear on this point. Since the time of Leo IX they had been energetically endeavouring to set the administration of the curia in order, to build up the papal state, to extend it and make it secure in Italy, and above all to increase their secular influence by a carefully-calculated policy of alliances. As an administrative officer of the curia, Hildebrand had taken a prominent part in this; we read, for example, that he had been greatly concerned to create a papal army. When he became pope, he followed the same policy as his predecessors, excelling them only in the passion and the political energy with which he pursued his ends. He sought out industriously every conceivable legal claim from which an increase in the power of the Roman church could be expected, and in several cases even tried to use his diplomatic · acumen to turn unpromising situations to the papacy's advantage; thus, for instance he built up a claim on the part of the Roman church to a tax from the whole of Gaul on the basis of a forged charter of Charlemagne, which established an annual grant for the Frankish school in Rome.

An increase in the immediate financial and military resources of the Church was, however, not enough. For centuries the popes had entered into special relationships with single bishoprics, churches and—in particular—monasteries, with the object of realising and strengthening their primacy and their general position of dominance inside the Church. They had made a practice of confirming possessions or granting privileges which had no particular legal effects but which nevertheless demonstrated their authority;

they had drawn still closer bonds by removing churches from episcopal jurisdiction and placing them under their own, and by acquiring rights of ownership over churches for themselves. No fixed principles had governed this policy, rather had the peculiar circumstances of each case decided whether moral or legal ties should be created between Rome and the particular churches. Similar objectives, pursued with a like realism, are to be observed in the policy of the curia towards the various European countries. Roman influence could chiefly be strengthened by an extension of common interests and by friendly intercourse —in short, by forming closer relationships. This aim was pursued with particular energy under Gregory, and it is plain that there was an unusually strong desire to set up legal connexions and to transform moral into legal ties; the contemporary method of securing this was the creation of feudal relationships. Gregory was not the first pope to adopt this method, but before him it had been used only occasionally and almost by accident; with him a deliberate purpose is clearly noticeable, and can be seen especially in his dealings with England, Denmark, Hungary and Germany. In so doing, however, he was simply using every opportunity of increasing papal authority, and had no intention of inferring a theory of complete feudal supremacy from the general authority deriving from the power to bind and loose.[1]

For Gregory VII the unity of the Christian world, with all its implications, became a deep-rooted conviction. The old attitude of mistrust towards the world, the long-preserved aversion from the wickedness of earthly affairs, found no echo in his vast creation; even if he did occasionally

---

[1] The latest summaries of Gregory's feudal policy are to be found in Fliche, *Réforme Grégorienne*, ii. 350 sqq.; Voosen, *Papauté*, pp. 306 sqq.; Wühr, *Studien*, pp. 48 sqq.; Hofmann, *Dictatus Papae*, p. 142, n. 3. Cf. also K. Jordan, *Das Eindringen des Lehnswesens in das Rechtsleben der römischen Kurie*, AUF. 12 (1932) 73 sqq. There is no thorough-going investigation of the whole problem. For England, cf. Z.N. Brooke, *Pope Gregory VII's demand for fealty from William the Conqueror*, EHR. 26 (1911) 225 sqq. (but cf. Caspar, *Reg.* p. 506, notes 2 and 3), and *The English Church and the Papacy*, (1931) pp. 132 sqq. On Germany, cf. R. Holtzmann, in HZ. 145 (1932) 334 sqq. and 350, and the references there quoted; on Saxony the references given by Caspar in *Reg.* p. 567, n. 3.

use condemnatory expressions about the world,[1] these
are but relics of ideas he had left behind, and are utterly
foreign to his thought. In reality he excluded nothing from
the purview of the Church. The old theory of the two
powers which should bear rule in the world consequently
lost its meaning for him and his supporters. For him, the
metaphysical precedence which, in the eyes of the spiritual
leaders of the Church, the priestly authority had always
possessed over the royal, had logically to be converted into
a complete supremacy. Gelasius' phrases about the two
powers continued to be quoted by the ecclesiastical party,
but their meaning had changed. Where earlier they had
been understood to involve the setting of the two powers
side by side, the point to which importance was now
attached was the superiority of the one over the other.
Room was still found for the secular authority, but it was
no longer independent, and was always open to such intervention as the pope might consider necessitated by spiritual
interests. In general, however, the theory of the two
powers only received from the Gregorians the scant consideration which innovators usually accord to the merely
traditional and customary, and was viewed with the same
coldness with which they had hitherto regarded those
holders of secular authority who, despite all theorising, had
continued to feel themselves to be the heads of Christendom.

Here we note with surprise that at the precise moment
when Gregory VII was giving up the theory of the two
powers in the old sense, Henry adopted it and made it what
it had anciently been for the popes and other ecclesiastical
princes—a defensive weapon. Henry IV now accuses the
pope in the same way that post-Gelasian popes had accused
the emperors: " Contrary to God's ordinance he desires to
be king and priest at once. He wishes to discredit the
king's sacred dignity, which derives from God, and can only

[1] Cf. the two letters to Hermann of Metz, *Reg.* iv. 2 (p. 295) and viii. 21
(p. 552). It is particularly interesting to see how the Anonymous of York
attempts to dissuade the clergy from interfering in secular affairs by means
of a similar disparagement of temporal power, which is equally irreconcil-
able with his general principles: cf. Böhmer, *Kirche und Staat*, p. 483, no.
xxx.

be taken away by God." The expressions used by the author of the *De unitate ecclesiae* show how passionately conscious the imperialists were of Gregory's intention of upsetting the theory of the two powers: " Behold, I beseech you, and see how Hildebrand and his bishops, resisting the ordinance of God in unheard-of wise, wish to destroy and bring to naught these two powers by which the world is ruled. They desire all bishops to be like themselves (who are, indeed, no true bishops at all), and wish for kings through whom and with whose consent they may themselves rule." " And they who, as servants of God, ought to have no part in worldly business, take it upon themselves to rule and govern kingdoms." It is a strange turn of history that in the formulation and application of the theory of the unity of the world and of the two powers the parts played by empire and papacy are exactly reversed in the critical year 1076.[1]

Gregory VII's contemporaries were also quite clear that in the pope's mind the old doctrine of the Christian Church's duty of non-resistance to the king by God's grace and God's anger was henceforth of no validity. " If, in earlier days," says the author of the *De unitate ecclesiae*, " the emperors acted wickedly, the popes begged for redress, since they had no idea that they could depose kings and emperors." Gregory of Catino asks: " What authority can, without contempt of God's commands, condemn him whom Almighty God, who rules both Heaven and earth, suffers in His inscrutable wisdom? " " The king," writes Hugh of Fleury, "is restrained from unrighteous ways only by the fear of God and Hell." Gregory is angrily accused of being the first not to be satisfied with the spiritual sword, the first to wage war against his opponents and to lead others to do the same. " It is novel, and was unknown in any past age," writes Wenrich of Trier, " for priests so easily to bring nations into civil strife, by a sudden act to shatter the name of king, which was discovered at the creation of the world and established by God, contemptuously to dismiss

[1] MGH. *Const.* i. 112 sqq., no. 63; *Lib. de unitate*, c. 15 and 26 (MGH. *Lib. de lite*, ii. 231 and 248).

the Lord's anointed as if they were mere bailiffs, and
to lay them under anathema if they do not instantly obey
the command to abandon the kingdom of their fathers."[1]

In actual fact the passive obedience of Christians to the
head of the state became ridiculous directly the Church
came to regard the state as merely a part of itself, for then
the head of the Church had the right and the duty of giving
orders to the king. It became equally absurd when the
ancient belief that the Church and its organs are the
absolute revelation of the divine spirit and the divine
purpose in the world were taken as literally as they were by
Gregory VII. Gregory was not making a dogmatic innovation, even though it seemed to many that he wished to be
the vicegerent of God on earth in a much stricter sense than
any previous pope, that he demanded a much higher
rank for the pope than hitherto, and a much greater degree
of identification with God. On the contrary: Gregory
merely grasped the idea of the papacy more logically than
any of his predecessors, and was therefore one of the truest
representatives of the spirit of Catholicism in the whole
course of history. He did no more than develop one-sidedly
a belief which the Church had long held: that Christ is God
manifested on earth; that he remains perpetually present
through the sacraments, by means of the priestly office;
that the purity and absoluteness of His nature is preserved
through all human errors and confusions because one
church, the Roman, has always remained the undisturbed
repository of divine action and of the purity of the true
faith, since its bishop, the successor of Peter, is, through
the prayer of Christ,[2] surety for the priesthood and bearer
of the spirit of God. If for Gregory the unity of the divine
Being and the divine Will in the Church is most perfectly
manifested in one human will, that of the pope, if he strives
for the sole leadership of Christendom and disputes the
possession by kings and bishops of an equally direct authority, for this very reason the Catholic Church remains for

[1] *Lib. de unitate*, c. 3 (MGH. *Lib. de lite*, ii. 187); Gregory of Catino,
Orthodoxa defensio, c. 8 (*ibid.* p. 540) and c. 10 (*ibid.* p. 541); Hugh of
Fleury, *Tract.* i. 4 and ii. 6 sq. (*ibid.* pp. 469 and 493 sq.); Wenrich, *Ep.*
c. 4 (*ibid.* p. 289).   [2] *Luke* xxii. 31.

him exactly what it had always been: the absolute, sole and established presence of the spirit of God on earth.[1]

Revolutionary changes in State and Monarchy were the result of his beliefs. Monarchical rule had in Christian times always been theocratic. God held the king's heart in His hands and guided it as He willed. The State had stood beside the Church, which was ready to accept the State's actions as a manifestation of the divine providence. Conversely, it was the sacred duty of every Christian king to serve the Church; the duty of obedience to God, Christ and the Church was never once disputed by any party. If the pope reminded princes that they had a Lord over them, and that it was right for a man whom God had set over so many thousands to be himself the servant of God, none would contradict him. Conflicts only arose when he used this truism to secure obedience for his own orders, when he presupposed a certain identity of his commands with those of God, and seemed to lay claim to an authority which no man had yet possessed. One of the profoundest thinkers among Gregory's opponents expressed what his age had experienced when he wrote: " But whereas Christ alone, who is one with God, gives and takes away authority to rule, and holds the hearts of kings in His right hand, we read that pope Hildebrand taught that he himself had power over kings and kingdoms, and could act as He alone can act, Who, as the Psalmist says, putteth down one and setteth up another."[2]

[1] Cf. Bernold, *Libellus*, ii. (p. 38): " Sedem Romanam veneror ut tribunal Christi, eius pontificem ut sacrarium spiritus almi, eius amplectens decreta, ut caelestis curiae edicta,' or Dieckmann, i. 437: " Est enim sicut Simon Petra ideoque fundamentum ecclesiae, Petrus qui nunquam moritur, vicarius Christi."

[2] *Lib. de unitate*, ii. 1 (p. 212). Similar expressions are common; e.g. Benzo, vii. 1 (MGH. SS. xi. 670); Hugh of Fleury, *Tract*. i. 1 (pp. 467 sqq.); Henry IV to Gregory VII, in MGH. *Const*. i. 111, no. 62: " Me quoque, qui licet indignus inter christos ad regnum sum unctus, tetigisti, quem sanctorum patrum traditio soli Deo iudicandum docuit." From Gregory VII's time onwards it was in fact held that of the two powers only the spiritual could claim to be judged by God alone: cf., for instance, Hugh of St Victor, *De sacramentis*, ii. 3 (MPL. 186 col. 418): " Nam spiritualis potestas terrenam potestatem et instituere habet, ut sit, et iudicare habet, si bona non fuerit. Ipsa vero a Deo primum instituta est et, cum deviat, a Deo solo iudicari potest." It is only a short step from this to Boniface VIII's bull *Unam sanctam*; cf. C. Mirbt, *Quellen zur Geschichte des Papsttums*, (1934) p. 211, no. 372.

EPILOGUE

THE age of the Investiture Controversy may rightly be regarded as the culmination of medieval history; it was a turning-point, a time both of completion and of beginning. It was the fulfilment of the early middle ages, because in it the blending of the Western European peoples with Christian spirituality reached a decisive stage. On the other hand, the later middle ages grew directly out of the events and thoughts of the decades immediately before and after the year 1100; as early as this the general lines, the characteristic religious, spiritual and political views of later times had been laid down, and the chief impulses for subsequent development given.

The great struggle had a three-fold theme. On the basis of a deeper understanding of the nature of the Catholic Church, an attempt was made to remodel three things: first, the relations of clergy and laity with each other; secondly, the internal constitution of the Church, through the imposition of papal primacy; and thirdly, the relations of Church and World. The first of these disputed questions, in which lay investiture played the most important part, has given its name to the whole period. The old state-controlled constitution of the Church and the proprietary church system, both of them factors of the first importance in the conversion of the Western European peoples and in the building-up of Church organisation, had originated in pre-Christian times and were at bottom foreign to the Church's real nature. Only after long and wearisome struggles did the Church succeed in restricting them or incorporating them in the structure of the canon law. Lay investiture and the whole proprietary system were, however, burning questions only for a few centuries during the earlier part of the middle ages; but the battle between episcopalism and papalism has, in spite of periodic interruptions, intermittently disturbed the Church from the earliest Christian era down to the present time, and the relationship between Christianity and the secular state is, for Catholics and Protestants alike, still a deeply moving and not yet completely solved question. The best-known and most violent conflict to which it ever gave rise, the struggle in which Church and State met each other in the pride of their strength and fully-armed with their natural weapons, was the Investiture Controversy.

It will never be quite possible to discover what were the real causes of the great eleventh-century crisis in Christian history ; many factors in the political life of the times which did in fact coalesce to form a developing situation the main lines of which are clear, might, it seems to us now, have operated very differently. It is just as difficult to explain why it was that men who were capable of great things came together in Rome at that particular time, and, above all, why at the critical moment the daemonic figure of the greatest of the popes occupied the throne of the Prince of the Apostles. Only a very wide-ranging view can make clear, even in part, the concurrence of events out of which the new age was born, for only thus will due influence be assigned to the advanced stage which the christianisation of the world had then reached. Ecclesiastical organisation had spread far and wide, monastic religion had taken a strong hold on men and made them more concerned for their souls' health, had spurred them on to greater conscientiousness and made them more anxious for the purity and right order of the Church. Thus a new and victorious strength was lent to the old belief in the saving grace of the sacraments and to the hierarchical conceptions based on their administration. Out of this arose the conviction that the Christian peoples of the West formed the true City of God, and as a result the leaders of the Church were able to abandon their ancient aversion from the wickedness of worldly men and to feel themselves called upon to re-order earthly life in accordance with divine precept. In the eleventh century the position had not yet been reached where the pope, the imperial Lord of the Church, appointed and confirmed the kings of the earth and watched over and

judged their actions, but the enormous advance made by
Gregory VII had opened the way for this, and he himself
had already realised more of it in practice than any single
one of his successors was able to do. Gregory stands at the
greatest—from the spiritual point of view perhaps the
only—turning-point in the history of Catholic Christendom;
in his time the policy of converting the world gained once
and for all the upper hand over the policy of withdrawing
from it : the world was drawn into the Church, and the
leading spirits of the new age made it their aim to establish
the "right order" in this united Christian world. In their
eyes, however, the most immediate task seemed to be that
of successfully asserting the supremacy of the " Servant
of the servants of God " over the kings of the earth.

Gregory VII was not particularly notable for his faithfulness to tradition. He was at heart a revolutionary[1] ;
reform in the ordinary sense of the word, which implies
little more than the modification and improvement of
existing forms, could not really satisfy him. He desired
a drastic change, and could be content with nothing short
of the effective realisation on earth of justice, of the "right
order" and of "that which ought to be." "The Lord hath
not said ' I am Tradition,' " he once wrote, " but ' I am
the Truth.' "[2] And yet, in spite of this reaction against the
merely traditional, Gregory himself embodied the essence
of Catholic tradition in a peculiarly characteristic manner ;
this fact shows, therefore, how instinctive and unreasoning
—in a sense, how primitive—his faith was. Catholicism
was to him the directive principle of life itself. For him the
age-old Catholic ideas of righteousness (*justitia*), a Christian
hierarchy (*ordo*), and a proper standing for everyone before
God and man (*libertas*), were the core of religious experience, and their realisation the purpose of life here on earth.
It would be incorrect to treat these and related ideas as the
personal discoveries of St Augustine or any other particular
individual among the early Fathers, or to attempt to trace

[1] Cf. E. Caspar, *Gregor VII in seinen Briefen*, in HZ. 130 (1924) 1-30.
[2] " . . . advertendum est quod Dominus dicit: ' Ego sum veritas et
vita.' Non dixit: ' Ego sum consuetudo,' sed ' veritas.' "—JL. 5277 (Jaffé,
Bibliotheca, ii. 576 no. 50).

out exactly the stages by which Gregory is supposed to have
inherited them ; they are in reality an inseparable part of
the Catholic faith, and can only be understood on that
assumption. It is just as wide of the mark to suggest that
ideas such as these were discovered for the first time by
Gregory and his contemporaries, or that they were in any
significant way remoulded during the Gregorian period ;
Gregory's real service was to leaven the earthly lump with
the principles of Catholicism, and to make the latter, in a
manner hitherto undreamed of, a really decisive force in
politics. His aim was to bring the kingdom of God on
earth, as he saw it in his mind, nearer to realisation,
and to serve the cause of order, justice and "freedom."
" He was indeed," writes Bernold of St Blasien, " a most
zealous propagator (institutor) of the Catholic religion and a
most determined defender of the freedom of the Church.
For he did not wish the clergy to be subject to the power of
the laity, but desired them to excel all laymen by their
holiness and by the dignity of their order."[1]

The unity of the Christian world, as Gregory and his
contemporaries wished to see it, could never quite be
established in practice; nevertheless, unity has always
remained an idea of the greatest historical influence, though
neither before nor after Gregory's time was it ever completely realised. Before the eleventh century, the principle
of unity was represented by the kingship ; but the persist-
ence of the old Christian feeling of indifference towards the
world, together with the remains of paganism, robbed
the monarchy of full co-operation and hampered its action.
Later on, the clerical claim to leadership was advanced with
such intensity that it provoked resistance of another kind :
belief in the Divine Right of kings and princes immediately
made itself more strongly felt, and was never quite overcome wherever monarchy was the prevailing form of the
state. But as Divine Right was no longer fully accepted
by the Church, tension and some impairment of the principle of unity was often the result. The assertion of their
own direct responsibility to God—put forward so forcefully

[1] *Chron.*, ad ann. 1085 (MGH. SS. v. 444).

by Henry IV—still remained for the kings of Europe their strongest argument against excessive claims on the part of the papacy, for the conception that the rule of one man over others can only be justified and made holy by direct divine intervention must always retain a certain moral value. It is further probable, as has often been pointed out recently, that the papacy's attacks on the Divine Right of Kings led directly to later attempts to set the state on new, and this time secular, foundations.[1] Conclusions such as this, the truth of which is difficult to demonstrate, must however be handled with great caution. The "order" which Gregory introduced remained dominant for centuries, and showed an astounding ability to overcome all opposing forces or to turn them to its own service. A similar picture is presented by Gothic art, which combined numberless powerful elements fundamentally at variance with each other, and yet was able to create out of them a stylistic unity in spite of the resultant stress and strain.

The enormous strength of the ecclesiastical claim to world-domination is only to be explained if we recognise how profoundly religious were its roots; it grew directly out of the fundamental tenets of the Catholic faith, and failure to realise this is the reason why many earlier attempts at explanation must be rejected as mistaken or insufficient. To derive a demand for world-wide power from asceticism and the flight from the earthly life, as some historians have done,[2] is to ascribe an improbable religious perversity to the Church; and there is equally little logic in the connected theory that the Church wished to reduce the world to subjection in order to be free from it. Nor is it possible to suppose that the emperor was deprived of the right of investiture simply in order that the clergy alone should represent the unity of the Church. Further, it is scarcely a half-truth to assert, as is sometimes done, that Gregory VII combated lay influence in order to increase his opportunities of carrying out moral reform and the internal

[1] Cf. A. Brackmann, *The beginnings of the national state in mediaeval Germany and the Norman monarchies*, in Barraclough, ii. esp. pp. 286-7, and Brackmann's earlier essays, there cited. Cf. also Kern, pp. 236 sqq. (=Chrimes, pp. 109 sqq.).   [2] Cf. Appendix V.

reorganisation of the Church. This was only part of his purpose ; as we have seen, the real reason for the action he took lies deeper : his moral principles were outraged by the mere fact that the laity were occupying a position which, according to the sacramental conception of the hierarchy, was not really theirs at all. A true understanding of the ideas of Gregory VII and of post-Gregorian Catholicism about the relation of the spiritual power to the world, and of the origins of these ideas themselves, can only be reached by going right back to the belief in the incarnation of God in Christ. This is the most fundamental of the Church's beliefs, for in the Church the saving grace of the incarnation has become an ever-present reality, and all the Church's institutions find in this belief their *raison d'être* and their ultimate justification. Mystical and hierarchical trains of thought arise naturally from the belief that God comes down from Heaven to man, and that the multitude of His priests serves as the steps by which He descends. If, therefore, the Church and the hierarchy of its servants have a part in the mediating office of Christ, if they exist in order to link Heaven and earth, then it is only just that the world should meekly accept their guidance and be subject to them.[1] This demand forms a principle the validity of which Catholicism is always bound to assert ; it is this principle which must ultimately decide its attitude towards the State, although in recent centuries it has been applied less in the purely political field than during the middle ages, and more as a claim to the care of souls and to moral leadership.

The superiority of the Church over the State derives, therefore, from Catholic belief in the Church and its vocation : nobody can admit the superiority if he does not share the belief. Hence Protestant Christianity immediately reoriented its attitude towards the state. Protestantism recognises no visible institution on earth which is infallibly entitled to speak in the name of God, or which possesses an unqualified claim to represent Him. For the Protestant there is consequently no authority which can issue commands

[1] Cf. *supra*, pp. 160–1.

to the State, since the dignity of the State is in his
eyes second to that of no other community on earth. On
the other hand, much as he may respect authority as a gift
from Heaven, he is forced to draw as sharp a distinction
between earthly kingdoms and the Kingdom of God as has
been drawn at any other time in Christian history. Protestant and Catholic Christianity are therefore at one,
though for totally different reasons, in the firm conviction
that the problem of man's existence can never find its
ultimate explanation in those sterile territories which are
all that a purely human understanding can ever penetrate
and all that a purely human activity can ever subdue.

APPENDIX I

HENRY III'S CHURCH POLICY

[*cf.* pp. 86, 106.]

1. Paul Kchr, *Vier Kapitel aus der Geschichte Kaiser Heinrichs III* (*Abh. d. Preuss. Ak. d. Wiss.*, 1930 no. 3) has pointed out that the popes chosen by Henry III, and Nicholas II and Alexander II as well, retained their German or Italian bishoprics. This fact, the meaning of which had never previously been investigated, is important enough to justify an examination of what the sources have to say about it.

Clement II, who was bishop of Bamberg before he was raised to the papacy in 1046, in 1047 still calls the church of Bamberg his *dulcissima sponsa*, and says expressly : " Sed nescio quo divino consilio evenit, quo matri tuae omniumque ecclesiarum consociarer et aliquid non tamen omnino a te separarer" (JL. 4149—MPL. 142 col. 588 no. 8). Lambert of Hersfeld (ad an. 1048) records the simultaneous succession of a new pope and a new bishop of Bamberg. Nothing definite is known of Poppo of Brixen (Damasus II). Leo IX retained his bishopric for a time (JL. 4224, 12 May 105ᴈ— Bénoit, *Hist. eccl. et pol. de Toul*, [1707] CXXIII), and in addition we are well-informed about Udo's succession to him in Augsburg. Kehr writes (p. 55) : " At Augsburg Leo seem's to have come into conflict with the emperor. . . He resigned his bishopric of Toul which, like his predecessors, he had retained for the first two years of his pontificate, and ceased thereby to have a place in the German Church." We do not know whether Leo and Henry made arrangements about the succession in Toul at their meeting in Augsburg, Feb. 1051 ; on the other hand, Wibert records (ii. 4, 19—AA.SS. Apr., ii. 660) that Leo was in Rome, when, " solicitous for the souls which had formerly been committed to his care," he secured the appointment of Udo. On Victor II, see the Altaich annals and Lambert in Kehr, p. 51 n. 2, and a deed of gift drawn up by Henry II in 1057 in favour of the Church of Eichstätt (*Mon. Boic.*, XXXIa. 336), with the clause : " Qualiter nos pro amore nostri spiritualis patris Victoris scilicet secundi papae. . . . ;" since the pope is referred to as beneficiary, he must at the same time have been bishop of Eichstätt. In the charters of Nicholas II the following two formulae frequently occur : " rationabile omnino ducimus speciali regimine nostrae curae commissae Florentinae ecclesiae congruentem provisionem impendere iugiter " and " ecclesiis omnibus sollertem provisionem incessanter debeamus, Florentinae tamen nostrae curae specialiter episcopali regimine commissae." In diplomas for the diocese of Lucca, Alexander II calls himself " sanctae Romanae ecclesiae praesul, Lucensis episcopus." Finally, it may be recalled that Sylvester (III) retained the bishopric of Sabina, Stephen IX retained Monte Cassino in spite of the election of Desiderius as his successor (cf. MGH. SS. vii. 702), Honorius (II) retained Parma and Clement (III) retained Ravenna.

2. Kehr writes of Henry's Church policy (p. 51) : " The purpose of this Church policy becomes clearer when we consider that all these German bishops, instead of cutting themselves off from the imperial Church, retained their bishoprics in the face of both law and custom, and so remained active members of it . . . ; there is a system and a plan in this procedure, and it is, I think, the key to an understanding of the ecclesiastical policy of Henry III, the ultimate aim of which was to bring Rome into the system of the imperial Church." Henry is thus supposed to have tried to secure control of the papacy by means of the synod of Sutri and his appointments to the Roman see ; Rome was to be made an imperial church, almost a royal *Eigenkirche:*

There seem to me to be many difficulties in the way of this interpretation. The emperor's influence on the papacy was of a political and moral character. The legal title which he created for himself—the patriciate—had nothing in common with his domination over the imperial Church, which was based on the theocratic conception of the state and on the proprietary system. Further, it is difficult to see how the retention of his bishopric fettered the pope, why his activities were thereby restricted, and how he was impeded in the fulfilment of his universal task. The French episcopate did not stay away from Reims because Leo was still bishop of the imperial diocese of Toul. Above all, if the popes' membership of the German Church was essential to Henry III's Church policy, what are we to make of Leo's resignation in 1051 and of Henry's immediate investiture of the successor whom he recommended? Leo—the most active and independent of all the German popes—was then only forty-nine, and might well have lived another ten or twenty years; yet he only held his German bishopric together with the papacy for a little more than two years. In view of this, can the personal union of the papacy and a German bishopric still be held an essential part of Henry's ecclesiastical policy?

It was not, it seems to me, altogether in the emperor's interest that the popes should retain their German or Italian bishoprics. From the emperor's point of view it was not so much that the popes were *compelled* to retain their bishoprics as that they were *allowed* to do so. In the case of the German popes it is easily understood as the conferment of an honour and—what is far more important—as a kind of insurance against difficulties in Rome. This was certainly so in the cases of Nicholas II and Alexander II: Nicholas had an anti-pope to deal with from the start, and Cadalus of Parma was soon set up against Alexander, who for part of his reign ruled from Lucca as Cadalus did from Parma. Did not these two popes at least retain their bishoprics in order to be the freer from party divisions in Rome? It is impossible to believe that the reform party chose Italian bishops who held imperial sees out of regard for the German court. Nicholas and Alexander could well have resigned their bishoprics like Leo, had it suited them to do so. See also Schramm, *Kaiser, Rom und Renovatio*, i. 228 sq.: " The papal elections under Otto III and Henry III had the object of freeing the papacy from the Roman factions; " also Jordan in AUF. xii. 44.

3. Henry III's Church policy is summed up by Kehr (p. 48) in the following words: " The whole nature of this *imperium* . . . entirely excludes thoughts of universal dominion, and the policy of Henry towards the papacy was also, in my opinion, controlled completely by the immediate political interests of the existing empire; " cf. the surprisingly similar remarks of Fliche, *Réforme Grégorienne*, i. 110: " En réalité, pour Henri III comme pour tous ses prédécesseurs, les ambitions politiques priment les intérêts religieux et peu importe au fond ce que deviendra l'Eglise, pourvu que le roi de Germanie règne sur Rome, sur l'Italie . . ." Kehr thus rejects the suggestion—made, for instance, by Haller, *Das altdeutsche Kaisertum*, (1926) p. 70—that Henry had a universal policy.

The emperor had in fact no intention of ruling the western Church through the pope; the universal ideas of the great period of the German emperors were in general far less political than is commonly assumed, and were rather moral, religious and literary. In Henry's case in particular, very little of such an expansive tendency is to be discovered. Kehr has further criticised the view put forward by Hampe, according to which Henry III was a poor politician who mistook the danger which the growth of the reforming party threatened. But can Henry really be taken for an egotist, a man who paid more attention to political advantage than to the moral well-being of the Church whose chief protector he was? Henry's efforts against simony and his motives in reforming the papacy in 1046 will be mentioned later. Hauck long ago remarked that after Sutri Henry withdrew to a greater extent from ecclesiastical affairs. Boye summarises the position very well in ZRG. *kanon. Abt.*, 18 (1929) 273: "At the synods Henry set aside the unreformed papacy, and then left the synods entirely in the hands of the reformed popes. When his task of reforming the papacy was accomplished, he withdrew and allowed the pope to ensure the continuance of the reform." The freedom which Henry left to the pope is made particularly clear by a consideration of the policy of Leo IX, who struck out a line for himself and yet found himself in no opposition to the emperor on matters of ecclesiastical policy. The emperor even helped to strengthen the political independence of the curia, as is well shown by the treaty of Worms of 1052, by which Benevento and imperial rights in southern Italy were exchanged for Bamberg and Fulda. The fact that the imperial court lent the popes no military assistance in prosecuting their Norman policy is not evidence of opposition between Germany and Rome. Appendix III (*infra*, p. 180) shows that the contrast between the policy of Leo IX and that of Victor II is frequently exaggerated. Both popes were in agreement with Henry, the one working in complete accord with the emperor's reforming ideas, the other in a more purely political fashion. They represented the two tendencies that were united in Henry: piety and caution combined with energy.

On the subject of the synod of Sutri, four points are
worthy of mention:—

(1) So many eleventh-century sources, both papal and
imperial, report that Gregory VI secured the papacy by
simony that the fact has hardly ever been doubted; cf. the
evidence collected by Giesebrecht, *Kaiserzeit*, ii. 411, and
Hauck, *Kirchengeschichte Deutschlands*, iii. 571, for example.
Fliche alone has suggested the contrary: " Il est donc
probable que la légende de simonie a dû être forgée dans
l'entourage de Henri III pour justifier après coup la déposi-
tion du pape par l'empereur " (i. 107, n. 2). This assertion,
which is in manner reminiscent of an anti-imperial pamphlet
of the eleventh century, is only made possible by an arbitrary
interpretation of the sources; and since it has recently (1932)
been fully disproved by the painstaking and exact researches
of Huysmans, *Wazo van Luik*, p. 111 sqq., and independently
by D. Feytmans, *Revue Belge*, xi. (1932) 130 sqq., it is the
less necessary for me to go into the question at length here.

Borino's arguments (*L'elezione e la deposizione di Gregorio
VI*, in *Archivio della R. Società Romana della Storia Patria*, 39
(1916) 208 sqq.) are more convincing than the special
pleading of Fliche. He does not deny that money played its
part in the abdication of Benedict IX and the election of
Gregory VI, but thinks that the wording of the earliest
accounts (Peter Damian: *venalitas intervenerat*; Hermann of
Reichenau: *ob avaritiam*) does not make it necessary to
assume that the papacy was simply bought and sold. It
does, indeed, seem possible that the legal crime of simony
was avoided in form though committed in spirit; cf. R. L.
Poole, *Benedict IX and Gregory VI*, in *Proc. Brit. Acad.*,
1917/18, pp. 219 sqq.: " Simony is understood to mean the
payment of money for a spiritual office which one desires;
whether it includes also the payment of money in order to
remove a scandalous holder of an office by a person who
does not desire it, I leave to those better versed in canon
law than I am to decide." The fact that Gregory VI was
commonly held at the time to be a simoniac is, however,
decisive; many neutral and anti-imperial writers of the
eleventh century, who would certainly have preferred not to
mention the subject, do in fact discuss it. Even a fanatic like
the Auctor Gallicus had heard of and believed in the simony
of Gregory VI. It is scarcely credible that it was only the

deposition of Gregory, which the Hildebrandine party condemned, which made current a false report of simony, and
that this was then accepted as true by the emperor's critics.
In view of Huysmans' work, it is needless to quote all the
sources in order to prove the correctness of the older opinion.
The famous letter of Odilo of Cluny (ed. Sackur, NA. 24
(1899) 734), written when Henry had just reached Italy,
must, however, be briefly mentioned, since it is of great
importance in determining Henry's attitude towards Cluny
and his intentions before Sutri. In the second part of the
letter Odilo advises Henry to deal cautiously with the
empire and to be particularly careful in his attitude towards
the pope, exhorts him to think more of the general good of
mankind than of establishing a severe government over his
own people, to love his enemies, and so on ; then, in
sharp contrast, follows the warning: "Econtra valde con-
trarium est et nimis inhonestum, ut hi qui fideles fuerint,
sentiant detrimentum." Shortly afterwards come the
decisive sentences: " Unum dicam apertius, quod si celatum
fuerit, ut multum timeo, diiudicabitur acrius: Quod ille
perdit qui totum dedit non debet ille possidere qui totum
tulit. Totum tulit, quantum in illo fuit. Si posset suum
velle, nil valeret vestrum posse." Sackur saw that this was
a reference to the Benedict-Gregory affair: " That which he
(sc. Benedict IX) loses who gave all (sc. the papacy) may not
be possessed by him (sc. Gregory VI) who took all. He took
all as far as he could. If he had been able to realise his wish
(sc. to establish himself permanently), your power (sc. to
depose him) would have been useless." This seems to me
the correct interpretation, in spite of an attempt by Borino
(pp. 376 sqq.) to read a reference to canonical principles into
the words, and to make them mean that if Gregory had been
canonically elected the emperor's power would have availed
nothing against him. I agree with Borino when he says that
before Sutri Henry had already thought of deposing Gregory;
but Odilo supported him in this, and was not, as Borino
thinks, an opponent of the emperor's policy. He was, after
all, probably in Sutri himself, and was certainly on friendly
terms with the imperial pope (cf. Jotsaldus, *Vita Odilonis*, ed.
Sackur, NA. 15 (1890) 119 sqq.).

(2) There is some question whether there was a schism in
1046 or not. Giesebrecht (ii. 412 sq. and 663 sq.) assumed

that there was a three-fold schism; Steindorff (*Jahrbücher*, i. 484 sq.) on the other hand attempted to prove that there was only a schism betwen Benedict and Sylvester, and that Gregory VI was no schismatic.   Hauck (iii. 584), Fliche (i. 108 n.) and Borino (p. 226) follow him, and the latter defends his point of view by quoting two charters from the *Regestum Farfense* of 1046, which are dated *temporibus domni Gregorii VI papae et viri venerabilis Johannis episcopi.*   To the mind of the writer there existed no schism, then; Gregory as pope and Sylvester as bishop of St. Sabina were, for him, living peacefully side by side.   Sylvester pretended to no more than his bishopric, and cannot have been attempting to exercise papal rights.   It is uncertain whether he had formally abdicated and submitted to Gregory VI, but that he was ready to renounce his claims appears to follow from the fact that he came to Sutri, whereas Benedict IX remained away, either for political reasons or because he feared punishment for his notoriously immoral life.   In any case the synods of Sutri and Rome deposed not only Gregory VI but also the other two former popes, probably in order formally to deprive them of any claim and to avert the possibility of future schism.   Later events showed how right this policy was, for after Clement II's death, as is well known, Benedict again assumed papal rights.

(3) Why did Henry cause Gregory to be deposed?   Some historians (e.g. Borino pp. 329 sq., Fliche i. 110 sq. and Kehr p. 50) assume purely political reasons.   There was certainly political friction between pope and emperor over small points like the choice of an archbishop of Ravenna; but two more serious hypotheses, commonly put forward, must be rejected. Gregory is supposed to have incited Halinard of Lyons to refuse the oath, and thereby to have shown his sympathy with the reform movement by opposing imperial control of the Church in the existing form.   I have explained elsewhere (*supra*, pp. 86, 100) what were Halinard's real motives. Secondly, the tendentious story of the Auctor Gallicus—that Gregory VI refused to crown the incestuous emperor—has been believed, and even Benedict IX is supposed to have put difficulties in the way of the coronation.   Would Gregory have met the emperor at Piacenza, however, would he have obeyed his summons to Sutri, if he had been immovably opposed to Henry and had wished to bring to nought the

whole object of the journey to Rome—the coronation and the settlement of Italian, and especially of Roman, affairs? (Schramm, *Kaiser, Rom und Renovatio*, pp. 237 sq., also suggests opposition between papacy and empire as early as 1046, and says that the assumption of the patriciate hastened the growth of the reform movement. But the patriciate, like the choice of German bishops as popes, was designed to free the papacy from the Roman parties. Imperial rights in papal elections did not conflict with the reform movement as it existed before 1058.)

These suggested reasons for conflict must therefore be rejected, and it can hardly be believed that the other points in dispute were sufficiently important to warrant Gregory's deposition. And why did Henry also have to secure the renewed deposition of Benedict and Sylvester? Would it not have been enough to remove Gregory and have an acceptable pope elected, if Gregory appeared politically dangerous?

The formal deposition of all three popes and the assumption of the patriciate by Henry III make the intentions of the emperor quite clear: he wished finally to lift the papacy out of the field of Roman party politics. What was his purpose in making the papacy independent of the Romans? Simony and schisms had had their origin in the fact that the papacy was the prize to be won by the victorious party in Rome. The popes who had been made in this way had hardly ever been chosen because of their suitability for their spiritual task, but they had been politically untrustworthy as well as morally unacceptable. Sutri was therefore not a victory for the Church alone, but for the empire as well. It is naturally impossible to tell whether Henry's motives were mainly those of political security or of Church reform. The sources report the Italian journey chiefly as an act of reform, but reform was the common topic of these years, and nothing certain can be deduced from the fact. But is the question whether Henry was led by religious or by political motives, justified in itself? Is not a question in the form " either—or " based on modern *raison d'état* and therefore false to medieval conceptions? The theocratic medieval king ruled Church and State, which were in the closest possible connexion with each other, both politically and spiritually, and besides this we know enough of Henry's positive religious feeling to be able to assert confidently that the moral as well as the political well-being of the first of all churches lay very near his heart.

(4) What form did the deposition of Gregory VI take? The accounts of Bernold, Bonizo, Desiderius and Leo, which speak of abdication, must be dismissed as tendentious falsifications of the proceedings at Sutri, for none of these writers is now regarded as trustworthy. The pope was far rather deposed by the synod which the emperor had, according to contemporary ideas, constitutionally called together and which he presided over or attended. Most of the sources speak in this sense, though some record that Gregory was deposed by the emperor alone; in any case, as Boye (*Die Synoden Deutschlands und Reichsitaliens von 922 bis 1059*, in ZRG. *kan. Abt.*, xvii. [1929] 273) rightly remarks, "Henry was both in fact and in theory the head of the synod."

APPENDIX II
PROPRIETARY CHURCH LEGISLATION, 900-1039
[*cf.* pp. 76, 91-2.]

The early history of proprietary church legislation has been made quite clear by Stutz in his *Geschichte des kirchlichen Benefizialwesens.* Stutz dates the first period of such legislation—when it was carried through by synods and capitularies—as extending from the middle of the eighth century until the death of Louis the Pious (840). " As contrasted with all this, the second period of legislation brought nothing new " (Stutz, *Eigenkirche*, p. 22 = Barraclough, p. 48). The rules which governed the *Eigenkirchenrecht* were received into the collections of capitularies and of the canon law—collections like those of Ansegis, Benedictus Levita, pseudo-Isidore and Regino of Prüm—and were frequently repeated at synods. I have brought together below such references to it as can be found in the scanty synodal acts of the tenth and eleventh centuries before Henry III's reforms, and in the two great *Collectiones canonum* of Abbo of Fleury and Burchard of Worms; these will at the same time provide the authorities for the sketch *supra*, pp. 91-2. The best starting-points for research on these synods are Hefele-Leclercq, *Hist. des Conciles*, iv. 2 and M. Boye, *Quellenkatalog der Synoden Deutschlands und Reichsitaliens von 922 bis 1059*, NA. 48 (1930) 45-96.

The numbers of the following paragraphs correspond to the numbers on pp. 91-2 :

1. Abbo, c. 11, 30, 32, and 37 (MPL. 139 cols. 482, 491 sq., and 495); Burchard, iii. 6 sqq., 20 and 146 (MPL. 140 cols. 675 sq. and 702).

2. Trosly (909), c. 6 (Mansi, xviii. 281); Koblenz (922), c. 9 (MGH. *Const.* i. 630 no. 434); Ingelheim (948), c. 4 (*ibid.*, p. 14 no. 6); Augsburg (952), c. 9 (*ibid.*, p. 19 no. 9); Seligenstadt (1023), c. 13 (*ibid.*, p. 638 no. 437); Bourges (1031), c. 22 (Mansi, xix. 505); Abbo, c. 32 (MPL. 139 col. 942); Burchard, iii. 111 sqq. (MPL. 140 col. 695).

3. Burchard, iii. 45 and 229 (*ibid.*, cols. 680 and 722).

4. Trosly, c. 6 (Mansi, xviii. 279 sq.); Koblenz, c. 17 (MGH. *Const.* i. 631 no. 434); Ingelheim, c. 8 (*ibid.*, p. 14 no. 6); Burchard, iii. 239 (MPL. 140 col. 724).

5. Ingelheim, c. 5 (MGH. *Const.* i. 15 no. 6).

6. Trosly, c. 6 (Mansi, xviii. 281); Hohenaltheim (916), c. 38 (MGH. *Const.* i. 626 no. 434); Burchard, iii. 116 (MPL. 140 col. 646).

7. Koblenz, c. 14 (MGH. *Const.* i. 631 no. 434); Burchard, iii. 42 (MPL. 140 col. 680).

8. Trosly, c. 6 (Mansi, xviii. 280); Rome (962; MGH. *Const.* i. 20 no. 10, note 3, and cf. Boye, p. 54); Burchard, iii. 52 (MPL. 140 col. 682).

APPENDIX III
VICTOR II AND STEPHEN IX
[cf. pp. 107 sqq.]

1. It is almost impossible to decide whether Hildebrand was present at the election of Victor II. On the death of Stephen IX he was probably still in France, but he may, of course, have taken part in the discussions at Rome and in the embassy which announced the election to the German court. The earliest authorities for the election of Victor do not mention him; the Anonymous Haserensis, for instance, only speaks of *primates Romanorum*, who, he says, asked the emperor to appoint his hero, the bishop of Eichstätt, as pope (c. 38, MGH. SS. vii. 265); if Hildebrand was really among them, it is remarkable that the Anonymous should not record the fact, for he hated Hildebrand—it is he who makes Leo IX say to Hildebrand after a dream: " Si tu unquam, quod absit, ad sedem apostolicam ascenderis, totum mundum perturbabis " (c. 37). Later sources, like Bonizo, mention Hildebrand; though they are too untrustworthy to justify any certain conclusion, there may be some truth in their story. Among modern authors, Giesebrecht, Hefele-Leclercq and Schmid have assumed the influence of Hildebrand, Hauck and Fliche have denied it.

2. The contrast between the ecclesiastical policy of Leo IX and that of Victor II seems sometimes to have been exaggerated. The commonly-held opinion that the election of Gebhard of Eichstätt as Victor II marked a departure from the policy of Leo IX really depends in part upon the conventional judgment of that policy. Points of opposition between Leo and Henry have been seen which did not in fact exist, and then Victor's attitude has seemed in comparison more friendly towards the emperor. Leo and Victor were certainly men of very diverse character—the one full of sublime enthusiasm for reform, the other more politically adroit—but their Church policy was essentially the same: both worked for a thorough reform of the Church, by means of synods and legates and in close collaboration with the emperor.

3. The leading feature of Victor's pontificate is not a new turn in Church policy, but his dealings with the Normans

and his changing attitude towards the brothers Godfrey and
Frederick of Lorraine.   As bishop and imperial adviser,
Victor had already protested against his predecessor's
Norman policy (Leo of Ostia, *Chron. Cas.*, ii. 81, in MGH. SS.
vii. 684); as pope he tried to come to an understanding with
the Normans, and succeeded in making peace with them in
1057.   Henry III had handed over Spoleto and Fermo to
the pope, as his friend, so that the latter might be able
effectively to support the imperial government in central
Italy against Godfrey, who could still be dangerous though
he had been expelled from the country.   For obvious reasons,
Henry distrusted Godfrey's brother, archdeacon Frederick;
the latter had to leave the curia, and became a monk at
Monte Cassino.   But the temporary withdrawal of Frederick
cannot be taken as evidence of disagreement on ecclesiastical
matters between him and the pope, as is clear from the fact
that when, through the pope's mediation, Godfrey had submitted at the end of 1055, Victor showed Frederick great
favour although Frederick disapproved of his Norman policy
(see *infra*), had him elected abbot of Monte Cassino and
raised him to the cardinalate.

It has also been suggested that Victor showed a certain
coolness towards the associates of Leo IX; that this was not
the case can be shown by an examination of the position of
Hildebrand and Humbert during his pontificate.   Hildebrand was again sent as legate to hold reforming synods in
France, he was for some time deputy-head of the papal
chancery, and was probably made a cardinal during Victor's
first year (he is first referred to as cardinal in June 1055—
JL. 4336).   It is doubtful whether any conclusions can be
drawn from the fact that Humbert did not receive the
chancellorship (cf. Kehr, *Vier Kapitel*, p. 59, with *id.*,
Scrinium und Palatium, MIÖG. *Erg.-Bd.* vi. [1901] pp. 74-5,
80); under Victor as under Leo he continued to draft important documents, accompanied the pope on his journey to
Germany in 1056, and was given the responsible task of
reforming Monte Cassino and securing the election of
Frederick.

4. Henry IV was not consulted at the election of Stephen
IX, but it is questionable whether this marks a conscious
step towards the emancipation of the papacy from imperial
control.   The attitude of the curia towards the German

court can be explained solely on the basis of the political situation at the time. Godfrey of Lorraine had—probably as a result of his agreement with Victor II—taken possession of Spoleto and the Marches, and it was with him that the curia had therefore to reckon first of all; the election of his brother was in consequence a clever move. The second most powerful factor was the Normans in the south. The young king took only the third place, and the regents' lack of energy provides the reason why they were willing to approve the election of Stephen *ex post facto* without making difficulties. The German government saw that the balance of political power had temporarily changed to their disadvantage, and was content with the payment of formal respect to the royal rights by the electors.

The increased influence of Hildebrand and Humbert shows that the pontificate of Stephen IX accelerated the development of the reform movement. Humbert received the important post of *bibliothecarius*, which was tantamount to the chancellorship of later days, and Hildebrand guided foreign policy. His importance is most clearly indicated by the story, reported by Peter Damian and Leo of Ostia, that on his death-bed Stephen told the Roman clergy and people to await the arrival of Hildebrand before choosing his successor. Yet it would be wrong to see no differences between Stephen and the three popes who succeeded him. He had become a monk even before his enforced withdrawal from the curia under Victor II, and his later friendliness towards the monks shows that in doing so he had other purposes besides that of escaping the enmity of Henry III; he made Peter Damian cardinal of Ostia and attracted him to his court, he kept abbot Hugh of Cluny by his side for a noticeably long time, he was on terms of close friendship with Desiderius (later Victor III), whom he made his successor at Monte Cassino. The fundamental opposition of Peter Damian to the Gregorians is well-known; and if Stephen was more than merely a supporter of Damian, just as little can he be identified with Hildebrand and Humbert. Had he lived, his policy would perhaps have been more like that of Victor III than that of Gregory VII.

APPENDIX IV

THE GREGORIAN IDEA OF FREEDOM IN RECENT LITERATURE

[*cf.* pp. 126 sqq.]

1. Many historians have remarked on the importance, during the Investiture Contest, of the cry for the " freedom of the Church," and the demand for *libertas ecclesiae* has even been understood as the programme of the reforming party or of its greatest leader, Gregory VII. The true meaning of *libertas ecclesiae* has, so far as I can see, none the less remained hidden from recent research. The aims of the Gregorians have been catalogued and described, but in terms of our ordinary modern use of the word " freedom; " and this has usually involved saying from what they wished to be free, to what they did not wish to be bound. In consequence, historians have constantly come to the conclusion that the Gregorians were working for the freedom of the Church from the State or from the world, although they themselves recognised the incorrectness of this assertion and either corrected it or tried to modify it. Since the work of Gierke and Hauck, however, the statement that the aim of the medieval Church was the separation of Church and State has become a great deal less common, and there has been substantial agreement on the fundamental importance of the idea of unity in the middle ages. Yet the view is still current that the Church wished to be free from the State's influence, from royal control of the episcopate, from the payment of taxes, from all kinds of secular services and in general from the world altogether. But how could this be reconciled with the demand for the supreme authority of the Church, which was also part of the cry for " freedom? " The two contradictory ideas were harmonised by saying that " Directly the cry for the ' freedom of the Church ' was raised, it was already plain that freedom from others was thought of as dominion over others " (Hauck, *Kirchengeschichte Deutschlands*, iii. 677). But " freedom from others " does not, in any ordinary use of words, mean " dominion over others; " and so a further explanation was added: dominion was demanded as a guarantee of freedom, since

the Church could not be certain that its freedom would be respected unless it was supreme over the secular authorities. This, however, is plainly a banal and inadequate explanation of the Church's pursuit of power. Yet side by side with all this we find, remarkably enough, the entirely satisfactory statement that the aim was " the establishment of a right relationship between the spiritual and the secular power." Most noticeable is the way in which Troeltsch (*Soziallehren*, pp. 213-4, trans. Wyon, p. 229) fails properly to understand the conception of *libertas*, and cleverly transfers his attention to *justitia*, with the help of which he arrives at a brilliant exposition of the Gregorian programme: " The claim for papal supremacy in the Church developed into the claim for the freedom of the Church from the State and for its supremacy over the State, a claim which Gregory VII summed up as ' righteousness ' . . . ' Righteousness ' requires the supremacy of the true ruler, of the spiritual authority, in order that in principle all interference with the true ruler may be excluded. In principle, however, such a possibility is only excluded if the State is theoretically subordinate to the Church, as an organ to be appointed by her for the control of secular affairs."

We shall avoid all the difficulties just described, and shall be clear of all possibility of false conclusions, if we use the word *libertas* in its correct medieval sense. As the text has sought to show, the freedom of the Church is that which is justly the Church's own: freedom from secular duties and the influence of the state, but also freedom to carry out its mission, the conversion of the world—and this last necessarily involves the leadership of the world.

2. Much that is valuable on the Christian idea of freedom is to be found in Johannes Lange's *Das Staatensystem Gregors VII auf Grund des augustinischen Begriffs von der libertas ecclesiae* (1913), which was written under Bernheim's direction, and still more in Bernheim's own *Mittelalterliche Zeitanschauungen*, pp. 43 sqq. and pp. 213 sqq. In their discussions of the idea of freedom, as of other subjects, however, Bernheim and his pupils ascribed much to Augustine which was in reality common to the whole of early Christian literature, and saw the effects of Augustinian influence in later writers where they did not in fact exist, even sometimes where no tradition of any kind had guided their thought.

These researches contribute almost nothing to our comprehension of the idea of *libertas ecclesiae*, since, through a strange logical error, they speak of *libertas ecclesiae* when what they are referring to is in fact only the freedom of others—of all Christians, of states, etc.—and not that of the Church at all. It is not necessary here to discuss the further point that neither Lange nor Bernheim can produce, as they promise, a specifically Augustinian conception of *libertas ecclesiae*, for the simple reason that no such conception exists. It will be enough to demonstrate their other mistake in one well-known example. In 1073 Gregory VII wrote to Geisa, the claimant to the Hungarian throne: " Notum autem tibi credimus, regnum Ungariae, sicut et alia nobilissima regna, in propriae libertatis statu debere esse et nulli regi alterius regni subici nisi sanctae et universali matri, Romanae ecclesiae, quae subiectos non habet ut servos sed ut filios suscipit universos." We have discussed the meaning of these words in the text (*supra*, p. 21); here they will serve to show that the *libertas* mentioned is of course not that of the Church but that of the kingdom of Hungary, and that it is a pure confusion to use the term *libertas ecclesiae* to describe this freedom or the analogous freedom of those monasteries which were independent of Rome.

APPENDIX V
CLUNY AND GREGORY VII
[cf. pp. 82, 166.]

In the text (cf. *supra*, pp. 82–5, 95, 166, etc.) Professor Tellenbach has sought to establish the exact nature of the relationship between the monastery of Cluny and the reform movement of which it was the chief source, on the one hand, and the Gregorian or Hildebrandine reform movement on the other. His conclusions, shortly put, are as follows: In its nature and for the first century and a half from its foundation, Cluny was essentially non-political; its main object was the moral reform of monastic life. The Cluniac movement, therefore, was not anti-imperial; it had at bottom no interest either in opposing or in supporting the imperial Church policy, for its own interests were different; but in so far as the Saxon and early Salian emperors wished, for reasons very like those which inspired the Cluniacs, to promote the moral reform of the Church, the great abbots of Cluny were prepared for friendship and co-operation with them (cf. *supra*, pp. 83–4, 86). It is important, however, to notice that the interests of Cluny, whether in co-operation with the emperors or not, seldom or never extended beyond monastic reform, and did not embrace the reform of the secular Church; this is explained by the essentially otherworldly outlook of monasticism and the "attitude of withdrawal" (cf. *supra*, pp. 45–6, 91).

From all this it must follow that the Cluniac movement cannot have been the source of the Gregorian programme, for the scope of the latter was far wider than that of the former, which it included as part of a much greater whole. The Gregorian programme amounted to a revolution, and one of Professor Tellenbach's main points is to insist on the novelty of its objects, while at the same time showing that it rested on traditional ideas—ideas which, be it noted, had dominated Christian thought long before the foundation of Cluny in 910.

Now the truth of all this has not always been recognised, and many historians, insisting on a closeness of connection between Cluny and Gregory VII which goes far beyond anything which is warranted by the evidence at our disposal, seem often to have followed one of two alternative lines of thought. Put in summary form, what some have written amounts to the argument: "Gregory VII was anti-imperial, therefore Cluny must have been anti-imperial; logically, therefore, the 1075 decrees against lay investiture, the humiliation of Canossa and Gregory's claim to supremacy were latent even before the meeting of the synod of Sutri, and it was only a question of time before they became the burning political issues;" others, on the other hand, seem to have argued: "Cluny was mainly interested in moral reform; therefore Gregory VII was mainly interested in moral reform, and this was the only essential part of his programme." There is perhaps also a small third class, a variant of the first, which will be dealt with below.

In his Appendix III (*Zur Beurteilung Clunys in der Literatur*, German edition, pp. 204–5) Professor Tellenbach attacked the former error and gave examples of the way in which it had misled historians, but the writers he quoted were nearly all German. For the purposes of this translation it has seemed that a useful service would be performed by extending the scope of Professor Tellenbach's note to cover non-German historians and also the second of the two errors discussed above, An attempt to do this is made in what follows, but it must be emphasised that for the greater part of it the translator alone is responsible.

I—"*Cluny was anti-imperial*"

(i) A real distinction in principle between the objects of the Cluniacs and the objects of the Gregorians was first made by Sackur in his *Die Cluniacenser*, published in 1892–4: cf. ii. 445 sqq. in particular. Sackur distinguished the tendencies of the two movements very clearly, and did not regard the Cluniacs as precursors of, or even leading protagonists in, the struggle against the secular authority; he regarded monastic reform as a predominately religious movement, and did not rate the Cluniacs' reforming activity very highly, even so far as the reform of the secular clergy was concerned.

Among more recent writers who have adopted a similar view there may be quoted:

L. M. Smith, *Cluny and Gregory VII*, EHR. 26 (1911)

20–33; see esp. p. 21: Cluny was purely monastic and " does not seem to have been especially interested in the secular Church; " p. 27: abbot Hugh was neutral in the struggle between emperor and pope; p. 33: Peter Damian was opposed to Hildebrand and yet a close friend of Cluny.

J. P. Whitney, *Hildebrandine Essays*, (1932) p. 11: "Above all, the Cluniac reformers must not be held opposed to royal or political influence upon the Church;" cf. also p. 26: even Gregory VII did not " start with the intention of subjugating the imperial power."

E. Caspar, *Gregor VII in seinen Briefen*, HZ. 130 (1924) 1–30, esp. p. 9: novelty of the reform programme of Hildebrand; p. 11: Gregory VII was not the embodiment of the Cluniac spirit in the way in which Gregory the Great, his chosen model, was of the Benedictine; his active nature did not fit in with the Cluniac " attitude of withdrawal; " he changed the Cluniac ideal of freedom from the world into the ideal of domination over the world; p. 30: " He is in fact, in spite of all forerunners, the great Innovator, and stands quite alone."

A. Hamilton Thompson, in *Cambridge Medieval History*, v. 665: " It is hardly surprising that [abbot Hugh of Cluny] preferred a cautious neutrality to a whole-hearted espousal of the cause of Gregory." The pope " looked for support to the great influence of the abbot. He found friendship and consolation . . .," but his letters betray " a tone of impatient reproach which shows that Hugh's regard did not go to the length of overt action. The voice of the abbot was not heard in the Pope's synods; Cluny was unprepared to throw its weight into the scales on his side."

A. Fliche, *La réforme grégorienne*, i. 39–60, esp. p. 39 : " On a souvent cru que la réforme grégorienne avait eu pour prélude la réforme clunisienne dont elle dériverait en ligne directe. Cette opinion est pour le moins exagérée . . .;" p. 41: " Le mouvement clunisien est exclusivement monastique et il ne pénétrera guère l'Église séculière. Saint Odon et ses successeurs ont remis la règle bénédictine en vigueur dans les abbayes qu'ils ont réformées; il ne semble pas qu'ils aient essayé d'entraîner l'épiscopat à tenter la même œuvre d'assainissement. . . .;" p. 43: Their ideal " a été avant tout de soustraire les âmes aux dangers du siècle en les jetant dans les monastères clunisiens;" p. 50 : " Sans doute,

Cluny a créé . . . une atmosphère favorable à l'éclosion de la réforme grégorienne, mais on ne saurait s'autoriser de quelques faits isolés pour affirmer que la réforme grégorienne est sortie de la réforme clunisienne."

See also E. Bernheim, *Mittelalterliche Zeitanschauungen*, i. 20 sqq., L. M. Smith, *Cluny in the eleventh century*, p. 58, Carlyle, ii. 50–1, Z. N. Brooke, *History of Europe*, 911–1198, p. 124.

(ii) In spite of the work of Sackur and, among others, the writers just quoted, the older view—that Cluny was in some way directly responsible for the development of the Hilde-brandine programme—is still frequently repeated. It rests in part, no doubt, upon the now entirely discredited legend that Hildebrand had been a monk at Cluny; for the over-whelming body of evidence against this, see EHR. 26 (1911) 30–31, Whitney, *op. cit.*, pp. 11–12, or Fliche, i. 377–8.

The incorrect view of the connection of Cluny and Gregory VII may be found in various forms, in differing degrees and with various modifications, in :

Viscount Bryce, *The Holy Roman Empire*, (edn. of 1922) p. 149, note t: " The abbey of Cluny was already the centre of a monastic movement in favour of the deliverance of the clergy from secular control."

E. Lavisse et A. Rambaud, *Histoire Générale*, i. 568 : " Les empereurs avaient voulu affranchir la papauté de la tyrannie des barons romains; l'ordre de Cluny l'affranchira de la tyrannie impériale."

H. Günter, HJ. 44 (1924) 5: " Everything which was produced by the Cluniac movement, from the *Dictatus Papae* to the bull *Unam Sanctam*, is the interpretation of the ascetic outlook in practice."

L. Reynaud, *Les origines de l'influence française en Allemagne*, pp. 54–66, 206 sqq., esp. p. 63: At the outbreak of the Investiture Contest " ' Rome n'était plus dans Rome ' ou plutôt Rome avait accepté la domination de Cluny, Rome était gouvernée par les Clunisiens, installés sur le siège de Pierre et coiffés de la mitre "; pp. 64–5: Hilde-brand " incarna la doctrine de la congrégation [de Cluny] dans ce qu'elle avait de plus intransigeant et de plus combatif, c'est-à-dire dans sa forme lorraine ou dijonnaise; " p. 212: " Le règne d'Henri III apporta la preuve décisive qu'entre

la Royauté allemande et la Réforme il ne pouvait y avoir qu'une lutte acharnée, éternelle."
L. von Ranke, *Weltgeschichte*, p. 250: ". . . the chief object of Cluny was to deprive the emperor of investitures."
C. W. Previté-Orton, *Outlines of Medieval History*, p. 201: The Cluniac monks "were the best propagandists and champions of papal supremacy in the Church. They had succeeded in their own ideals by a revolt from the decadent local authorities. They aimed at a similar remedy for the whole Church."
Similar views may be found in A. Dempf, *Sacrum Imperium*, p. 178 (Cardinal Humbert was the chief representative of Cluniac ideals); R. Sohm, *Kirchengeschichte im Grundriss*, p. 89 (in the person of Gregory VII, Cluniac monasticism occupied the papal throne); A. Harnack, *Das Mönchtum*, p. 45: E. Troeltsch, *Soziallehren*, p. 207 (trans. Wyon, p. 224); M. Manitius, *Geschichte der lat. Literatur de Mittelalters*, iii. 3; H. A. L. Fisher, *History of Europe*, i. 198; D. J. Hill, *History of European Diplomacy*, i. 203–4, 210–11, 218; G. H. Sabine, *History of Political Theory*, p. 230.
E. Voosen, *Papauté et pouvoir civile à l'epoque de Grégoire VII*, (1927) pp. 60–64 is critical but inconclusive; e.g., p. 64: ". . . s'il est excessif d'écarter totalement l'influence plus générale des mouvements réformateurs monastiques. . . ."

(iii) Finally, there appears to be a third school of thought, composed of writers who, after full and serious consideration of the view, expressed in (i) above, that Cluny was mainly interested in monastic reform and that Gregory VII's ideas marked a radical advance on its original principles, yet reject it and return to something very like the older view, that of section (ii). The chief representatives of this third group are A. Brackmann, *Die politische Wirkung der kluniazensischen Bewegung*, HZ. 139 (1929) 34–47 (see also the same author's article *The beginnings of the National State*, translated in Barraclough, *Mediaeval Germany*, ii. 281–299, esp. p. 284, where the same view is expressed more briefly), and U. Berlière, *L'ordre monastique*, (1924) pp. 243–5.
Typical statements are:
" The Cluniacs . . . never forgot the great difference between their own ecclesiastical outlook and the outlook of the dominant classes in the various countries of Europe, and they were consequently as politically-minded as those with whom

they came in contact, the leaders of secular society and of the opposition party in the Church."—Brackmann, *Wirkung*, p. 34.

" The political significance of the Cluniac movement has been denied, its effectiveness has been limited to the influence which the strict Cluniac rule exerted over western monasticism. But this view is wrong. The great abbots of Cluny were politicians and strove to realise a concrete political objective."—*Med. Germany*, ii. 284.

[But cf. also Brackmann's article *Die Ursachen der geistigen und politischen Wandlung Europas*, HZ. 149 (1933) 229–239, where he expresses the more moderate opinion that "the Cluniacs respected the secular power and contented themselves with offering it advice and guidance " (pp. 231–2).]

" . . . on a parfois mis en doute qu'il y ait une relation nécessaire entre les idées grégoriennes et le programme clunisien. On a répété que Cluny n'avait d'interêt que pour la vie claustrale à l'intérieur de ses murs et ne s'inquiétait guère de l'Église séculière. . . . Profonde erreur. . . . Rien que le concept clunisien de l'indépendance monastique vis-à-vis du pouvoir laïque et de la soumission directe au Saint-Siège heurtait de front le concept impérialiste et régaliste et constituait, à lui seul, un programme."—Berlière, *op. cit.*, p. 243.

Cf. also *Mediaeval Germany*, ii. 136, 141, 183.

It is perhaps worth while to make two comments upon this view :—

(*a*) It is true that the Cluniacs did attack secular princes; but they also took Peter Damian's view of the monarchy— that it was not secular, that the king was more than a mere prince, etc.—and so these attacks did not touch the monarchy (cf. EHR. 26, p. 23); further, they looked to the king to free the Church from the secular control of the aristocracy. It is, of course, no accident that reforming centres like Cluny, Gorze and Brogne grew up in Burgundy and Lorraine, where central control was weakest.

(*b*) On the other hand, Cluniac reorganization did seek papal, not royal, protection, and so from the outset did aim at freedom from the royal or state-Church; but if this point can be succesfully urged against the extreme " neutrality " of, for instance, Smith, *loc. cit.*, it does not really go very far towards proving that Cluny was, originally and in any true sense of the word, politically-minded, especially in face of the evidence (friendship of abbots with emperors, etc.) which can be quoted against it.

II—"*Gregory VII was mainly interested in moral reform*"

This view is a good deal less common than the one which has been examined above; the reasons for rejecting it are explained in the text, *supra*, p. 166. It has been expressed, for instance, by

Ch. Petit-Dutaillis, *La monarchie féodale en France et en Angleterre*, p. 99: " Le but de sa vie a été de détruire la simonie et d'assainir les moeurs du clergé. Le reste, pour lui, était accessoire."

A. Fliche, *La réforme grégorienne*, ii. 111, 119 note: " Grégoire VII, préoccupé avant tout d'en finir avec la simonie et la nicolaïsme. . . ."

H.-X. Arquillière, *Saint Grégoire VII*, (1924) p. 113: The Augustinian *justitia* " est foulée aux pieds par les abus criants de la simonie et du nicolaïsme. Il s'attaquera à ces deux fléaux, comme à l'objectif principal de sa mission "; p. 120: " En résumé, réformer l'Église ravagée par la simonie et le nicolaïsme,—restaurer l'unité dechirée par le schisme oriental,—collaborer avec les princes . . . maintenir les droits acquis, et, s'il est possible, les étendre . . . tels sont les premiers linéaments de la pensée pontificale de Grégoire VII . . . dans les premiers temps de son pontíficat."

Finally, it is worth while repeating Professor Tellenbach's warning that a productive source of error has been the fact that the whole of the monastic reform of the tenth and eleventh centuries has too often been called the " Cluniac movement," in spite of the many important points of difference which distinguished its manifestations in France, Germany and Italy.

INDEX

Abbo of Fleury, 5, 83; (and proprietary system) 94; 104, 178
Adalbero of Metz (Bp., 929–964), 95
Adalbert of Prague, St (Bp., 982–997), 83, 90
Adalbold of Utrecht (Bp., 1010–1027), 102
Adelaide (empress, wife of Otto I), 83
Ado of Vienne (Abp., 860–875), 89
Alcuin, 41, 58, 59 n., 64 n.
Alexander II (pope, 1061–1073), 15, 112, 121, 123, 142, 143, 169, 170–1
Alfonso VI (king of Castile, 1072–1109), 83
All Souls, Feast of, 79
Amatus of Oléron (Bp., 1073–1089), 122
Anastasius I (emperor, 491–518), 33, 35
Anno of Cologne (Abp., 1056–1075), 51
Anonymous of York, The, 136, 142, 146, 149, 158 n.
Anselm II of Lucca (Bp., 1073–1086), 115
Arnald of Ager, 123
Asceticism, 27, 42–7
Athelstan, king of England (924–940), 90 n.
Atto of Vercelli (Bp., 924–961), 67, 105, 115
Auctor Gallicus, The, 103, 104 n., 105, 110, 173, 175
Auctoritas, 12, 35

Bamberg, 107, 172
Bardo of Mainz (Abp., 1031–1051), 51
Bavaria, 76
Beatrice of Tuscany, 107
Benedict of Aniane, 76–7
Benedict V (pope, 964), 103
Benedict VIII (pope, 1012–1024), 78, 98, 139
Benedict IX (pope, 1032–1045), 173–6
Benedictine rule, The, 77
Benevento, 107, 172
Bernard of Besalù, 123

Bernold of St Blasien, 46
Berthold of Reichenau (and proprietary system), 119
Boniface of Albano (Cardinal-bp., 1049–1067), 98
Brogne, 76
Bruno of Toul (Bp., 1026–1049), *see* Leo IX
Burchard of Worms (Bp., 1000–1025), 99, 102, 104, 115, 178
Burgundy, 76, 124
Byzantium, 140

Cadalus of Parma (Bp., 1046–1071), *see* Honorius II
Calixtus II (pope, 1119–1124), 122
Cambridge Songs, The, 53
Canonical election, 100–2, 113, 123
Canon Law, vii, viii, 24, 94, 101 sq., 115, 117
Charlemagne (king of the Franks, 768–814, emperor, 800–814), 58–9, 62, 64 n., 156
Charles Martel, 80
Charles the Bald (king, 840–877, emperor, 875–877), 76
Cicero, 5 n., 10, 11
Clement of Alexandria, 5, 8
Clement II (pope, 1046–1047), 98, 103, 129, 169, 175
Clement III (anti-pope, 1080–1100), 121, 144–5, 170
Clermont, Council of (1095), 114, 116
Cluny (Masses at), 46, 76–8; (and politics), 82, 91; (and proprietary system), 93–4; (and Gregory VII), 186–92
Conrad II (emperor, 1024–1039), 18, 59, 83–4, 103–4
Constantine I, the Great (emperor, 306–337), xii, 9, 30–32, 62
Constantius II (emperor, 337–361), 32

Damasus II (pope, 1047–1048), 98, 169
Denmark, 157
Desiderius, abbot of Monte Cassino, *see* Victor III
Deusdedit, Cardinal, 115

Dictatus Papae, 141, 142 n., 151, 153-4, 189
Dietrich of Metz (Bp., 964–984), 95
Dionysius the Areopagite, 8, 38, 53
Diversorum sententiae patrum, 115
Divine Right, 10, 60
Donation of Constantine, The, 110
Dualism, 43

England, 59 n., 90, 157; (Investiture Contest in), 123-4; *and see* Athelstan, Offa, William the Conqueror
Eigenkirche, Eigenkloster, vii, viii, 20, 70-7, 80, 170, 178, *and see* proprietary system
Einsiedeln, 76
Episcopalism, 139 sqq.
Ernst, duke of Swabia, 18
Exorcist, 148

Felix II (pope, 483–492), 138
Fermo, 107, 181
Fleury, 51, 76, 94, *and see* Abbo
Florus of Lyons, 48
France, 120; (proprietary system in), 122; (Investiture Contest in), 113-4, 124, 142; *and see* Philip I, Robert II
Frederick of Lorraine, *see* Stephen IX
Freedom, 2-25, 38, 127 *and passim*
Frotard of St-Pons-de-Thomières, abbot, 118
Fulbert of Chartres (Bp., 1007–1029), 40, 59, 90
Fulda, 107, 172

Gauzlin, abbot of Fleury, (Abp. of Bourges, 1014–1029), 95
Gebhard of Eichstätt, *see* Victor II
Geisa, 21, 185
Gelasius I (pope, 492–496), 33-6, 62-3, 138, 158, *and see* Two Powers, theory of the
Gerbert, *see* Sylvester II
Gerhard of Brogne, abbot, 95
Gerhard of Cambrai (Bp., 1013–1048), 68
Gerhard of Toul (Bp., 963–994), 90, 95
Gisela (empress, wife of Conrad II), 84
Godfrey, duke of Lorraine, 86, 107-8, 181-2
Gorze, 76, 95
Gregory I, the Great (pope, 590–604), 8, 9, 13, 38, 40-1; (and celibacy), 49; 67, 138, 142, 151, 188
Gregory V (pope, 996–999), 98
Gregory VI (pope, 1045–1046), 103, 106, 173-4, 176-7
Gregory VII (pope, 1073–1085), 21, 40, 49, 52, 98; (and Leo IX), 101; (and Lorraine law-schools), 102; 103, 107-8, 110, 112·sqq.; (aims of), 137, 164-8; (not a Cluniac), 189; *and passim*
Gualbertus, Johannes, 76
Guibert, *see* Clement III
Guido of Pomposa, abbot, 82, 84, 86
Gunther of Cologne (Abp., 850–864), 89

Halinard of Dijon, abbot (Abp. of Lyons, 1046–1052), 86, 91, 100, 175
Hammerstein, count and countess of, 139
Henry I (king of the Germans 919–936), 89
Henry II (emperor, 1002–1024), 57, 83, 169
Henry III (emperor, 1039–1056), 59, 67, 83-4; (character of), 85-8; (aims of), 97; 99, 101; (and Wazo), 103; 105-8; (and Humbert), 110; 136, 148, 169-74, 176, 181-2
Henry IV (emperor, 1056–1105), 18, 64, 70, 113 sqq., 121, 133, 143-4, 151, 158
Henry V (emperor, 1105–1125), 117
Heriger of Laubach, abbot, 102
Hermann of Metz (Bp., 1073–1090), 70
Hezilo of Hildesheim (Bp., 1054–1079), 143
Hierarchy (ascetic), 42-7, 148-51; (sacramental), 47-50, 154; (royal theocracy), 56-60, 69-71; *and passim*
Hildebrand, *see* Gregory VII
Hincmar of Reims (Abp., 845–882), 41, 49, 66-7
Hirsau, 119-20
Honorius II (anti-pope, 1061–1064), 15, 121, 170-1
Hosius of Cordova (Bp., 296–357), 32
Hugh of Cluny (abbot, 1049–1109), 52, 83, 133, 182, 188
Hugh of Die (Bp., 1074–1092), 113
Hugh of Flavigny, 52
Hugh the White, Cardinal, 98

Humbert of Silva Candida (Cardinal-bishop, 1057–1063), 15 n., 16–7, 98, 107–8; (*Libri adv. simoniacos*), 109–11: 133, 135, 181–2
Hungary, Hungarians, viii, 21, 75, 85, 157

Investiture, v, 90, 99, 112–15, 122–5, 129, 135–7, 145, 162
Isidore of Seville (Bp., 599–636), 23; *see also* pseudo-Isidorian forgeries
Italy, 76, 82, 124
Ivo of Chartres (Bp., 1090–1115), 145

John X (pope, 914–928), 90
John XVIII (pope, 1003–1009), 140 n.
John of Salisbury, 14
John Scotus Erigena, 38
Jus gentium, 23
Justitia, 23, 184

Laity, subordinate position of, 42, 56, 70–71, 111–12, 115–17, 134–7
Land-peace, 85
Leo I, the Great, St (pope, 440–461), 138–9
Leo VIII (pope, 963–965), 98
Leo IX (pope, 1048–1054), 51, 62, 68, 86; (policy of) 98–107; 121, 140, 142, 156, 169–72, 180–1
Lex regia, 13
Libertas, 12–25, 41, 183–4 *and passim*
Liemar of Bremen (Abp., 1072–1101), 143
Lietbert of Cambrai (Bp., 1049–1076), 67
Liutpold of Mainz (Abp., 1051–1059), 142
Lorraine, 101–5
Louis II (emperor, 850–875), 65 n.
Louis I, the Pious (emperor, 814–840), 59, 62, 65, 76, 112, 178
Lotharingian law-schools, The, 101–2

Macedonians, 128
Mainz, 54
Majolus of Cluny (abbot, 954–994), 39, 83, 86, 91
Manasses of Reims (Abp., 1068–1080), 114
Manorial organization, 72
Marriage of priests, *see* Nicolaitism
Mass, 46, 50, 76–8
Melchisedek, 35, 58

Merit, 45, 50, 78
Monasticism (characteristics of), 42–47; (reform of), 76–85; (reform of, and proprietary system), 93; *and passim*

Natural law, 22–5, 27, 39
Nellenburg, count of, 123
Neoplatonism, 8, 38
Nicholas I (pope, 858–867), 65–6, 89, 141
Nicholas II (pope, 1058–1061), 112, 123, 169–171
Nicolaitism, xiii, 131, 192
Nilus, 83
Non-resistance, xvi, 67 sqq., 160
Normans (invasions of), 75; (popes and), 106–7, 172, 181–2
Notker of Liège (Bp., 972–1008), 101

Odilo of Cluny (abbot, 994–1048), 79, 83, 93 n., 174
Odo of Cluny (abbot, 927–941), 41, 49, 67, 86, 188
Offa, king of Mercia (757–796), 59 n.
Olbert of Gembloux, 102
Origen, 3, 8
Otto I (emperor, 936–973), 103, 105
Otto II (emperor, 973–983), 83
Otto III (emperor, 983–1002), 83, 171

Paschal II (pope, 1099–1118), 117, 119, 124, 145, 150 n.
Patarini, 155
Patriciate, 101, 111, 170, 176
Patronage, 118
Peter Damian of Fonte Avellana (Cardinal-bp. of Ostia, 1058–1066), 49–50, 67–8, 82, 84, 86, 98, 111, 116 n., 133, 140, 173, 182, 188, 191
Peter of Substantion, 116
Philip I, king of France (1060–1108), 80
Pippin, king of the Franks (751–768), 57 n., 62
Plato, 8
Poppo of Stablo, abbot, 83, 86, 91, 95
Precedence and superiority, distinguished, 36
Privilegium, 16–17
Proprietary system, The, (in hands of the Church), viii, 74, 91–7, 117–20; (and monastic reform), 82–4; (in England), 123–4; 170, 178; *and see Eigenkirche, Eigenkloster*

Pseudo-Isidorian forgeries, 49, 99, 104, 139, 140 n., 141, 178

Ratherius of Verona (Bp. of Verona, 932–954, 962–968, Bp. of Liège, 954–956), 102, 105
Remigius of Lyons (Abp., 852–875), 41
Richard of Capua, 122
Richard of St Vannes, 83, 91, 95
Robert II, king of France (996–1031), 83, 93 n.
Roman law, 12
Rome, Romans, 11–12, 14; (parties in), 88, 105–6, 108, 176; (primacy of), 138–147; (schism with Constantinople), 121
Royal theocracy, 56–60, 89–91, *and passim*
Rufinus, 9

Sacraments, validity of, in hands of impure priest, 49, 85
St Ambrose of Milan (Bp., 374–397), 13, 32
St Anselm of Canterbury (Abp., 1093–1109), 119, 124
St Augustine of Hippo (Bp., 395–430), xii, 4–10, 28–31, 37–8, 164, 184
St Cadroe, 95
St Cyprian, 130
St John Chrysostom, 32, 36
St Paul, xii, 3, 5–6, 26, 67
St Peter, 133, 138
St Romuald, 76, 83
St-Bénigne-de-Dijon, 76, 95
St Evroul, 96
St Trond, 95
St Vannes, 76
Sallust, 18
San Benigno di Fruttuaria, 76
Saracens, 121
Sewin of Sens (Abp., 977–999), 93
Siegfried of Mainz (Abp., 1060–1084), 54, 143
Simony, xiii, 75, 82, 86, 93, 100, 110, 128, 173, 176
Spain, 120; (Mozarabic rite in) 141
Spoleto, 107, 181–2
Stablo, 76, *and see* Poppo
Stephen IX (pope, 1057–1058), 98, 102, 108, 142, 170, 180–2
Stoics, Stoicism, 5–6, 26
Subjective right, 15
Superiority and precedence, distinguished, 36

Sylvester I (pope, 314–336), 139
Sylvester II (pope, 999–1003), 15, 98, 104, 139
Sylvester III (anti-pope), 1045–1046), 170, 175–6
Symmachus (pope, 498–514), 36
Synods:—(Gerona, 1078), 122; (Quedlinburg, 1085), 145; (Reims, 1119), 122; (Rome, 1059), 121–2; (Rome, 1078), 119, 122; (Sutri, 1046), xv, 87, 97, 103, 170, 172–7; (Tours, 1060), 122; (Vienne, 1112), 146 n.; (Worms, 1076), 143–4

Theocracy, 26, 34, 56–60, 69–71, 89–91, 93, 161, 170, 176
Theodosius I (emperor, 379–395), 13
Theodosius II (emperor, 408–424), 31
Theutgaud of Trier (Abp., 847–868), 89
Tithe, institution of, 72, 75
Truce of God, 68, 82
Two Powers, Theory of the, 33–7, 64, 68, 158–9

Udo of Trier (Abp., 1066–1078), 143
Ulrich of Augsburg (Bp., 923–973), 90–91
Unam sanctum, 189
Urban II (pope, 1088–1099), 52–3, 116, 121–3

Valentinian III (emperor, 424–450), 31
Venantius Fortunatus, 58
Victor II (pope, 1054–1057), 107–8, 142, 169, 172, 180–2
Victor III (pope, 1086–1087), 121, 182
Villein, 19

Waulsort, 95
Wazo of Liège (Bp., 1042–1048), 87, 102–5, 129, 148
Wenrich of Trier, 115
Widger of Ravenna (Abp., 1044–1046), 104
William of St Bénigne, abbot, 39
William the Conqueror, king of England (1066–1087), 40, 120, 123, 155
Wolfgang of Regensburg (Bp., 972–994), 90
Worms, Concordat of (1122), 122, 124